CARROTS DON'T GROW ON TREES

BUILDING SUSTAINABLE AND RESILIENT COMMUNITIES

ROBERT TURNER

A FARMER'S VENTURE INTO THE AGRIHOOD

Discovery Books
Published by Discovery Books, LLC.
P.O. Box 186
Skyland, NC. 28776

www.discoverybooksllc.com

First published in the United States by Discovery Books, LLC

Copyright © 2019 by Robert Turner

The Library of Congress has cataloged this paperback edition as follows:

Turner, Robert
Carrots Don't Grow on Trees - Building Sustainable and Resilient Communities
p. cm.
Includes bibliographical references
ISBN 9781946412454
1.Sustainable development. 2. Food Habits   3. Food Security   1. Title
Library of Congress Control Number: 2018908219

Printed in the United States

Book design by Discovery Books

For Kara

CONTENTS

INTRODUCTION

THE FAR-DISTANCE COMPANY

In the year 1602, spice traders gave us the earliest example of a powerful, multi-national food corporation...

The ship's crew worked for The Far-Distance Company, which had the financial backing and support of The New Company for Voyages to East India, and when they returned from their long journey they were paraded through the streets of Amsterdam as the church bells tolled throughout the city, and then given as much wine as they could drink.

Most of the city turned out for the celebration and the parade and lined the streets along the route. The parade was led by a marching band that included trumpeters and a drum corps, followed by politicians and prominent local officials. Behind them were the managers of The Far-Distance Company dressed in their finest silk. The ship's crew came next, numbering about 300 men, and all of them looked quite thin, missing some teeth and showing other signs of scurvy.

Behind the crew came the stock holders and investors, gleefully cheering and shaking hands with each other and with citizens along the street, very happy about the success of the enterprise and the huge return on their investment.

The leader of this second expedition to the Spice Islands

was the fearless and intrepid explorer, Admiral Jacob Van Neck. Van Neck and his crew had just returned home with nearly 1 million pounds of pepper and cloves, as well as half a shipload of nutmeg, mace, and cinnamon. Many men were lost on this voyage to the East Indies, but the venture was considered a resounding success, earning a 400% profit.

It did much better than the first expedition to the Spice Islands, organized solely under the direction of The Far-Distance Company, which took two years and three months to complete the 25,000-mile round trip voyage and suffered serious setbacks along the way, including storms at sea, deadly clashes with Portuguese war ships and hostile natives in the islands. Three of the four ships that sailed were lost in the venture, with only 87 men left alive from an original crew of 248 when it returned to Amsterdam. Still, that first expedition made a reasonable profit for its investors, even accounting for the lost ships, bringing back 245 bags of pepper, 45 tons of nutmeg, and 30 bales of mace. Profit, after all, was why the company was formed, and there was no column on the balance sheet to account for the lives of men.

So it was determined that a second expedition should be organized under a combined venture by the Far-Distance Company, and the recently established New Company for Voyages to East India, who joined forces and between them managed to raise more money than had ever been raised in the Netherlands for a private venture, and this time they sent eight ships off to Indonesia and the Spice Islands. The year was 1598.

Soon after Van Neck and his crew returned from the successful second expedition, in 1602, another company was formed by the merger of these two companies and several others and included investors from across Holland. The purpose of this great merger was to form a cartel that could completely control the spice trade supply, and thus the prices that could be charged, and the new consolidated company called itself the United East India Company, or as we know it today, The Dutch East India Company. That company was to remain in business for almost 200 years.

The Dutch East India Company was the first multi-national food corporation in the world, dealing mainly in high value spices and tea from far-away places. It was also the first publicly traded stock corporation in the world; the first corporation to be listed on any official stock exchange where an average citizen could buy stock and invest in a company. It was the first corporate-led global corporation and at one point the most valuable corporation ever formed; the Google or Microsoft of its day, only much bigger. The company's might and power in corporate history dwarfed any corporate entity that we know of today. The company was all-powerful.

The company also deserves notoriety because of some of its other 'firsts'. It was the first joint stock company, for instance, to practice corporate espionage by sending a company spy and inside man, Cornelis de Houtman, to competitors in Portugal in order to steal closely guarded marine charts and other trade route secrets to the Spice Islands. Portugal had a virtual monopoly on the spice trade, and wanted to keep it that way, so marine charts, maps and the trade routes to India and beyond to the Spice Islands were closely guarded trade secrets and stealing them or divulging any information to outsiders or foreigners came under the strict penalty of death.

The Dutch East India Company also gave us the first example of a hostile corporate take-over, of sorts, when an early expedition attacked and captured a Portuguese trading port at present day Jakarta in Indonesia, and took warehouses, ships, crew and cargo. By taking Jakarta in 1619 the company established its stronghold in the region, and over the next several decades it continued to establish or take by force other ports that allowed it to expand its control of the region and the spice trade. The company might also be considered a pioneer in foreign direct investment, building forts, towns, and warehouses in many countries, but like most ventures into distant regions during the Age of Discovery, the cultures of indigenous peoples were often decimated.

The company came heavily armed and with a fleet of military ships. Many native groups were relocated or simply wiped out and replaced with slave labor. The company was also known to burn or destroy trees and crops on islands that were not under their control in order to reduce or eliminate supply to a potential competitor. Van Neck and his men were the first Dutch fleet to reach the 'Spice Islands' of Maluku, cutting out the Portuguese and middlemen in Java. The atrocities came later, after him.

The Dutch government gave the Dutch East India Company a monopoly on the spice trade, and it opened the door for globalization as we know it. It's corporate logo, using the letters VOC (from the Dutch language and spelling of United East India Company) became the first recognizable worldwide company brand and logo. The corporate logo was seen and immediately recognized by peoples around the world, much like an apple with a bite out of it.

But it was much more than just a brand identity, it represented power. In foreign ports and colonies, the company possessed quasi-governmental powers, including the ability to wage war, negotiate treaties with foreign states and kings, imprison, hold trials and execute convicts, mint its own money and coins, and establish colonies or take-over existing colonies by force from its competitors. Most of these hostile corporate take-overs were aimed at established Portuguese ports in Africa and Asia, but hostilities were also directed toward other competitors from France and England.

At various times in history, many spices were worth their weight in gold. But it takes money to make money, and the managers of the Far-Distance Company benefitted from a new class of citizen investors that gave them the capital to build ships, hire crews and labor, purchase trade goods, and begin a military conquest. The capital investment helped the company finance the "Spice Wars" which began in 1602, shortly after Van Neck returned to the Netherlands, and that lasted another 60 years. To the company, war was just a cost of doing business, and it was investor financing and corporate capital that allowed the company to capture and take control of the important ports of India and the East Indies and eventually dominate the spice trade.

With its increasing importance and growing number of foreign posts and offices, the company became what many consider the world's first true transnational corporation based on the importing, processing and distribution of food products, and it wielded more power and military might than most nations at the time.

Spices and other food additives are so prevalent and inexpensive today that it's hard for us to imagine what spices meant to the middle ages. Many foods are fairly bland and boring without spices and flavorings, and spices were particularly helpful at a time when meats and other foods were not always fresh because of the lack of refrigeration. Spices can certainly make foods much more interesting and enjoyable, and spices give many countries and regions their food identity and food culture. Spices make Italian food taste Italian, Indian taste Indian, Thai taste Thai, and British taste boring. Our processed food today is so full of food additives and flavorings, like heaps of salt and sugars derived from corn, that we really have no idea what it would taste like without them. They most certainly wouldn't be as enticing and delicious as a Twinkie.

Spices were believed to have medicinal purposes, and nutmeg was believed to be the only cure for the plague. Many spices were believed to help with digestion, some were thought to be a sedative while others a stimulant or stringent, and some were considered an aphrodisiac. Clove was considered, and still is, an antiseptic.

The sole source of nutmeg was the tiny speck of an island called Run, located in the Moluccas Island group of Indonesia. Run was rumored to be the home of a tribe of head-hunters and cannibals, which is perhaps where it got its name. Run is also spelled 'Rhun' on some old maps, so Run was probably used more often as a noun than a verb. But It's funny to think that some early explorer landed on Run, took a look around and said, "This is a nice island, what do you want to call it?" Just then some headhunters came out of the jungle and someone yelled "RUN!", and the name stuck.

While the Dutch eventually took possession of most of the Spice Islands, Run became an English hold-out. The island's nutmeg made it one of the most lucrative of all the Spice Islands, and a rag-tag band of British adventurers were determined to keep it from the Dutch East India Company. Led by a courageous young man named Nathaniel Courthope, this small group of men working for the British East India Company and their native allies fortified the island with cannon from their ships and held it for a few years through several brutal and bloody attacks and near starvation conditions, but Courthope was finally killed and the small island fell under the VOC control. Remember the island of Run, because I'll come back to it with another story at the end of this book that may surprise you. It's a little bonus for reading this introduction and not jumping right to Chapter One.

Rumors that nutmeg cured the plague were good for business and probably added greatly to its price and profits. This could also be the early story of Big Pharma. Rumors of headhunters and cannibals probably helped reduce some competition by discouraging sea captains from planning a stop there. And like Big Pharma, exorbitant prices could be justified because of the high cost of R&D; Risk and Decapitation for those that ventured there.

Like any start-up, The Far-Distance Company had challenges to overcome, including setting up supply chains half a world away. Just finding the suppliers represented a major obstacle, with far flung islands in the most remote and uncharted region of the world. A round trip voyage was equal to a trip around the world at the equator, over 25,000 nautical miles.

For over a hundred years, explorers had been trying to find a sea route to India and the East Indies. The riches of the spice trade inspired Christopher Columbus, who had the daring idea of going west to get to the east in 1492. So it might be said that the discovery of America was all about food additives and flavorings.

Ferdinand Magellan sailed west for Spain in 1519, made it

around the bottom of South America and across the Pacific, but was killed on Mactan Island in the Philippines in 1521 and never actually circumnavigated the planet himself, but some his crew did. Of the five vessels that left Spain under his command, only one, Victoria, circled the earth for the first time and returned to Spain. Most of the crew had perished. Onlookers at the Spanish port when the ship finally returned were horrified at the appearance of the skeletal crew that remained; men starving and half dead laying on the deck of a tattered ghost ship. Of the 280 crew members that left on the five ships destined for the Spice Islands, only 18 men returned on the one remaining ship.

But almost three years exactly from when the expedition started, Victoria returned with 26 tons of cloves and cinnamon on board, and so their venture was viewed as a remarkable success, whatever the cost in human lives.

Arab traders dominated the spice trade between Europe and southeast Asia and carefully guarded the secret sources of the spices they sold for hundreds of years. To protect their business and market share, and to discourage competitors, they spread fantastic tales of dangerous and far-away places where the spices came from. Stories were told of mythical beasts, strange human-like creatures of enormous size, man-eating tribes of cannibals, and tribes of warrior 'Amazon' women that existed in these far-off distant lands in the southern hemisphere. The spice Cassia, stories told, grew in shallow lakes guarded by winged dragons, and cinnamon grew in deep glens infested with gigantic, deadly poisonous snakes. Horrible sea monsters waited for unsuspecting sailors in the Arabian sea, the route to India.

The stories became so fearful and outrageous that at one-point Pliny the Elder (AD 23–79) ridiculed the stories and declared, "All these tales…have been evidently invented for the purpose of enhancing the price of these commodities." But the stories did discourage competition. Many 16th and 17th century maps still depicted sea serpents, cannibals, and other mysterious creatures in the otherwise blank regions of the map.

Meanwhile, Arab traders were sailing directly to spice-producing regions in India since long before the time of Christ. Spices would make their way from India across the Arabian Sea, up the Red Sea and across Egypt to Alexandria and the Mediterranean, and on to Europe. That supply line fell into jeopardy when Christians started fighting Muslims with the Crusades.

Although the origins of spices were known throughout Europe by the Middle Ages, there was no way to break the Arab and Muslim hold on the trade routes that went through Muslim territory in the Levant, the lands along the eastern Mediterranean shore. The Ottoman Empire controlled the spice trade through the Levant in the 15th century and finally cut off all trade with Europe.

Another way to India had to be found. Near the end of the 15th century, intrepid businessmen and brave explorer partners began to build ships and venture out into the oceans in search of new ways to reach the spice-producing regions. So began the voyages of the Age of Discovery, and the era of corporate governance.

Admiral Van Neck would navigate by the sun and the stars. He had a compass for direction and an astrolabe to judge his relative latitude north and south by the position of the heavenly bodies above. But like all explorers at the time and for another 175 years, he had no way of judging his longitude, or relative position east and west, so no way of knowing how far he had traveled or how far he still had to go.

Van Neck would follow Vasco da Gama's route around the bottom of Africa in a wide sweeping arc toward the coast of Brazil that would loop around the bulge of Africa and far out to sea before turning back to the southeast. While it may have added hundreds of miles in distance, he was able to catch the currents and favorable trade winds and make very good time, reaching the tip of South Africa in only three months at sea. He still had another 10,000 miles to go.

As Van Neck rounded the Cape of Good Hope he was suddenly hit by a terrible storm that separated his ships and split his armada in half. Van Neck and three ships made it to a safe harbor on the eastern shore of Madagascar for repairs and to resupply the ships. He eventually regrouped with his other ships four months later on the Island of Java.

After just seven months at sea, cutting the first Dutch expedition time in half, Van Neck made it to Bantam, a trading city on the western edge of present day Java. He quickly formed an alliance with the Bantamese and had four ships loaded with pepper and other spices within a month. With pepper loaded and some assurance of profit for the company, he sent the four other ships on to the Spice Islands for Cinnamon and other spices that would add to their haul.

When the ships finally returned to Amsterdam, many of the investors in the Far-Distance Company became rich men. Enthusiastic investment, the dot-com explosion of its age, followed as many more people purchased stock in the new corporation, the Dutch East India Company, hoping to get rich quickly themselves. The atrocities of war and conquest, the subjugation of people, the decimation of entire cultures, and the lives of men, were not accounted for on the corporate balance sheet. It all went sight unseen to the investor buying stock. The management of the corporation was held accountable only to its share-holders and no one else, and its performance was judged solely by profit and loss.

The Far-Distance Company set the stage for an empire in the food industry. Like most multi-national corporations today, the Dutch East India Company took advantage of opportunities and became involved in other lucrative ventures like the silk and porcelain trade, but its primary business was always food additives and flavorings. Van Neck and The Far-Distance Company gave us the humble beginnings of the multi-national food corporation.

FOOD INC. IN A NUTSHELL

To give you some idea about how far Food, Incorporated has come since those early days, the current status and major problems with the global, industrial food complex follow now in rapid-fire succession. Get ready, I'm going to throw a lot at you in a dozen short paragraphs. In the coming chapters, you're going to learn about the important trends in the grow local, eat your view movement, but first we need a quick overview on the current state of things under our global food web. Hopefully you can use some of this stuff at your next "farm to table" dinner party (as if the swashbuckling stories of the early spice traders wasn't enough!).

Today, just ten multinational food corporations control most of the food that you eat or find in the local supermarket. These ten mega-corps, like Kraft and General Mills, own almost all the brands that you recognize and buy in the grocery store. There are roughly 138 people who sit on the boards of these ten global corporations and make all the decisions about the food we'll be having for dinner tonight.

Twenty percent (20%) of the food that Americans eat now comes from a foreign country. That's one out of every five bites that you take. Food now travels on massive container ships, trucks and airplanes thousands of miles, from all over the world in a global food web, to finally get to your dinner table. The average vegetable in your grocery store traveled 1500 miles to get there. That's the distance from New York City to Dallas. But a lot of it comes from much further away, like asparagus flown in from Argentina, blueberries from Chile, and beef from New Zealand. The food miles associated with one meal can equate to 25,000 miles, or the circumference of the earth.

If all the ingredients that really went into your supper were laid out on the table, there would be a hefty bowl of jet fuel and a jug of truck diesel sitting there, and plenty of CO_2 emissions for dessert. A couple cups of pesticides, herbicides, and fertilizers (made from fossil fuels) would also take their place at the table. It all goes sight unseen. We don't even think about it, but it's in there.

The modern, corporate-industrial food complex is like a well-oiled machine, with standardized, mechanized and controlled inputs and outputs, and centralized processing and distribution centers that deliver us human beings our daily allowance of protein, carbohydrates, vitamins and minerals. Truck- and train-loads of corn enter the massive machine at one end, and brightly colored pipes spew food products out the other end, like high-fructose corn syrup, modified corn starch, mono-, di- and triglycerides, xanthan gum, maltodextrin, lecithin and lactic acid. Even the glue used to seal the box that all this stuff goes into comes from corn. We eat and drink bushels of corn without even knowing it. God help us, it's even in beer. These easy sugars from corn in our processed foods are contributing to a serious obesity problem in the U.S. and around the world.

Like the clothing industry (and most other industries), the global corporate food industry chases cheap labor around the world, looking for ways to increase scale, reduce costs and improve profits. Capital flows from one region to another, and like migrant workers, capital can be easily picked up and moved to where resources and profit can be more efficiently extracted around the globe.

Just four companies produce almost all the chicken that we eat. Your chicken doesn't come from a pretty farm like the one pictured on the packaging. It came from a warehouse-looking structure where it spent eight short weeks growing up. Some chicken is now grown and slaughtered in the United States, then frozen and shipped on container ships to China where it is ground up and processed into chicken nuggets, with a little corn added for flavor and texture, and then sent back to us. These chickens have circled the globe, twice, and have traveled further than most Americans (lucky chickens).

Cattle are shipped to massive confined animal feed operations, or CAFO's in Kansas, where corn from other parts of the country is trucked in to feed them. Thousands of cows stand closely confined in knee deep mud and manure when it rains in this the far-away and mysterious land where almost all our meat comes from. Your hamburger might also come from Argentina or New Zealand, both huge exporters of beef to the United States. Meanwhile, the US ships a lot of our beef to a rapidly growing market in China.

There is one large processor that cleans, processes and packages almost all the spinach grown in California. It may package the spinach with different labels for different brands, but it all flows through this one massive facility. The risk of salmonella or other bacterial contamination at this one plant instantly becomes a national crisis if just one farm ships contaminated product to the facility, because from there, it goes everywhere. Because we've concentrated food processing and production, national outbreaks are becoming more frequent with regular food alerts and recalls in the national news; a big scare for Americans that can involve anything from swine to salads.

The centralization of food processing is a key to efficiencies of scale and reducing costs for food corporations in America. So is the growing of certain food commodities in centralized regions, like corn and soybeans in the Midwest. And while there used to be thousands of mills scattered throughout the US that could simply grind wheat for making bread, now just a few large facilities strategically located around the country grind most of the wheat. Small local and regional food processing centers, like facilities to grind wheat, process beef or make dairy products, have all but disappeared.

Farmers in the fields of the Midwest grow nothing but corn and soybeans, and generally can't support their families from it. Most farmers in America have working spouses and work other jobs themselves off the farm to pay the bills, and many are up to their eyeballs in debt. And they're getting older. The average age of a farmer in the United States is now almost 59 years old. Just 5.7 percent of American farmers are under the age of 35, and they face steep challenges accessing land, capital, knowledge and credit.

Corporate food processors, who do most of the bulk purchasing of farm products, along with the United States Department of Agriculture, started demanding that farmers "get big or get out" back in the 1960's and 70's, and thousands of small farms were swallowed up by larger corporate farms. It became a farm economy of size and scale, with the gathering of farm land into fewer and fewer hands. With the loss of thousands of small family farms, small towns and communities around the country were decimated. Without all the working farmers and families to shop in downtown stores, small towns began boarding up store fronts; a picture of rural, small town life that we're all accustomed to seeing now. And with the specialization of mono-cropping farms we abandoned the ancient knowledge, techniques and principles of diversity, of plants and animals and crop rotation, and we became a corn and soybean nation highly dependent on fossil fuels to do what nature used to do.

Our mono-cropping system of agriculture in America depletes the soils to such an extent that we are completely dependent on massive amounts of fertilizers (again—made from fossil fuels) to grow anything now. We need oil as much as we need food, must have it in fact even before we can eat. Food and fossil fuels have become locked in a dance where one is absolutely dependent on the other, and in turn our nation is dependent on other nations for that oil, and so our food. Over 60% of the oil that we use in America (and in our chemically intensive agricultural system) comes from a foreign nation. That has ramifications to our food safety and security.

While I can go without cinnamon, and even coffee for a while (I'd be a bit grumpy about that), I can live without it. But our complete and total dependence on a global food web is creating some serious risk if supply chains or distribution channels are ever disrupted. Threats exist that can take out oil refineries or the power grid, and whether that threat is a series of hurricanes, a solar flare, Russian hackers, or terrorists, certain events could be devastating to our national or regional food supply. The Pentagon has been conducting research related to another threat, and here's a new word, "agri-terrorism".

Americans are discovering that the industrial food complex is harmful to the planet and to human health, and it's simply not sustainable over the long term. It causes soil and water degradation with chemical run-off; it's fossil fuel intensive; and it consolidates power into just a few hands. Unhealthy processed foods are causing an obesity epidemic and a health care crisis. What all the above points to is this: All communities should regain some local capacity and the technical know-how to grow some food locally. It's called food sovereignty, food security and community resilience, and it's the prudent thing to do in an ever-changing world.

EAT YOUR VIEW

One hundred years ago a community could feed itself from local farms. With the growth of the industrial food complex, we're just not that self-reliant or resilient anymore when it comes to our food supply and food security as a nation, and much less so at the regional and local level.

We've all become completely disconnected from our food and where it comes from, and that's happened by corporate design. Just as Arab traders kept secret the source of the spice trade, Corporate America doesn't really want you to know where your chicken or your apple juice comes from. It can be a messy business, and many people don't want to know.

Most communities have lost the capacity (the farm land) and the technical know-how to grow and process food locally. But if we can just grow something locally, at least some small part of what we eat, we'll learn how to do it again as a community and retain some of the knowledge and food producing capacity for future generations. We can take back some power and control in our lives, and that improves our psychological health. It creates feelings of independence, freedom, self-reliance and self-esteem in the individuals growing the food and in entire communities sharing the food. We can change, as a community, ever so slightly, from just being consumers to becoming growers and producers.

We can gain more control simply by starting a backyard or community garden, purchasing local food at restaurants and the farmer's market, joining Community Supported Agriculture (CSA) programs, and just supporting local farmers in general. It's a way of standing up and becoming less dependent while we build strength at home, locally. If we do nothing, then we accept that we are vulnerable, helpless, dependent, and unable to provide for ourselves and our own basic needs for survival. Many now believe that is risky, irresponsible and short-sighted behavior, and that we need to take more responsibility for feeding ourselves and building our community resilience. Besides all that, it helps preserve and protect some of the pastoral beauty that we like to drive by.

What started with the Far-Distance Company has grown into a massive and complex industry that has removed food production from the local hands of the people and made us all vulnerable and dependent on far-away people and places for the basic necessities that support life. It's also made us unhealthier. An alarming 20 % of US children are now considered clinically obese. With diabetes and heart disease on the rise due to our unhealthy diets of processed foods, this is the first time in history that we can predict that our kids can expect a shorter life span than their parents.

Many people around the world are concerned about the globalization of our food supply, and the industrial food complex that controls it all, and this is one big reason for the organic, grow local and farm-to-table movement that is changing the way we eat in this country and around the world. It's also starting to determine where we choose to live.

Where we live and how we live can have the greatest impact on our health and life expectancy, and the built environment is just as important as modern health care facilities to our national health. We spend trillions on health care costs that keep rising and that are quickly becoming unsustainable for the long term. As the saying goes, an ounce of prevention is worth a pound of cure, and parks, walking trails and walkable communities are more important than pills when it comes to our overall national health. Education and access to healthier food is more important than innovations in open heart surgery over the long term. We can spend more on prevention through education and the built environment and save trillions in future health care costs.

As we're about to see, positive change is happening and it all started with a grass-roots movement. Well, actually it was kale, which kind of looks like grass, and tastes a little better.

CHAPTER ONE

THE AGRICULTURAL COMMUNITY

Agriculture is our wisest pursuit, because it will in the end contribute most to real wealth, good morals and happiness.
                    -Thomas Jefferson to George Washington, 1787

The organic, farm to table, "eat your view" movement has gone from niche to mainstream and changed restaurant menus across the country and around the world. Here's just one example from pop culture.

On an episode of the television show Portlandia, a young couple sits in a Portland restaurant about to order food from their waitress. The young woman asks the waitress a question about the chicken on the menu.

"Is it USDA organic, or Oregon organic, or Portland organic?"

The waitress replies, "It's all of that, across the board."

She leaves briefly and returns with piece of paper that includes a picture and a short bio on the chicken.

"This is the chicken that you'll be enjoying tonight," says the waitress. "His name is Collin."

She continues to describe the chicken's happy life roaming freely with his friends on a four-acre pasture 30 minutes outside of Portland. Collin ate sheep's milk, soy and hazelnuts.

The young man asks, "Were the hazelnuts local?"

He later asks, "Do you know these people? This farm isn't run by some guy on a yacht in Miami, is it?"

The couple then asks the waitress to hold their table while they leave to go check out the farm.

While Portlandia pokes fun at Portland's long-standing reputation for liberal environmentalism, this little skit highlights a trend that is influencing our national food culture. The organic and grow local movement has gone mainstream everywhere.

In the town where I live, Asheville, North Carolina, a sizeable proportion of the restaurants now promote local and organic food on their menus. They may not post a picture of the chicken you'll be eating (thank goodness) but they often list the name of the farm that supplies the meat and produce, and sometimes show a picture of the farm and farmer that grew the food.

One evening in July of 2014, as I sat eating my organic-free-range-local-chicken, let's call her Stella, at a trendy Asheville restaurant, I had to ask myself, "Why was all of this happening?"

What's more, I paid $32 for my chicken. Other people were obviously quite willing to pay that because the restaurant was popular and always busy. But it was happening all over the place. In fact, there are over 100 restaurants and bakeries in Asheville and nearby that promote locally sourced food, which usually comes with, if only slightly, higher prices.

The rapid growth of Whole Foods and stores like it also gives evidence to this movement. Farmers markets are part of the same trend, and they're sprouting up everywhere. The number of farmers markets across the United States has skyrocketed. The US in 2016 had an estimated 8,669 farmers markets in operation, which represents a fivefold increase since 1994, when there were only 1,755 of them.[1] The Asheville area has fifteen farmer's markets operating on different days and at various locations.

Community Supported Agriculture (CSA) programs are a newer trend, and there are over 40 of them operating now around Asheville. In a CSA, people buy a "share" from a farmer at the beginning of the season and pick up a box of fresh, organic vegetables from the farm or a pick-up location every week.

Yes, it's about healthier organic food without all the chemicals. And yes, it's about supporting local farms and farmers. But what's behind it all? What's really driving it? It didn't make economic sense.

I've spent my career in business developing and selling hundreds of products for different markets, but I would never have had the nerve to slap a price sticker on a carton of eggs that was more than double the competition. This trend didn't seem sustainable from a business economics standpoint, not for the long run anyway. To use less efficient production methods to produce product at a significantly higher cost and retail runs contrary to the normal business principles that I'm familiar with.

I was about to learn some different principles were at work here, and clearly a lot of people are perfectly willing to pay a much higher price for an egg, a tomato, or a chicken. I have noticed that sometimes the chicken at Whole Foods comes with a pretty picture of a farm on the packaging, and I started to wonder if the organic chicken farmer wasn't really selling chicken. He's selling an idea, or a lifestyle, or a principle, or beliefs and values, or something else.

How do you price that? The question throws economists for a loop. They don't have a model for that. People who shop at

Whole Foods jokingly refer to it as "Whole Paycheck", but they still shop there. This must drive economists nuts.

Take everything that you know about the local food scene and the farm to table movement and stretch it to the extreme. What do you end up with?

Rather than bringing food to where the people are, save the 1,500 miles and bring the people to where the food is. In fact, plant them right in the middle of it with the tomatoes and onions. Call it "hyper-local." This is where the local food movement is going, and it's called the agricultural neighborhood, or agrihood. Why bring the farm to the table when you can bring the table to the farm?

It's been twelve years since Michael Pollan published The Omnivores Dilemma and first opened our eyes to the modern problems of the industrial food complex. Over that time the grow local and farm to table movement has exploded and changed our food choices and is now affecting our food culture and even determining where and how we live.

This is the story of my journey through the process of trying to create a new type of agricultural community where an organic farm takes center stage and residents gain a closer connection to food, nature and the environment. I wasn't trying to build Utopia; just a community that was a little more connected to food and farming. I had been lucky and successful in my business career but had no experience in new urban planning or design, only a desire to find a more sustainable way for people to live closer to nature and food production, and so I risked everything, including millions of dollars, in this new model for living called the Agrihood.

While doing research for this new community I met an extraordinary group of farmers and growers who perfectly illustrate what sustainable living close to the farm looks like. I discovered that the growing, processing and celebration of food creates the connection points that build healthy communities. Living closer to food production, the community becomes immersed in the working organic farm and intimate with the farmers who work there. I'll describe the pains and pitfalls of trying to create such a food-centric community, and the beauty and joy of finally achieving a more sustainable community model with a little help from neighboring farms and farmers.

The grow local movement in America is a sign that people are recognizing the health and environmental perils of corporate agri-business (and other extractive institutions) and we're now beginning to establish new forms of food webs and lifestyles based on different values and connections. Those involved in the grow local crusade give us a better understanding of how to create a healthier and more sustainable planet. They define a values-based and principle-centered approach to food that can restore our health and create a more robust food system for future generations.

We'll see the importance of developing the infrastructure and human capital that is at the root of healthy, sustainable living, and the result is a guidebook to creating more connected communities. And while this book describes in some detail the concepts related to building an agriculturally-based community, it also describes in some detail the reasons for it. Our current global, industrial food web needs to change, must change in fact, for it to endure and feed a growing global population over the next 30 to 50 years. We are going to hit our planetary limit at some point, sooner or later, because the current global, extractive food system is not sustainable for the long term simply because it's highly dependent on fossil fuels. The good news is that there are other healthier ways to grow food, healthier for humans and healthier for biological ecosystems that support the process.

This book describes a new agricultural community that is closely connected to an organic farm and the farming lifestyle in the Appalachian Mountains of Western North Carolina. I didn't come up with the idea for building an agrihood. Others had already started to blaze that trail. And really, I just saw it as the natural extension of an already booming grow local, farm to table movement going on everywhere around the world. I saw good reasons for building it and for taking on the financial risk. They were the same reasons people shop at farmers markets, and they are directly related to a concern over our current industrial food complex and the desire for long term safe, secure and healthy food systems. I just didn't know at the time if the concept would work and if people would actually buy into it and move there. It was risky business.

And while this book describes in some detail the nuts and bolts of building a full-blown agricultural community, the ideas and principles behind it can be applied to your own backyard garden or starting a small community garden in your neighborhood. It has been proven in study after study, including a 2018 report by the World Health Organization, that the two most important things that affect health and a longer life are diet and exercise. The modern, industrial food complex that includes processed foods and harmful additives is having a devastating affect on our national health. Obesity rates are skyrocketing along with diabetes and heart disease in an unsustainable health care system. Rather than treating symptoms, we need to focus on the solution; healthy diets and a little exercise. It all starts in a garden.

While the average vegetable in the produce section of your grocery store travels 1,500 miles to get there, a lot of our food comes from much further away, like asparagus from Argentina or chicken from China, and one-fifth of our food is imported from outside the country. As surprising as it may seem, we're not that self-reliant as a nation when it comes to our food, and much less so at the regional or local level.

Just one hundred years ago, most communities could feed themselves from local farms in the area. That's not true today. Food production and processing centers are now centralized in faraway places. The growth of multi-national food corporations and the industrial food complex over the last half of the 20th century has completely disconnected most of us from our food and where it comes from. Most people today, and most communities where they live, are incapable of growing their own food anymore on any kind of scale.

Even in largely agricultural states like Iowa, 80 to 90 percent of the food they eat there is imported from outside the state.[2] Most farmers in Iowa can't even feed his own family off the farm because he's growing a huge monocrop of corn or soybeans, and nothing else. It's becoming more and more evident with the rise of Big Ag that we need more local food security and food sovereignty over the basic commodities of life, and this is driving the grow local movement.

As we begin to understand the failings and health problems associated with the food and agriculture systems that were developed in the 20th century, it's become increasingly evident that we need an entirely new approach to food, and how and where we grow it. At the same time, we need to develop community infrastructures so that they can withstand the threats related to climate change. Entire regions of the country are completely disconnected from food production and entirely dependent on importing food from across the United States and other countries around the world.

This is the story of my three-year journey, as a novice farmer-developer with more money and passion than brains, trying to build a more sustainable and resilient, agriculturally-based community. It presents a business model for building an agrihood and describes the reasons or motivations why some people might want to live there. It's not a book about development. It's about mindful development. Justifiable development. It's about protecting and preserving some farm land and the food producing capacity of a region.

Here's one reason why some people might choose to live there. Our current food system is controlled by a surprisingly small number of individuals (fewer than 150) who sit on the boards of a very small number of multi-national corporations (just 10) and is based on massive inputs of petroleum (a limited resource), chemicals and corn. This small group of people likely come from the same educational, economic and social circles, and their decisions and actions are driven by one concern; profit for shareholders. The same is true in every industry, and we shouldn't really expect anything else.

Many people believe now that we need more people involved in the decisions and production of food for our own health and food security. Grass-roots, alternative food systems were first developed in response to the concern over Big Ag and included the rapid growth of organic food and the means to distribute that food through the "grow local" and farm to table channels at restaurants, farmers markets and CSA programs across the country. These efforts helped to build some food security and put food sovereignty back into the local community and economy. People began to understand that we need to bring food production closer to where it is consumed, and more under the control of those consumers.

People also began to understand that local food is much healthier and better for the environment. Transportation makes up over 30% of the harmful CO_2 levels in the atmosphere. Local growers under the watchful eyes of the people who will be consuming that produce are less likely to dump tons of chemicals onto it unnecessarily. If it's organic, that problem is solved, and just about all small farms growing for local distribution are growing organically. And the food of course is much fresher and healthier because it didn't travel the 1500 miles to get to you.

The goal of sustainable agriculture is to meet society's food needs now in the present without compromising the ability of future generations to meet their own needs. Conventional farming is fossil fuel intensive and uses massive quantities of chemical pesticides and herbicides that kill more than just a targeted pest, they kill just about everything in the soil. They deplete the soil of valuable organisms and nutrients, rendering it lifeless, dead. Sustainable agriculture works to improve the quality of the soil by building up organic matter, helpful organisms and nutrients. Sustainable agriculture is farming based on an understanding of ecosystems and the study of relationships between organisms and their environment. It's about building the long-term health of the soil and surrounding environment in symbiotic relationships that benefit all life.

Perhaps the biggest benefit to local food is that it protects local farms and our local farming capacity, and it preserves the technical knowledge and capability of growing food for future generations. It also preserves much of the rural, pastoral beauty of the region because a working, profitable farm is at less risk for development and the effects of suburban sprawl. A community closely connected to farming and nature is also a happier place to live for many people that might enjoy connections to a more agrarian lifestyle.

The grow local movement is not exactly new, but the trend has gone from niche to mainstream over the last decade. It's time urban planners and developers realized how big and important the trend is and got on board with it. As we'll see, they can play a big role in the future of farming and food, as surprising as that may sound.

As part of my initial research into developing a more food-centered community that would be closely connected to farming and agriculture, I went to a place where small communities have been living this lifestyle for hundreds, even thousands of years.

During the summer of 2015, I went on a farm tour through Italy with my friend Alberto. Alberto Cirri is an opinionated Italian environmentalist, avid hiker, foodie, and part-time organic gardener. One day we stopped in a small café in the Tuscan town of Greve in Chianti. I don't speak Italian, so I just sat quietly and watched my friend Alberto get into an argument with the waiter over what wine to bring us for lunch.

The discussion started off cordial and pleasant enough, and

I knew they were friends because they man-hugged each other when we came in and chatted for a few moments at the front door with big smiles on their faces.

For lunch, Alberto and I each decided to have a simple margarite pizza, and I could tell this part of the order was placed without incident. The waiter wrote it down without further discussion. But when it came to ordering some wine, I could hear their Italian get louder and faster and I could tell things were starting to escalate by the tone of their voices.

It was hot outside, although it was nice and cool in the café, but still it was hot outside, so that might have had some play in this conversation. It was about two o'clock in the afternoon, so a late lunch, which also would probably have some effect on the outcome here, I don't know. A margarite pizza should have made it a no-brainer, but too many variables were coming into play with the heat outside and the time of day and the pizza and a wine book that was four inches thick.

They each took turns flipping pages and pointing at the wine menu and using some sort of superlative. I think the real problem was that they knew many of these wineries personally, because many were local, and they knew the owners, and knew the soil types and weather patterns, and had intimate knowledge of the operations, and so the discussion involved too much information (and opinion). They would not take this decision lightly, but thankfully, after several minutes, they settled on a cold prosecco before things got out of control, and the waiter walked away a little angry. This is what it's like eating with Alberto in Italy.

There is no question that Italians know how to eat. And they eat a lot differently than Americans; they take food very seriously. Dinners with Alberto could last two hours or more, which left me plenty of time to get up from the table to stretch my legs and step outside to check out the street life while Alberto chatted in Italian with a waiter or the restaurant owner. I always enjoyed just hanging out in some doorway watching life go by in another language.

We usually stopped to eat in small rural farming villages off the beaten path and away from most of the tourist traffic. Between courses or after dinner, I would step outside to observe the goings on and I would almost always spot a farmer on a tractor up on a hillside above the village or somewhere off in the distance. Sometimes I'd see a truck in a field not too far away and workers bringing in grapes or some other produce.

Standing on a street corner at the intersection of two narrow cobblestone streets, in the smallest Italian village, a farmer would inevitably drive by me on an old tractor pulling a cart or trailer full of vegetables or hay or something else. In late summer and fall, in the wine country, the cart was always full of grapes. These were agricultural communities, and the main street was an artery for farm traffic between fields and barns and wineries, and probably had been for hundreds of years. These were also food resilient communities. If the gas pumps stopped working, plenty of food could still easily make its way into town.

I was traveling with Alberto through the rural parts of Tuscany and Umbria researching a new trend in tourism, called agricultural tourism, or in Italian, the Agritourismo. Over the past several years vacationers have been spending a great deal of money to stay on a farm in this region of Italy. It's also popular now in many other places around Europe. Hundreds of small farms in Italy have set up B&B's for guests, and some farms have accommodations that can be likened to three-star hotels with comparable prices.

There are now several web sites that cater solely to agricultural tourism in Italy, and these sites can help you book a room at a perfect little farm, with rolling fields and wonderful pastoral views, an old barn, chickens and all the trappings of rural farm life. I wanted to understand why this crazy trend was happening and why it was becoming so popular, and Alberto volunteered to be my guide.

On several occasions Alberto and I ate meals at small farms in the countryside. Many farm owners in rural parts of Italy prepare meals with produce right off the farm. Providing meals and accommodations for visitors to spend the evening is a smart way to supplement income on a farm in some of the more picturesque regions of Tuscany. At places like this we'd have a chance to walk around and watch the old farm workers with their big hands working in the fields nearby. At the end of the day the farm workers would sometimes join us for a glass of wine and maybe have dinner, and we would talk about the weather, what was coming up in the fields, and what projects they were working on.

The farm workers hands were always big and dark and wrinkled from the sun, and the hands always looked much older than the man who owned them. After watching them hard at work in the fields, I could see that farming, the kind of farming that they did, small scale with a lot of hand tools, was not an easy occupation. It was labor intensive for sure, and I would ask myself, "Why would people do this work? Wouldn't it be easier doing something else? Who in their right mind would want to be a small-scale farmer?" Most of these farm workers that we met joked and laughed a lot, and they all seemed happy enough and I guess that is all that really matters.

In agri-tourism, it seems some people want to enjoy a simpler lifestyle down on the farm, more connected to food and to nature, even if it's only for a weekend holiday. As it turns out, this same trend toward paying and staying on a farm is growing quickly in the US, where it's often referred to as "Farm Stays."

The agri-tourism trend is also closely related to the farm to table movement at restaurants and farmers markets around the world. People are trying to find connections to food and where it comes from, and they're doing that in a myriad of different ways. I think it's probably because we've become so disconnected from our food in modern society.

As I traveled with Alberto through so many of these small Italian farming villages, many of them dating back a thousand years or more, I began to look at these places a little differently. I began to see these ancient little towns as really nothing more than big food machines. For hundreds of years, village life was all about the growing, processing, distribution and preparation of food that came from the fields that surrounded the village. The farmer, the butcher, the grinder of wheat, and the baker were cogs in the machine, and you could witness the wheels turning as you walked down the street.

Food is the one key consumable that we can't live without, the most important product a town or village could produce and distribute, and so its primary function. People crammed inside the city walls for protection, and farms circled the town, from where farmers would bring their produce into town for processing and distribution. People weren't that far removed from it, like we are now.

Just a couple hundred years ago, one farmer was able to feed about 10 people, and depending on how many kids he had, that freed up as many as nine other people to do other stuff. Today an American farmer feeds an average of 129 people. What has also radically changed is the distance that food travels to get to your plate.

The good news is that the current industrial food complex is at odds with another more positive trend that is happening now in America. The rapid growth in the organic and 'farm to table' movement at restaurants, farmers markets and community supported agriculture programs is a sign that people are waking up to the problem and beginning to understand the importance of healthy, local food. The growth of Whole Foods and grocery stores like it is another positive sign of change. But how far would this movement really go? Would it actually begin to determine where people choose to live?

BUILDING THE AGRIHOOD

The agricultural neighborhood, or "agrihood," is a new concept in urban design where an organic farm and agriculture are built right into the community as a central feature and amenity. And for the people who want to reconnect to the farm and the bucolic lifestyle that it represents, this newest trend, the agricultural community, is a way to help them to do just that: plug in instantly.

When I first heard about the agrihood concept, I must admit that I thought the idea was a little crazy. It was so new and novel that it seemed way out there in the stratosphere. I'd seen how hard small-scale farming was in Italy and elsewhere. And at first, I couldn't see a connection between urban planning and this hard work of growing food. I couldn't yet see agriculture as any kind of real estate amenity, like a swimming pool, golf course or tennis courts. That was until I learned what the agricultural community is really all about. In an agrihood, you don't actually have to do any work, because farmers do it for you; you just sit on the porch, drink a glass of wine, and watch the corn grow. Now that's different. That's pretty cool, I thought, I could do that; I did that in Italy and I got pretty good at it.

You can always help out on the farm if you want to or stroll through the vegetable garden to see what's coming up, but the heavy lifting is done by people who know what they're doing, and they get paid to do it. There's no commitment from residents, other than just buying and eating the food through a CSA program.

The agricultural community promises fresh air, pastoral views of beautiful rolling farm land, a connection to nature and to where our food comes from, a clean and healthy environment, and fresh, healthy organic food. Most importantly, it offers closer connections to the environment and a more sustainable food web. If that's not your thing, then you probably wouldn't want to live there.

An agricultural community can have other amenities, of course, like a pool or tennis courts. You're not moving to the middle ages, for goodness sake. And yes, there can even be a pool bar. In fact, an organic farm can be added to the other amenities that might be planned in any wellness development, like the hiking trails and the exercise center. But it's the newest trend in urban planning and design because it's the natural progression of a much larger food trend happening in America. It's the other half of the health and wellness equation that most wellness communities are missing—the food. Total wellness is about a healthy diet and exercise, not just the exercise.

A true agricultural community has a working farm at its center, with all the activities related to organic farming going on in real time in and around the community for all to see and partake in, if they wish. Real farmers do all the hard work, but residents are welcome to help out in the vegetable gardens for exercise and enjoyment. Or they can just walk down to the garden to sit and chat with neighbors or the farmer for a while. It's entirely up to them.

THE GROWING TREND

The trend toward building the agrihood is new, but there are some good examples of agricultural communities already under development. There's somewhere between 150 and 250 agrihoods that are built or under development, depending on how you define an agrihood, or to what extent farming is a central feature of the development. While there have been several stories in the media about the agrihood concept, probably because of the novelty of the whole idea I suppose, I liked one article that describes some of the 'high-end' properties in a Wall Street Journal story by Amy Gamerman in March 2018. I think it's just interesting to see where the high-end is for a life on the farm. Think of it as an episode of "Lifestyles of the Rich and Famous Farmers" where you'll meet glamourous people in fabulous places, and eat squash.[3]

While my little agrihood at Creekside Farm is a smaller example of the agrihood concept, one of the largest agriculturally based communities is at Rancho Mission Viejo in California that is a booming 23,000-acre project and includes organic fruit orchards, vegetable farms, and a large-scale cattle ranching operation. Over 17,000 acres are being preserved as open space, with 6000 acres under development for residential and mixed-use villages and towns. The scope of the project is enormous.

Eventually some 14,000 homes will be built. Schools, parks, clubhouses and retail centers are planned. The first phase of this development includes over 900 homes and two communal farms, and yes, they even have chickens. The homes are already sold out in the first phase. The second phase is underway and includes over 2,500 homes, with home prices ranging from $400,000 to over $1 million. This may be the largest agrihood development so far.

Perhaps the first real agrihood to be purposely built was a community outside of Chicago called Prairie Crossing. Located in Grays Lake, Illinois, the project started in 1992, and a 100-acre working, organic farm has been in operation on the property since 1993. The land that is Prairie Crossing was purchased in 1987 by a group of neighbors who wanted to preserve open space and agricultural land. They formed a company with the goal of developing the 677 acres responsibly, with a total of only 359 single-family homes and 36 condominiums (as opposed to 2,400 homes that were planned by another developer).

Probably the best known agrihood is Serenbe, outside of Atlanta, because it's been featured on NBC Nightly News, CBS Sunday Morning and numerous print media including The New York Times. Serenbe is a 1,000-acre development that currently has over 200 homes with a lot more on the way, and includes village like town centers that include retail, art spaces and three restaurants. The project has plans for a total of 1,200 residential homes, and a 25-acre farm, professionally managed, is the centerpiece of the community and operates a farmer's market and CSA program. Housing is condensed on smaller lots leaving more room for open space and walking trails through wooded landscapes. Lots range from $150,000 to over $400,000 with finished homes from $470,000 to $1.4 million. The development has already proved very successful and shows that people are willing to pay a premium for nature, open space and a working, organic farm in the neighborhood.

At the very high end of agrihood developments is the Kukulula Resort on the Hawaiian Island of Kauai. It's a "luxury agrihood" with a pick-your-own 7-acre orchard including mangos and other tropical fruits and a 6-acre organic farm at its center. Homes can range from $1.5 million to $15 million. I'd call that high-end.

This upscale agrihood project gives residents unlimited picking rights of fruits, microgreens, berries and flowers. At some of the newest upscale agrihoods like Kukulula, where people may want their own garden but don't have the time or inclination to keep it up, concierge watering and weeding services are provided, for a fee of course. Resident chefs give cooking lessons and demonstrations on how to prepare the bounty of the garden, which also could be private affairs in your own home.

Kukulula is a 1,010-acre development that grows five different types of bananas that you won't normally find in the grocery store, along with a lot of other tropical fruit. Want a smoothie? Go pick it. The farm also includes raised vegetable beds, chickens and a "superfoods" garden area with goji berries, gotu kola and turmeric among other healthy and unique plants. Residents are even provided rubber boots and bags to pick their own food in the orchards and gardens, or they can just stop by a refrigerator near the farm and pick up any fruits, veggies or flowers that they want from there. Residents pay a one-time $50,000 membership fee and about $26,000 in annual dues. Yes, I just said that. That's definitely high-end.

The project begs the question, how high is high-end when it comes to developing an agrihood, and who is the customer base for this kind of connection to farming and food. It shows us that it's not just poor, young, free-spirited homesteaders. The customer base can be diverse and varied at all income levels and backgrounds.

Miralon is another upscale agrihood development in Palm Springs, California that is turning an old golf course into agriculture. That's right, plowing under the fairways to grow 45 acres of olive trees that will be pressed for olive oil for the residents living there. The development will include 1150 homes and the old golf cart paths will be repurposed as walking trails through the orchard.

The list of agriculturally-based communities goes on with many creative people getting involved in the planning and development of projects like this. At many agrihoods, residents can pick from a menu of services or "agrarian upgrades." For instance, at Hudson Woods, a 131-acre development in the Catskills, residents can have their own small orchard for about $16,000 that includes 10 fruit trees, planted, mulched, irrigated and fenced off. And for $15,500 they can get a master gardener to plant a 20 x 30 organic garden on their own property with three months of complimentary weeding and watering services.

A new community called Harvest is a $1 Billion (I capitalized the "B"), 12,000-acre master-planned development in Argyle and Northlake, Texas. The development will include 3,200 single-family homes with 120 acres set for mixed use and high density living. It will include a professionally managed farm and two community garden areas for residents to play in the dirt. Harvest will also rent raised garden beds to residents so they can have their own rich spot of earth. Harvest's farm currently sells food to over 30 restaurants in the Dallas-Fort Worth area, so the farm is already very productive and generating revenue. Homes range from $300,000 to $550,000.

The Creekside Farm agricultural neighborhood is incorporated into a high-end wellness community, The Cliffs at Walnut Cove, and deserves to be included in this survey of high-end agrihoods. Walnut Cove is a 2000-acre, 600-home development started in 2005 with home sites ranging from $180,000 to more than $1 million, and homes and townhomes ranging from $850,000 to $5 million and up. Walking trails inside the community wander past pristine creeks and waterfalls, and if that's not enough, the famous Blue Ridge Parkway is right outside the gates and offers easy access to hundreds of miles of walking trails and waterfalls scattered through the southern Appalachian Mountains. A wellness center includes indoor and outdoor pools, hot tub, tennis courts, massage and sauna rooms, state of the art weight and cardio equipment, and various yoga, pilates and fitness classes and programs. A signature Jack Nicklaus golf course offers terrific views of the surrounding mountains, and the development includes two restaurants that feature food grown within the community. It's mountain country living that happens to be just 4 miles from Biltmore Park Town Square with restaurants, shopping, and movie theaters. It's also just 15 minutes to hip downtown Asheville.

Six acres of vegetable gardens and an adjacent 45-acre farm with livestock creates the farm living experience at Walnut Cove. The farm and vegetable gardens are supported through a CSA program that costs resident members $750 for the growing season, and they pick up their fresh veggies every week at a community center that includes a commercial kitchen for cooking and canning classes and regularly scheduled farm to table meals.

All these communities are good examples of how a developer can leverage food as a community feature and create jobs for farmers at the same time. It's a win-win for everyone. Investments in food related business can support a developer's bottom line. It just takes a little creativity and the right partnerships with farmers, growers and food groups in the broader community.

Because I used some high end agrihoods as examples above, the question will naturally arise, is this concept just for wealthy people? Are the well-to-do the only ones who can afford healthy hyper-local food? Local and organic food is going to be more expensive than industrial produce because it's more labor intensive, so, can middle-class and low-income people afford it? I'll answer these questions more thoroughly later in the book, but here are just a couple of points related to the subject.

A garden can pop up anywhere, in any community, if there are people to work it and the infrastructure to support it, including in middle class neighborhoods or even on vacant lots in inner-city neighborhoods. You'll get to visit some of these gardens, and meet the people who work them, a little later.

People at all income levels shop at farmers markets and Whole Foods. A lot of those decisions on where to shop are based on values and what people believe is important. Many are spending a higher percentage of their disposable income on higher priced food, but for their own good reasons.

I'll use craft beer as an example from the food and beverage world. Many people are choosing to spend a little more on local and craft beers. The local and craft beer industry is exploding, and local breweries have popped up in most mid-sized towns. The trend is hurting the large conventional breweries like Anheuser-Bush and brands like Budweiser. It has to do with taste for certain, and it's usually a bolder, more vibrant and fuller flavor with craft and local beers, but the rapid rise in craft beer is also based on the belief in supporting a local business and taking some pride in that local brand. The same can be applied to locally produced food, and the value-added flavor and freshness that comes with it. People willingly spend a little more on craft beer, and a lot of people spend a little more on healthy, fresh, local food. They take pride in their community of growers.

Local food is a booming business now. Sales grew in the US from $5 billion in 2008 to over $12 billion in 2014, more than doubling in just six years. Sales are projected to hit $20 billion by 2019.[4] The National Restaurant Association has reported that 68 percent of consumers would be more likely to eat at a restaurant that offers locally sourced and produced food.[5] A survey of professional chefs found that locally sourced meat, fish and produce, tied to environmental sustainability, were the top "menu trends" in 2016.[6] Millennials are a key driving force in this local, healthy food movement. They prefer spending their money on experiences, like dining out, rather than on just buying stuff, and they typically dine out 3-4 times a week.

Local food strengthens the overall local economy as money circulates several more times through the community rather than going straight off to some corporate headquarters. And while local food only accounts for about 2 percent of the total food purchases right now, food in general is big business. Even in economically stressed Detroit, for example, the food system accounts for $3.6 billion in revenue and employs over 36,000 people, making it the third largest industry in the city. If the number of people now buying local food increased by just 30 percent, the food system would become the second largest industry in Detroit because of the increase in jobs and revenue for the growers, suppliers and distributors. But what's really striking about Detroit is that the public-school system now buys 22 percent of its produce from Michigan farms, and has been working with local producers and growers to build supply chains and the infrastructure that includes helping small farmers learn how to package and sell their products to larger institutions.[7] Food plays an important part in the local economy everywhere, and it takes an entire community to raise a farmer.

More people are now growing their own food at home. In a five-year period, from 2010 to 2015, the number of households growing food at home or in community gardens more than doubled, from 17% to 35% of households. It's a growing hobby and interest for about a third of all households.[8] It makes sense for developers to set aside some common area for a community garden simply because it would appeal to a third of their client base.

The number of farmers markets across the United States is now approaching 9,000. If a developer does nothing else, build near a farmer's market, or allow one in the parking lot on Saturday mornings. Leverage the demand. It's a key benefit for potential home buyers.

Having a "third place" to go (after home, 1, and work, 2) is more important to more people now given the way the internet has changed our shopping experience and the time we used to spend doing that. People aren't going to the shopping mall like they used to. A farm or community garden can be, and is for many communities, that third place, a place where people want to spend time enjoying the outdoors and socializing with others. It can change the entire culture of a neighborhood, and certainly is a tool to differentiate a developer's real estate product.

Some studies show that property values of homes and lots adjacent to parks and open space, which could include organic farms or community gardens, are 15 to 30 percent higher than similar lots without these amenities nearby.[9] Once again, a developer can leverage food-based amenities to create real estate value, at the same time promoting economic development for the local food industry, improving environmental sustainability and community resilience, and, last but not least, improving overall public health by creating access to healthier food. It differentiates your project from all the rest and creates a market advantage. It's smart business to go green. Leverage the demographics and market trends.

Let me stop here and explain something. I use coarse terms like real estate product, market advantage and leveraging demand in a discussion related to agrarianism and agrarian values that will probably shock and dismay some environmentalists and lovers of nature, but unless a project is profitable, and we put it in terms that investors and developers understand, it won't get built. The goal is building communities that are more connected to nature, farming and healthy food production, but it has to make financial sense.

SAY GOODBYE TO IOWA

The agrihood is all about protecting and preserving farm land, and I will propose later a minimum of farm land that should be set aside in a project. For years, many people have watched as farms in their communities have turned into new housing developments and strip malls. Most people have seen farmland vanish before their eyes as a new development sprouted up, but there's not been a lot of hard facts about the demise of the family farm; mostly just a lot of anecdotal evidence.

But now, with the release of a recent study called "Farms Under Threat: The State of America's Farmland," we have some proof and hard evidence about the disappearance of America's farmland. This study by American Farmland Trust (AFT) gives us some pretty clear evidence about the loss of farmland over the past 20 years.

In the most comprehensive study ever undertaken about America's loss of agricultural lands, using current technologies like high-res satellite imaging, the researchers show that nearly twice the area of farmland was lost over two decades than was previously thought or known. The study shows that between 1992 and 2012, the United States lost nearly 31 million acres of land to development. That's 175 acres an hour, or 3 acres every single minute.

That 31 million acres is equivalent to losing most of Iowa or all of New York state to development in a 20-year period. And importantly, 11 million of those acres were among the best farmland in the nation; land that is classified as the most productive and most versatile land, like the rich farmland in the Midwest. That equates to losing half of Indiana.

The study also showed that development disproportionately occurred on agricultural lands, with 62 percent of all development occurring on farmland (versus wooded or unfarmed open space). It also showed that expanding urban areas with higher density housing accounted for 59 percent of the farmland loss. Low-density residential development, or the building of houses on one to 20-acre parcels, accounted for the other 41 percent of the farmland loss.[10]

With suburban sprawl and the growth of major metropolitan areas, the U.S. is becoming more urban—at an average rate of about 1 million additional acres a year. That's the equivalent of adding a new urban area the size of Los Angeles, Houston and Phoenix combined, every year. Urban areas in the United States have more than quadrupled in size since

1945. Most of the land used for this growth came from farm land as cities spread out.[11]

I don't proclaim here that the agrihood concept is the only way to save some of this farm land. It's just a model of development that might, just maybe, protect and preserve some of it. It might encourage young farmers to take up the trade. It might help to build communities centered around healthy food production. But unless you put the concept into business and financial terms that a developer or planner can understand, and show that there's profit in it, it won't get built, and the land in its entirety will get developed with no consideration of the possible amenity of farming and local food production.

The agrihood model is one way to set aside some of that open land for future generations of farmers and provide a valuable amenity for current residents. With a growing US population, and an exploding population in some regions of the country, you can't stop development. People need a place to live. But we can offer an alternative to developers that includes the preservation of some farm land and food production.

Building a true agrihood doesn't just mean setting aside a large chunk of land and throwing some seeds out. It means building a place around food, and includes the planning for processing, sales and distribution of food. It requires a new way of thinking about food and economic development at the local level. It includes not just small scale, artisan agriculture and the growing of healthier food that tastes better, but the project must include a plan for the cleaning and washing, processing, packaging, refrigeration, storage/warehousing, marketing, promotion, distribution, wholesaling and finally retailing the product. It's a lot to handle for a small grower or farmer, and developers can help because they have the people, planning and building experience, and most importantly, the capital to make it all happen.[12]

The agrihood requires an entirely new system that includes building infrastructure, purchasing equipment and facilities, and developing sales and distribution channels that include farmers markets, restaurants and institutional buyers at schools, hospitals and other food wholesalers and distributors. Developers have the financial wherewithal and business experience to help growers navigate the obstacles of setting up a new kind of farming operation. And most importantly, they can bring a new segment of customers in the form of the residents of a new community who have an interest in local food.

The developer is instrumental in weaving the sustainable agriculture feature into the social and economic fabric of the community through urban planning and design. It's a way to invite people back into the agricultural framework to participate in food and agriculture as an important and satisfying part of lifestyle, and not just for sustenance, but for psychological health and well-being; let's call that happiness.

So it is that the real estate industry finds itself in a unique position to affect the natural environment in a different way. It's in a position to affect food production, sustainability, safety and security. Who would have figured that 10 years ago? The real estate industry can actually do something good for public health and the environment. It can preserve farm land. It can give farmers a job. It can help to reduce the use of fossil fuels and limit CO_2 levels in the atmosphere. It can support sustainable agriculture and it can turn a profit.

The investment in food production and distribution can affect the developer's bottom line, while improving and beautifying the environment. An investment in agriculture and food production adds value while building a sense of attachment to the land and the project, and it builds community social ties at the same time. The project can go further to provide nutrition and cooking education programs with the goal of improving public health. It can be a place that demonstrates how communities can be built to adapt to the threats of climate change and reduce our dependency on fossil fuels. It can help to provide some healthy food options to low income households through the sharing of produce from the farm and gardens. By financially supporting the start-up of a farming operation the project can have a lasting impact on a much wider region in some very positive ways.

An integral aspect of the agrihood is the farm and the farmer. In most regions around the country, it's quite easy to find young farmers willing to do the work necessary in an agricultural community. It happens to be many of the same people that you see at your local farmers markets. They're the leaders in the healthy food, grow local movement, and they want to do this work because it represents a lifestyle choice that they're looking for. Because of land prices and startup costs, it's very difficult for these young farmers and growers to get started in the business of producing food, and this is where the developers of an agrihood can really help, because they can offer the farm land at no cost and attract the customers.

Farming and growing food are not just about making a living for many of these local growers, but it's really about making a life. The two things can be intertwined, and many people with deep connections to the earth and agriculture are learning how to do that. Agriculture in the end is really a lifestyle choice. The agrihood can offer young farmers or people willing to learn the trade an opportunity to make a living while living this agrarian lifestyle. It gives them the land to work and the customers and income to support themselves. The financial difficulties of starting a small farm business are significant for a new, young farmer, and the agrihood concept can help get someone going.

To be clear, it's possible to simply add a vegetable garden to an existing wellness community plan, and hire a farmer or gardener to work it, but if it's not large scale enough to support all the residents who might want to partake in the vegetable program, it can't really be considered a farming community or agrihood. Unless the development is attached to a real, working farm with plenty of acreage in agricultural production, and perhaps some pasture farm animals, it loses some of the luster of a true farm experience and the communion with nature that comes from a real farm.

This is not to say that adding vegetable or herb gardens, or adding edible landscaping, is of no value or benefit to any community, because it certainly is. But to be called a true 'agrihood', farming must take center stage and occupy a good portion of land that cannot be developed for other purposes.

THE FULLY SUSTAINABLE AND RESILIENT COMMUNITY

There will be detractors to the agrihood concept because there are people who don't want to see any kind of development whatsoever, period. They would rather see no farm land or open land of any kind developed in any way. But that is just not realistic, particularly in areas where there is high growth and a need for more housing to accommodate people moving to the region. I would also suggest that where many of these detractors live, the very spot of earth where their own home or neighborhood sits, was at one time open land. You can't stop growth, but you can look for ways to create growth that preserves farming and food production, and thus protect much of the open space and rural feel of a region.

Many people want to homestead or find a way to live off the land, but just don't know how to do it, and most already have a full-time job. The agrihood gives them an alternative. A way to plug in and connect with nature, and a farmer that can grow the food and teach them a thing or two about gardening, food production and even animal husbandry. It's an agrarian life-style that can bring deep meaning and life satisfaction to many people. At the bear minimum, you become more attuned to the seasons and the weather, to the sun and the rain, because you begin to understand what it means to the fields and the crops that are coming up. And you begin to know and antici-pate what vegetables are in season and what's coming next. Asparagus in the spring, tomatoes in the summer, and melons after that. You're connected to all of that.

But because people won't expect the farm to produce all their food needs, and because they'll still eat at restaurants and go to the grocery store, there can (and should) be excess capac-ity to produce food that is sold outside of the community which helps to recover costs and perhaps even make a profit on the farming operation. With the excess capacity a portion of the production could also be donated to food-insecure households, and that helps to build good-will in the broader region.

Imagine a self-sustaining agricultural community with a dome over it that required no inputs from outside the dome and that can meet its own basic requirements for food; one self-contained unit, like all small communities throughout human history. I like the way this concept puts a target on preserving agricultural land to differentiate it from other projects. It's my opinion that this should be the goal of a true agri-hood—self reliance.

Because diet is so important to health, the best wellness communities will offer community gardens within the development and promote healthy food at restaurants and dinner events. Even if it's not a true agricultural community, all wellness communities can and should include fresh healthy food choices, and allow space for vegetable gardens, herb gardens, and a regular farmer's market on weekends.

Any community can also start a community supported agriculture (CSA) program simply by reaching out to local farmers in the region. A CSA program helps young farmers because shares are purchased up front at the beginning of the growing season when the cash is needed most. Members also share in the risks of the crops being grown. These are good things that can happen in any community.

But the agrihood is the newest trend and sign of the times. Here, an entire community is built adjacent to a large working farm and immersed into all the activities related to farming and growing food. Farmers on tractors out in a field. Green things coming up all around at different times and seasons. Growers with hand tools tending to the weeds that always come up in organic gardens. Cows in green pastures. Chickens of different colors roaming around scratching in the dirt looking for bugs. It's all of that.

These communities are a reflection of a simpler time when people knew their farmer and knew where their food came from; a time when people gathered with their family and neighbors to enjoy and celebrate food and the bounty of a harvest. An old barn, the gardens and pastures are the central features of the community, and the agricultural community is purpose-built around those features and the growing, gathering and sharing of healthy food.

CHAPTER TWO

———

CARROTS DON'T GROW ON TREES

We had some fourth graders from a local elementary school scheduled for a farm tour which gave me the perfect opportunity to test their knowledge and mess with their heads.

Before they arrived, I pulled some carrots from the garden and tied them by the green tops to a young maple tree growing near the vegetable garden. As part of our tour, which was like herding cats and much harder than cattle, we walked over and I showed them 'the carrot tree'. No one questioned it. It makes perfect sense to a little kid that a carrot could grow on a tree, like an apple. Why not?

We eventually walked over to a row of carrots and I pulled one out of the ground and let them in on the gag. I don't think pulling a carrot out of the dirt made it any more appealing to them. A few of the kids scrunched up their noses and were a bit concerned that food came out of the dirt like that. I think they preferred food from trees because it was cleaner, and they like trees. My generation of course had the benefit of watching Bugs Bunny cartoons on TV, and we saw Bugs Bunny pulling carrots out of the ground just as fast as Elmer Fudd could plant them. Kwazy wabbit.

We're all a little disconnected from our food and where it comes from, and especially kid's today. Here's a couple more fun ideas. Throw some bunches of bananas out in the garden on top of leafy greens and call it a "banana patch." Or there's the all-time farmer favorite; pull out a couple Hershey's chocolate bars and tell the kids that you feed them to the cows, which they love, and that's how you get chocolate milk. What fun.

A nutritionist friend of mine often meets with school groups about healthy food and where it comes from, and she usually brings vegetables with her for the talk. She says that a lot of kids at all age levels, even into middle school, have difficulty identifying common vegetables, like an onion or a potato. She'll hold up a potato, and ask the simple question, what is the name of this vegetable? Even in rural farming communities, kids have a hard time answering that question even though they eat potato chips and French fries all the time.

We as a nation have already raised one or two generations on processed and fast food; the baby-boomers all grew up with it, and they're now feeding it to their kid's and grandkids. America has become a fast food nation and that says a great deal about our culture and where we're headed. Food also relates to many economic and environmental interests, and it happens to be a very big business in America with a few massive corporations supplying most of the basic ingredients that we need to survive.

Food shapes our lives and our bodies. The way we grow, process, and eat our food, and how and where we eat it, says a lot about our culture. Food can make us healthy, or it can make us fat and sick. Food creates patterns that determine how we live in society, how and where we eat, how we treat animals, and how we relate to each other, to our families, our neighbors and our community.

It's no wonder that kid's today have a hard time identifying the name of a common vegetable. They're not seeing it get chopped up for dinner at home or on a plate. Americans now eat more meals away from home (50.1%) than prepared at home, and most of the time that means fast food that includes lots of fats, carbohydrates, sugars and salt. The meals that we do prepare at home often include processed foods with lots of starch and salt. We've dramatically increased our calorie intake from sugars (derived from corn) and fat (from soy) which has led to significant weight gain across the United States. The Center for Disease Control (CDC) says that 9 out of 10 people don't eat enough fruits and vegetables. The cost for fruits and vegetables has gone up 117 percent since 1980 while the cost of soda pop (with high fructose corn syrup as the second ingredient on the label, after water) has gone down 20 percent. Corn subsidies paid by the federal government (using our tax dollars) are a major contributor to an obesity epidemic now occurring in our nation. Farmers are finding it much easier and more profitable to plant corn and soy, so that less than 3% of our farm land is planted with other fruits and vegetables.

The $30 billion dollars that the U.S. government now spends on corn and soy subsidies will end up costing hundreds of billions to the health care system because of weight related illness and disease like diabetes and heart disease. Prevention is so much smarter and cheaper than paying for treatment, but our agriculture policies seem to be going in the opposite direction and subsidizing the problem (sugars from corn). But rising health care costs are just a piece of the puzzle. By one estimate, weight related illness costs businesses in Texas over 9 billion in worker absenteeism right now, with estimates that it will rise to 50 billion in the next couple of decades as our obesity rates continue to rise. If we don't take the obesity problem very seriously as a national priority right now, we're going to pay a heavy price later.

One thing is for certain, food can transform a family as easily as it can transform a nation. As just one example to stress the point about the transformative power of food, the Center for Disease Control (CDC) released statistics in October 2017 that a full 20% of our adolescents in America are now clinically obese. Not just overweight, but obese. 40% of our children are overweight.

Our younger generations now have a shorter life expectancy than their parents. This is the first time in history that we can predict and say that. Overweight and obese children have a higher risk to stay obese and childhood obesity is clearly linked to a higher chance of early death in adulthood. Our kids are fighting an uphill battle with junk food placed at kid height in every gas station and convenience store in the nation and bombarded with corporate advertising for tasty cereals and snacks at every turn.

The truly sad thing is that kids are acutely aware of their own body image, and their excess weight causes significant emotional and psychological stress. They know that they're heavy, they get teased about it all the time. They know that they can't run as fast or as far as the other kids, and the excess weight affects their self-image and self-confidence at a very early age. They feel the weight physically and emotionally and it's very difficult to break the chains of our processed food culture that is at the root of the problem.

Educating our young people about the importance of eating the right foods, and what that food looks like and where it comes from, and limiting the junk foods, is a step in the right direction. It's a major focus and goal for our farm and the adjacent Education Center. Hopefully the grow local, farm to table movement is a sign of a cultural shift now happening in America. Just as smoking has become 'uncool', so is eating junk food all the time. We're starting to build a culture of healthy food from the ground up.

I called this new agricultural neighborhood that I was going to build Creekside Farm at Walnut Cove. It started with a 55-acre farm in a beautiful cove tucked into the mountains of Western North Carolina near the lively and vibrant town of Asheville. I believe it's about the prettiest piece of land in the Blue Ridge Mountains, with rolling green pastures and long-range views of the surrounding blue-grey hills.

An agricultural community, as discussed in this book, is a planned and purposeful development where farming and agriculture are a significant feature within and around the community. Food production is a key element and an important amenity for those who choose to live there. This type of community would probably be located in a rural or less densely populated area on the outskirts of cities and suburbs where there is still some available farm land. The problem is that farm land is disappearing quickly in some regions of the country and getting harder to find.

As more people try to connect to the land and the farming way of life, without really having to do all the work or buy all the equipment, the agrihood is an emerging and rapidly growing trend right now. There is some appeal to this kind of country living that is drawing people to it. Most of the residents will have jobs that employ them elsewhere but they like the idea of coming home to the farm.

Many residents may choose to help and do some actual

work on the farm where they can, but strictly for the aesthetic pleasure, or the exercise and health benefits. Most will not do any real work but would rather just look out onto the fields and tool around, or perhaps wander down to the gardens to pick a perfect pepper for dinner.

Most of the residents will either be retired or will have regular jobs outside of agriculture and pay the farmers and those with agricultural experience to farm the land and produce the food grown around them. The farmer gets paid either through HOA dues, community supported agriculture (CSA) programs, and/ or by selling produce through a community farmers market. Because CSA programs provide a necessary steady and reliable income for the farmer, this seems to be the best way to manage the food production within the community.

In the food production and distribution model of the CSA, shareholders and farmers freely tie their fates together. The community supports the farmer's financial needs and the farmer in turn takes care of the land and feeds the community. The health of the community and the health of the land become woven together and bound in a new food web that benefits both and improves both. It is based on social and environmental values and principles that strive to create a new and sustainable food economy where community health and farming becomes everyone's responsibility.

But it's very tough, and I'll get into the numbers later, growing food on a smaller scale and making a decent living at it, especially when trying to compete with Big Ag. Food is going to cost a little more, but the health benefits of locally grown, organic food are proven beyond any reasonable doubt. Most commercial vegetable varieties available in the supermarket we're developed and grown for traits that help them endure a cross country trip. These varieties were not developed for taste and nutrition, but endurance. Most are picked early so that they ripen on a truck, and not the vine. The difference in taste between truly fresh, organic vegetables and varieties grown commercially (to endure) is incomparable, and in my opinion certainly worth a little more.

The fact is, we currently spend less than half what our grandfathers paid for food as a percentage of income, or about 9% of our income on average, and we spend less on food than any other nation in the world. People in France and Spain pay twice what Americans spend on food as a percentage of income. Many people can certainly spend a little more for healthier, fresher food, and do so. It's really just a matter of redirecting a small portion of the household budget. And as we'll see later, we need to make certain that farmers are making a decent living growing this local food or it can't be sustainable. They'll burn out.

CSA's are thriving around the world in countries as diverse as the United States, Japan, France, China and India. People everywhere are forming communities around locally grown food. Community Supported Agriculture is called by many names around the world, including Teikei, AMAP, Reciproco, and ASC. And while the names may be different, the essence of the programs are the same; people pay a farmer to farm food for them directly, and they share the risks and the bounty of the farm. The outcome is also the same; these programs help small farmers make a living in a world of corporate food giants and a global economy.

Fields and gardens can also be incorporated into any public spaces or common areas within the agricultural development, and fruit trees and berry bushes can and should be used to create an edible landscape throughout the community. Residents should be encouraged and helped to keep their own kitchen gardens close to the back door of their home for easy access to herbs and spices and some frequently used vegetables like tomatoes. The entire community can be one big food village. The sky's the limit, and the community is only limited by the creativity of the planner, architect, developer and residents. A building or common space can be created and dedicated to make salsa, bake bread, make cheese, pickle vegetables, or grind wheat; you name it, if it's related to food, it can be in there.

Unless the costs to run the farm and pay the farmer is paid through HOA dues, then it's important to convince residents to participate in the CSA program, which is voluntary, so the key to the agricultural community becomes convincing people to spend their discretionary dollars on hyper-local food production. The farm operations can and should be self-sufficient; residents just need to participate and buy the food. One of the most important aspects of community food systems is that they increase community participation and involvement. Without the people, the whole system breaks down. Organic, local food can be more expensive than food produced by big agribusiness, but organic food grown in a CSA program can and should be comparable to prices at Whole Foods and the local farmers market.

It's important to note, so I'll say it again, that even with a slight increase in cost for fresher, organic, locally grown food, we're still paying far less for our food than our grandparents did as a percentage of our income. We're paying less than half what they did just 40 years ago for food, and significantly less than their parents at the turn of the 20th century. So clearly there is some room for many people to pay a little more for healthier food. It's also important to consider the external costs of industrial food production on our environment, and the real costs on our wallet through taxes that we pay in subsidies to support industrial agriculture, not to mention the billions of dollars that we spend on health care because of poor diets.

The agricultural community is not simply an attempt at recreating the 19th century lifestyle because of some nostalgic belief in the good old days. It's an attempt at creating a healthier lifestyle for the long run. It uses some of the modern machinery and technology to reduce the more difficult and labor-intensive tasks, such as tractors for plowing and tilling the earth, but it uses significantly less petroleum and no chemicals harmful to the environment.

The food is certainly much fresher, and because of the farms proximity to the community, where most people can walk to it, food is usually distributed the same day it was harvested. You can't get any fresher than that. The agricultural neighborhood also protects farm land that might be at risk of further development, and it preserves the knowledge of farming for future generations. It creates jobs and trains young farmers in the knowledge and skills of farming and helps them get a start in this valuable occupation.

All these points above need to be expressed in some manner to potential buyers and residents of this new type of community. And how do you do that? Marketing. Yes, another crass word for such an agrarian utopia, but unless people know about it and understand the reasons for living here, it won't become economically viable and self-sustaining. It's important to tell people what it is, and what it isn't.

The agricultural community isn't like a commune or a kibbutz, both of which have been generally failing propositions because some people don't always pull their own weight or do their part out in the fields, which leads to conflict with those who are willing and do their share of work. Here farmers do it all.

The model of a "community garden" doesn't always work

either. People are generally excited about gardening in the spring time, and they make lots of plans for a big garden. But come July, when it's hot outside and there's weeding to be done, nobody shows up to work. The community garden often ends up looking overgrown with weeds and unattractive. In an agricultural community, the hard work is done by farmers who are paid to do it, and the gardens should be as attractive to the eye as they are productive.

The agricultural community is a way for people to enjoy country living, but in many cases, it can be located close enough to a town with jobs, shopping, restaurants, movie theaters and the other joyful benefits of modern life, like the dentist and auto repair shop.

Urban Land Institute researcher Ed McMahon has often been quoted on the agrihood trend in the media on shows like CBS Sunday Morning. He says the purpose of the agrihood is to integrate the farm and agriculture back into the community as a "wellness feature". It becomes a selling point that differentiates one real estate product from another. He's probably not surprised that 200 of them have popped up around the country over the past few years. People want to re-connect in some way to the land again. They want to get to know their neighbors at and around the farm, and the farm becomes something that binds them all together into a community.

McMahon says that for the last several decades we've "designed physical activities and green space out of our communities;" he calls it "nature deficit". Many urban planners now agree that the old model of development from the '50s through the '90s isn't working anymore. We need a better way to connect with others, enjoy nature and the outdoors, and connect with food as a way to enjoy nature. This is what the new agrihood is all about—food, nature, community.

Urban designers and planners of these new agricultural neighborhoods have discovered that food can indeed bring people together and build a sense of community. And whether you're helping in the garden, taking a canning class or a cooking class to learn how to prepare this week's garden vegetables, learning about and collecting heirloom seeds, or just sharing the bounty of the garden with your family and friends in a true farm-to-table experience, it's all about using food to connect with each other.

The successful land planner and one of the early leaders in agrarian urbanism, Andres Duany, suggests that "it's a new kind of village – agriculturally productive even if inhabited by people who work elsewhere." But as Duany says further, it must be "profitable, popular and reproducible" for developers to invest in and build them. This book answers some of those questions. Is it financially viable? If you build it, will they come? And why would they come?

The appeal of a rural lifestyle has surprisingly deep roots in history and human psychology. Ancient Romans spoke of getting back to the agrarian lifestyle. Philosophers wrote about getting away from the crime, corruption, congestion, dirt and grime of the city, and returning to the rural, pastoral beauty of nature and a wholesome agricultural life outside of Rome.

It's funny to think that 2,000 years ago, one Roman would say to another Roman, "It took me 30 minutes to park the chariot, I circled the coliseum three times, some guy cut me off, I stepped in dung twice, and some barbarian tried to sell me a fake sundial. I'm moving out of this craziness. I'm moving to the country." As funny as that sounds, ancient writers often praised the agrarian lifestyle outside of Rome as a relief from city life.

The agricultural community isn't for everyone, but it is a

way of life and a chance for many to 'dwell in the land' if they choose to. It's a slower, more peaceful pace surrounded by nature and a farm. It's quiet at night.

Of all the places in the Appalachian Mountains, even the world, I think Walnut Cove is special. Long range views of multicolored farms in various shades of green and gold are scattered in the distant view. In the foreground, orderly fields of vegetables in rainbow colors, with rolling pastures and green hills behind. Avery Creek meanders down from the hills past an old, grey and weathered barn. These visual clues touch the soul in subtle and sublime ways.

The cows come down at sunset to graze on the rich bottom land, and you find yourself, subconsciously at first, counting them to make sure they're all there. Twelve momma cows, seven calves, two miniature donkeys. Yes, all accounted for, and the world is in order.

For some reason, to me anyway, looking at a large garden growing food brings a sense of peace. It's almost like it answers a question from deep in our human evolution because we know, and can see, where our next meal is coming from. It's as if, at some deeper level, it takes away some worry or stress that has plagued us for tens of thousands of years. I don't know why, but there is something calming about it. It's pretty to look at, for sure, but there's something more to it. Something deeply satisfying, in the colors, in the orderly rows, in what it means. I can't quite put my finger on it, but I know what it feels like. I don't get the same feeling in a grocery store, not even close. Food feels different when it's out in the field.

Rolling green pastures run uphill to a forest of deciduous trees that light up in the fall in miraculous colors of red, orange and yellow on the surrounding hillsides. Coyote and bear still roam these mountains and remind us of the wild nature close at hand. Thousands of acres of national forest abut Walnut Cove, and this cove has become the last reach, the last encroachment, the final outpost of civilization, before natural and undisturbed nature and the forest takes over. A high ridge closes it off and says go no further. Avery Creek Road ends here, where the mountain ridge gets steep and impassable. And beyond that, the Pisgah National forest, and beyond that, Smokey Mountain National Park.

I'm not a poet, and a picture is worth a thousand words, so I'll throw up some images of the farm and Walnut Cove on the web site at www.eatyourview.com. It's a beautiful, inspiring place nestled in the southern Appalachians and it fills you with a sense of place that is clearly defined by the high hills and ridge tops that surround it.

In the end, the agricultural community is a more sustainable way of life for the long run, and for the moral and ethical implications alone I think it should be built. Whether or not it will be successful over the long term, I can't tell you. But I built it anyway, because it should be built. And if the idea will work anywhere, it should work in Asheville.

Andres Duany is a visionary architect and land planner, and one of the first to design and write about the agrihood concept. "Because of its mitigating effects on climate change," says Duany, "the agrarian way of life should be made available to as many people as possible- for ethical reasons no less than practical ones." Duany was the first to open my eyes to the possibilities of building this agrarian lifestyle, and I am greatly indebted to him.

All ethical and moral reasons set aside, the obvious reasons for living in an agricultural community are also closely related to the enjoyment of the pastoral beauty and peaceful nature of the farm itself. It's about living closer to the land, more aware of the cycles of the seasons, the rain, the sun, the animals in the pasture, and the green things coming up on the farm and in the garden. I believe this is the main reason why people would choose to live there; connections to nature and to get out of Rome.

For me as the developer, I just had to stick my neck out and start building it. I said earlier that by some estimates 200 of these types of communities were popping up but most were still in the planning or early stages of development. Very few were up and running and selling lots or homes. Duany had a warning for me.

"Because of its benefits," says Andres Duany, "Agrarian Urbanism could be idealized to the point that it remains another unbuilt utopia." Duany knows what he's talking about. He worked for years planning an agricultural community near Vancouver called Southlands that, now, after more than 10 years, is still in the planning and approval stage, and nothing has been developed.

As many scientists and experts argue, we need to change our food production system. We can't give up entirely on the massive industrial food complex or large-scale farming that has developed over the past 70 years and which helps to feed much of the world and its expanding population, but we can try to enable more of the smaller scale and sustainable farms to grow more food locally and with less damage to the environment. The agricultural community is an attempt to enable some of that small-scale food production. It also means less food importing, and more local food security, which is important to a lot of people, not just survivalists or preppers.

My experience with farming and agricultural communities answered questions that had been bothering me for some time. A big question for me was always "Why is our American food system so damaging to the environment, and what can we do to change it so it's healthier and more sustainable for the long term?" Hopefully I'll answer some of those questions in this book.

CREATING THE MODERN AGRICULTURAL VILLAGE

Detractors of the agricultural village might say that we're trying to re-create a village of yore or some idealized past. But I don't think we're trying to recreate a 19th century village or go back in time at all. This is the future, sustainability almost to the point of self-sufficiency, as Duany calls it. And anyone who doesn't understand where the sustainability movement is going, far beyond green homes and fuel-efficient cars, shouldn't be in urban land planning or development. It's the wave of the future. It is the future.

What we are creating is a lifestyle choice that is connected to living simpler and leaving a smaller footprint. It means living a little more in tune with the soil and how our food comes to us, and more in tune with the seasons because we eat seasonally what is coming up in the garden at any given time, spring, summer and fall. We're not flying in asparagus from Argentina. We're eating asparagus in the spring when it comes up. It doesn't mean you can't eat asparagus from Argentina in the winter if you choose to, but why not at least eat it in the spring from your own backyard. It's healthier and it tastes better, and once you understand how difficult it is to grow asparagus, that it's a perennial, and that it can take a few years before you can get your first harvest from it, you begin to appreciate it all the more.

Local organic food production is based on the recognition that we only have one planet, and we can't continue to extract resources and pollute the environment like we've been doing for decades under the current industrial food complex. We can try to limit our impact a little.

This book is an attempt at illustrating one possible development model that can benefit from the sustainable food movement, and it's based on my own experience of trying to create the agrihood. I wasn't trying to reproduce some medieval village that I had visited in Italy. We can use modern science and technology to reduce some of the burden and labor in food production, storage and preparation. We can use modern equipment like small tractors and best organic practices, and in the end two or three people can still feed one hundred.

But it takes a community to support a farm and a farmer. The gardens in an agricultural community are presented as an amenity to the residents who live there, but it is the awareness, understanding and participation from the community that will have the greatest impact on the success of the farm. It will also determine the successful health benefits and well-being of those residents living there.

Even if someone just eats fresh vegetables more often, say two or three times a week, there is benefit and some good being done within the community, for the farmer and the resident. The ease of access to fresh food within the community, and in fact just seeing it out your front door all the time, should help to keep healthy food top of mind and on your plate.

But in the end, the agricultural community is a transaction between a developer and a lot or home buyer, and as with any commercial transaction, it must be seen as a fair deal, a fair trade, for all parties, even those people living outside of the community. The local residents in the surrounding region must understand that there is a tradeoff, that some open land will be lost, but they will know also that the development is condensed housing on a smaller portion of the open space, leaving the bulk of the land open and productive.

People are funny. Once they move to an area, particularly a fast growing and popular region of the country, they often think to themselves, "OK, I'm here, now shut the door!" But you can't stop growth and development, so this type of urban planning can be seen as a 'fair trade' to the surrounding region. If the food production and the economic value of that production can be increased because of this new community's participation and support of farmers using more intensive organic practices, all the better for everyone in the region.

This book is not intended to encourage developers to start plowing under farm land in order to create new communities; it is intended to protect as much farm land as possible, particularly where there is rapid growth. If a farm is economically productive and financially healthy, great, there is no reason for a farmer to sell any of it; just pass it down to future generations. The problem, as we'll see later on, is that many small farms (I should say most) are not profitable and can't compete with the large corporate farms that produce the bulk of the nation's food today. Most farmers are finding it extremely difficult now to support their families on a small farm. Most small farms, over half of them, are not profitable.

Particularly in fast growing regions like Asheville, North Carolina, the value of the land has far exceeded any profit the farmer can ever pull from the land farming it. But rather than just cash in and sell it all to a developer, which is what many farmers around Asheville are doing, this book offers another option to farmers that can allow them to cash in on some of the land, perhaps to have some money for their retirement, but keep the bulk of the land productive and in farming.

I've met a lot of farmers. I know farmers don't want to see

their land, the land that they've worked and loved, turned into a housing development. But with the average age of farmers in the Asheville region now 59 years old, many of them are getting close to retirement. And because a farmer's children may not want to follow in their parent's footsteps and farm the land, and many have gone off to college or moved on to other occupations that promise a higher income level, the farmer must figure out what to do with the land and how he will support himself in old age.

The farmer in Asheville also must ask himself, "Do I want my son or daughter to work so hard, like I did, making a living out of the earth, or do I just cash in, make millions of dollars, and we all live more securely and better off, including me in my retirement." That's a very tough question to answer honestly. The farmer, and his son or daughter, will never get rich farming the land, but might by selling it.

Because land values in Asheville have skyrocketed in recent years, no other farmer can pay current market land prices and make enough money farming that land to pay the mortgage on it, let alone make money on it. The profitability of a farm is tied directly to the cost of the land. So, it either stays in the family, or it gets sold off for other development purposes. As one example, I paid roughly $30,000 per acre for my farm in 2015, which seems to be the going rate for farm land now in Buncombe County. You can find land cheaper as you get further away from Asheville, perhaps as low as $10,000 or $15,000 the further you go out and depending on the slope and the quality of the land. But it's simply not possible to pay the going rate in Buncombe County for land and farm it and pay the mortgage on it or get any decent return on the investment from farming. The cost of the land is critical to the profitability of a farming operation, and no other farmer in the area would have considered paying $30,000 per acre because they would know it's not financially viable to farm it. Call me crazy.

In some areas of the country, you can still buy good farm land for $8,000 or $9,000 per acre, when you're buying a lot of it, even in rich soil country like Indiana or Iowa. But you'll likely be a hundred miles away from any city of a reasonable size. We're talking rural America. At those land prices, using conventional farming practices, you have a chance at making some money, if you include the government subsidies (more on that later).

Under the agricultural community model proposed in this book, the farmer can work with a developer to develop a portion of the farm, perhaps a portion adjacent to a road, for a limited number of home sites that the developer can market and sell as an agrihood. With an agreement to protect the remaining land and keep it in farming, the farmer can continue to work the land himself or allow it to be farmed by others. The farmer could also sell all the land to the developer with an agreement that the bulk of the land will remain in farming under the agrihood model. There are many ways to structure a deal between the farmer and the developer, using industry terms and concepts like common area, conservation easements or farming easements or long-term leases.

Another important underlying principle behind the agricultural community is breaking the long food chains in the current food production and distribution system. It involves building a community immersed in a new kind of food web.

While all towns and villages of the past were really just an apparatus to grow and distribute food and nine out of ten people farmed the land, urban land planner Andres Duany says, "Circumstances are different."

"Then people had little choice but to put shoulder to plow," says Duany. People today can have a choice to live an agrarian lifestyle on or near a farm but with all the modern conveniences of life. And the burden of the plow has been greatly relieved by modern equipment, like my brand-new John Deere M Series 5085 tractor (which I love, by the way); a husky little 10-year-old farm kid with a round face talked me into it. You'll get to meet him later.

What makes the agrihood possible is the fact that there are many young Millennials eager to get into farming and willing to do the work. Many Millennials seem to have values and motivations that differ from their parents and grandparents. Many young people are not so eager to sit in a cubicle or climb the corporate ladder, and they have different values and expectations from life and work. If I run and ad today on Craigslist in Asheville for farm help, I'd get at least 10 replies to it, all from young people wanting to learn and try working on a farm, and many of them with college degrees.

The farming infrastructure in this type of settlement is key, as are the farmers making it all happen, as are the residents willing to pay for it through the purchase of produce or the CSA shares that support it. In some cases, a homeowner's association might support some of the costs. The costs to run a small farm are greater than the traditional costs of lawn maintenance in common areas that are usually covered by the HOA, but it may be possible to redirect some of that landscaping cost to the farm and food production. Fortunately, the farming aspect of the agrihood should become, if well managed, a self-sufficient amenity with costs offset by products sold, and it might even become a profit center. It's not really all that different from managing the costs associated with a golf course or swimming pool as an amenity. Here's an example for that type of amenity.

The Cliffs at Walnut Cove, like many private golf clubs, charges residents $50,000 to join the golf club (if they choose to), and about $10,000 per year in dues. There is also a cart rental fee every time you play of $18 (unless you choose to walk and get some exercise). The golf course also makes money in the pro shop from selling golf balls, clubs, shoes, gloves and apparel. It all adds up to the revenue stream that will support the maintenance of the golf course. It's a beautiful Jack Nicklaus designed course, and expensive and labor intensive to maintain. And like our CSA, without enough members joining the club and playing rounds on the course, the golf course can lose money. A golf course costs millions of dollars to develop and can be a risky investment. Fortunately, there are plenty of avid golfers out there who truly love the game.

Because the development cost for the farming operation in an agrihood is much less than a golf course, it's much less risky to develop as an amenity for residents. And our CSA is charging $750 for a season's worth of fresh vegetables, which is less than one month's golf dues at the club. I think that's reasonable for this type of amenity, I mean since it's food, a basic necessity for survival, but some of my golfer friends would say the same thing about golf.

The agricultural community must compete with all the other "real estate products" out there and available to home buyers. As noted, marketing is key to the success of the community. How the word gets out about this new lifestyle choice can of course use the same marketing approach and toolkit that already exists and that real estate professionals already use. This again may seem like harsh commercialism for such a real estate concept as the agrihood, but it's necessary to make people aware of this real estate option. Otherwise, as Duany warns, it becomes another "unbuilt Utopia."

The only way buyers will know there is a choice is through marketing, and the marketing plan needs to discuss the unique features and amenities. A good marketing plan first needs to understand the customer: Who are you trying to appeal to and why? The agricultural community may have some positive affect on the environment as it compares to other development options, but are we just going to say, 'Come live here because it's good for the environment?' This is a big investment for a home buyer, and she needs to understand all the reasons and benefits for living here.

Pricing is also part of the marketing plan. Because a developer of an agricultural community buys land with the intent of just developing a portion of it for resale as home lots, the cost of the land that is left open space for farming must be offset with higher prices for the individual lots that are sold. It's an uncommon thought for a developer to buy land and not develop all of it; usually he would try to place as many lots on that land as conceivable or allowed by local regulations and spread out the cost of the raw land by as many homes as possible. But like the golf course example above, the developer could add a "farm membership" fee to the cost of the lot and an annual fee to maintain it and produce the food. There's a lot of options to consider in how to manage and cover the costs of food production in an agrihood.

This book will hopefully convince some land planners and developers that there is another way, that you can save some farm land and the pastoral beauty of an area, and still make a reasonable profit. The key is to see that open farm land as an amenity that is viable and sellable in today's marketplace. The pastoral beauty and open space are what drives many people to a region in the first place. It's not in the best interest of a developer, particularly if he wants to keep doing business in the same area or region, to fill up all that open space with unbroken chains of housing developments.

For the client buying a new home or lot in the agrihood, he or she must be willing to pay a premium to live in this new model of an agricultural community, and they must feel that there is value in this premium price. The amenities of fresh, hyper-local food and the lifestyle choice of living close to the farm with its produce, and perhaps farm animals, as well as the pastoral beauty of looking at open pastures and farm land, makes the premium price a fair deal.

The agrihood gives the home buyer another choice in terms of how to live and where to live based on a preference of lifestyle, among many different choices and development concepts out there. The developer of course must make a profit for his risk, time and investment to be a fair deal for him, or it won't get built.

AUXILARY FACILITIES TO SUPPORT THE AGRIHOOD

The agrihood needs to have facilities for social interaction and all the necessary operations of a working farm. We saved and restored an old barn that the centerpiece of the Creekside Farm neighborhood because, mainly, it was just a cool old barn. But it also became vital infrastructure and we use it for the storage of tools, equipment and farm supplies. Built in 1932, the old barn has become the centerpiece of the agrihood and ties the community to the history of the place and its long-standing farming tradition and heritage. The land has been a working farm for over 100 years, and the old barn ties the community to that history. And those bales of hay piled up next to the old barn are not a decorative art installation.

In the late fall of 2017, my wife and I took a bold step and purchased an old red school house that was adjacent to the community vegetable gardens and repurposed it as a community center and for food processing, preparation, storage and distribution. The old, three-room schoolhouse was built in 1924 and so also ties the community to the history and rural past of the region, but we knew that the building could serve a deeper purpose. The building now has a large commercial kitchen that can be used for cooking and canning classes, and it can be used for processing and production of canned goods like salsa or pickles which can then be resold at farmer's markets. We allow some other local farmers and producers to occasionally use the commercial kitchen to prepare and package their products for resale at farmers markets and small shops in the area. It's another way to support small growers and local food producers and keep vibrant the grow local movement in our area. Administrative offices are also housed in the building.

The old red schoolhouse is also used for regular farm to table meals and gatherings for our residents. A large dining hall (the old main class room) is used for these meals and other larger events like our annual Fall Harvest Festival. I think that the key to the agricultural community is creating spaces and events for people to gather to share and celebrate food together. Like the Fall Harvest Festival, these events should be regularly scheduled every year so that they become a tradition. Traditions build community.

One of the important goals for Creekside Farm, from the beginning, was educating young people on the importance of eating healthy food, where it comes from, and how to grow it. With so many of our adolescents now overweight, this is perhaps the biggest challenge our society faces and the biggest health risk to our younger generations. For this reason, the old red schoolhouse has been renamed "The Creekside Farm Education Center," and one of its main social functions is to become a place for elementary, middle and high school students to visit for classroom and field instruction on healthy food and where it comes from. The education center invites teachers and students to visit any time throughout the year. Our farm manager Melissa and her helpers from the community have simple lessons and projects for groups of all ages, and students can take projects or seeds with them to continue working on back at school or at home.

While we may have a worthwhile vision and goals for the community, in the end the agrihood is just another lifestyle choice among a myriad of choices the average home buyer has these days. We still had to figure out who the customer really was.

The agricultural community might appeal to retiring Baby Boomers looking for a hobby or interest and something to do with part of their newly gained leisure time. Certainly, the social networking opportunities within the agrihood is a benefit, and there are many opportunities for interaction and engagement in the gardens and at various events and classes.

Younger Millennials who have been educated more than previous generations in the environmental problems that our society faces, and the looming threats, would probably find the agricultural community appealing because it limits our footprint and environmental impact. There is also a growing segment of the population who take climate change very seriously and would look at the agricultural community, with its self-sustaining food production capability, as a smart choice for their family and an insurance policy against some possible crisis in the future.

"It's not enough that a certain way of dwelling on this earth is sensible," writes Andres Duany, "people are not so rational." In the end the agrihood must appeal to different people and different niches in the market for different reasons. Whether those people are trendsetters, environmentalists or survivalists, there must be an appeal and message for each of them. And we had to figure all that out. Who are these people? Who's the target market? And for all the different groups that might be attracted to the agrarian lifestyle, each of them wants to know that the value of the property will increase or at least hold its value. Every big decision has a practical side, no matter how idealistic.

CHAPTER THREE

COSTS FOR CARROTS

Asheville, North Carolina is booming. The natural beauty and the climate are the key draws to the area, and it seems to be included in everyone's list of the best places to live or retire in America. Asheville was named among Forbes' 15 Coolest Places to Go in 2018 and one of CNN Travel's 18 Best Places to Visit in 2018. Asheville has also won praise from Fortune (Best New Cities for Beer Lovers), U.S. News & World Report (Best Foodie Destinations in the USA), Lonely Planet (#1 Best in the U.S. Destinations for 2017), and plenty of other media outlets.

The population of Buncombe County, where Asheville is located, is expected to grow by 20% in the next 10-12 years, up from 250,000 to 300,000. Developers can't seem to build apartment buildings fast enough, so there's currently a shortage of apartment housing. New single-family housing developments are sprouting up everywhere, including one that is just now breaking ground and that will include 150 homes on 50 acres located only a quarter mile down the road from my farm.

Farm land was disappearing quickly all around us, and we wanted to save this old farm; we just didn't know what we were doing. My friends started calling me Eddie Albert, a reference to the 1960's TV show Green Acres, because here I was, a city boy, trying to be a farmer. I'd tell them I was thinking about buying some pigs, and they'd laugh and say, "You're Eddie Albert!"

They would laugh and add, "You don't have a clue what you're doing, and you're going to kill those pigs." I have been the subject of much humor and many jokes among my closest friends, but there was some truth to it, and my biggest fear was that I might accidently kill a poor animal that through no fault of his own ended up on my property.

The first time that my wife and I went "shopping" for animals, in this case it was goats at the Canton Live Auction, I parked my Range Rover next to a bunch of old pickup trucks. My wife Kara stepped out of the car in dress shoes with heels and a Coach purse (I think we were coming from a meeting at the bank), and that's when we realized that we weren't exactly dressed or prepared for the occasion. Everyone else was wearing a flannel shirt, jeans and a baseball cap (men and women). We felt just a little out of place, even though no one said or did anything to make us feel that way. Neither one of us had ever been to a live auction before, and we couldn't tell a good goat from a bad one, so we didn't dare bid on anything. Except at one point when the auctioneer tried to sell a momma and baby goat as a set, and there were no takers for them, so he was going to split them up and sell them separately. Kara was a little shocked and dismayed by this and wanted to buy them just so they didn't get split up. I held her hand down so she couldn't raise it and said, "We're not ready for this, and you can't just buy any old goat because you feel sorry for them. And how are we going to get them home, put them in the back of the Range Rover with us?" We came to the auction totally unprepared, and Kara was sad on the ride home. There's a learning curve to farming, but fortunately I had some help from some other farmers in the area. Here's the story of how I first came to be a farmer.

Gilbert Alexander is a soft-spoken, thoughtful, kind and gentle man, born and raised on a small farm off Avery Creek Road in Arden, North Carolina. He lived for almost 70 years in or nearby an old stone house that his father built out of the larger river rocks that came from Avery Creek and that ran close to the house. He didn't talk a lot, just not naturally gabby I guess, but when you asked him a question he would think carefully about the answer for a few seconds, and slowly, honestly give his opinion on the subject.

He spoke ill of none, and never was caught gossiping. He would talk about the weather and his beans. He loved to grow different varieties of beans, and he was most proud of the beans that came from his little kitchen garden out his back door. He planted those beans early and made sure they were well-watered and got covered if a frost was expected. He was especially proud if his beans were the first to come up, a full week before anyone else's in the neighborhood, maybe even the county, and then he'd talk at you about those beans, the different varieties, which did better, and which tasted better.

Gilbert's father died young, when Gilbert was just 11 years old. His mother, Clementh Alexander, was a strong Appalachian woman who raised her son and kept up the farm as a single mother for the next 50 years after her husband Avery died, until she died herself in the old stone house at the age of 80. We named the old barn The Clementh Alexander Barn in honor of this brave woman who loved her son, loved her farm, and loved stock car racing, in that order.

In 2012 Kara and I bought ten acres of rolling pasture land on a hilltop adjacent to Gilbert's farm, and over the next few years we became friends, not just neighbors. It was a small farm, but we had chickens and a large vegetable garden that provided enough produce for our family and some for friends and neighbors. Kara would bring Gilbert chicken eggs every week, which he loved, and I'd help him till his kitchen garden with my tractor, and we'd all keep an eye out for the cows in his pasture. We'd often see him out riding his four-wheeler around the property, and he'd stop by occasionally to chat. His knees were giving out on him after a lifetime of throwing hay and other farm chores and he was often in some visible pain from that. We tried to convince him to get his knees replaced, but he'd never been to the hospital and the whole idea of knee replacement was a bit radical to him, which it is. But he was still a strong man and not afraid of hard work.

Years ago, Gilbert gave up the old rock house and lived in a newer double-wide nearby. He rented the old rock house to some local boys who weren't very good tenants, never paid rent on time, and always tore through the corn fields on a very loud 4-wheeler without a muffler. They pretty much trashed the house. I guess it was hard for a man of his quiet and thoughtful disposition to be a tough landlord.

One day in the fall of 2015 Gilbert alluded to the fact that he might be considering selling his 45-acre farm next to us. It was getting harder for him to keep up with it, he said, and I offered to buy it immediately. The last thing we wanted was for some developer to come in and bulldoze it all for a bunch of tract housing that we'd have to look at. Enough of that was already going on all around us.

Kara and I took a big chunk of our cash, and some of the bank's money, and bought the land for $1.3 million dollars. I kicked the no-good tenants out the week after we closed on the place, and we knocked down the old rock house because it was now, unfortunately, beyond repair and not worth saving.

Eventually we would have to figure out how to pay for the farm and get some of our retirement money back so that I might be able to retire someday too, like Gilbert. But buying this working farm is what started my education in being a farmer. It also started my education in why people who are close to the earth look at things a little differently. I think it comes down to certain character traits that people have, or that they learn or develop working close with nature, and that has a profound influence on what they think is important.

Now begins the section "How to Build an Agrihood." Later in the book, we'll go deeper into the reasons for building it given the current food system that has developed since the 1950's. But the following section is written primarily for the benefit of three groups of people. One group is the farmer who is thinking of retiring and needs income for retirement. The argument that I present here is that the farmer may not have to sell all his land. He may be able to develop a small piece of it to get the money he needs for retirement under an agrihood model but keep the bulk of the land productive and in farming.

The second group is developers, land planners and city officials. The argument that I'm making to them is that there is value in keeping land in farming as an amenity for potential home buyers and residents, and the land gives the developer an opportunity to create something unique and different, but still profitable.

The third group is the people who might consider living a more agrarian lifestyle within an agricultural community. It's for those people who may want to connect to nature and to the farm. Creekside Farm, at the heart of this book, is that kind of place. I must say up front that we didn't buy this farm to develop it, we wanted to keep the farm intact but needed to pay off debt from the farm purchase. From that, the agrihood concept took on a life of its own.

Many of the principles discussed in this book may also be used by anyone who wants to create a more agriculturally based community within their own neighborhoods. All it takes is a little organization of your friends and neighbors. Schedule group outings to the farmers market. Work with a local CSA program, or get with a farmer and start one for your neighborhood. Start a community garden. Have farm to table meals with your neighbors in your backyard. There are plenty of ways to connect your neighborhood to farming and healthy food. The first step is educating them about the importance of it. The goal is to support local farmers and local food production, and the sharing and celebration of food with friends and family is a necessary benefit.

To begin, here's what I think is a critical point related to the term "agrihood." You can't just add a 20 by 30-foot vegetable garden to a development with 500 homes and call it an agrihood. With the rapid growth in popularity of the agrihood concept, the word 'agrihood' might begin to be used a little too loosely by some real estate marketers, so we need to clarify concepts a little more. We need to define what an agrihood really is, or should be, and we need better descriptive terms for the varying degrees of agriculture within a community to have a meaningful conversation on the subject and so that home buyers can differentiate real estate "products". We need to define what really should be considered a true agricultural community.

Ultimately, it's about food production, and it is my opinion that a true agricultural community should have the farming capacity to feed every household a full year's supply of food calories. That doesn't mean it has to grow enough food to feed residents everything that they will eat from the very beginning, or that it will ever accomplish that, but I think an agrihood should attempt to be agriculturally self-sustaining, and so should set aside enough farm land (the capacity) to meet that requirement. I will propose here a minimum of one-quarter acre of land set aside for farming per home in the project, with the ideal target goal of one acre of farm land per home. A full acre of land could feed a large portion, if not all, the dietary needs of each household in the community. It's a hefty goal for a developer, but it at least places the bar somewhere.

Having some measure or expectation on the land that is in agriculture allows us to differentiate a true agricultural community from another development using the term agrihood (just because they added a small garden to a project of 500 homes). The agrihood is all about protecting and preserving farm land and farming capacity, and a minimum should be established to meet a certain level of production. The whole idea is about reclaiming our traditional food ways and being able to eat locally, and in this case, hyper-locally.

I will save the subjects of community food security and resilience for a later chapter, but the concepts relate to the food producing capacity of a community and its self-sustaining ability to feed itself in case something bad happens that might disrupt our normal, conventional food distribution. If the goal is to meet all the food needs for all the residents, the farm land and production capacity must be large enough so that it could feed everyone living there. People will still go to restaurants and grocery stores for food, but the capacity to produce enough food is there and that defines the community. If an agrihood can't accomplish this, and have the capacity to feed all its residents, how is it really different from any other development with a community garden?

Early on in our agrihood project we determined that to meet the community's total food needs, we would develop just one-fifth of the land for homes and leave four-fifths in agriculture. At the same time, we planned to increase overall food production from the farm by five times using organic and intensive farming methods. But there may be another straightforward way to measure and calculate the food production capacity of an agrihood project.

Several researchers have analyzed the average American diet in order to determine how much land it would require to feed the average American. Although estimates between researchers have varied widely on this subject, and it's difficult to accurately measure given varying soil and climate conditions and the methods of farming, one group came up with an average 20,000 square feet of land per person, or .45 acres, with the bulk of the land necessary for cattle and meat production. (There are 43,500 square feet in one acre of land). A vegan diet would require significantly less land at about 7000 square feet, or roughly one-sixth of an acre. More agriculturally intensive farming would require even less land. But because most Americans are meat eaters, we'll use the conservative .45 acres per person for farm land in our calculations.

The average US household in 2017 was 2.54 people, so to feed one average meat-eating household would require at least 1.14 acres of farm land. Let's round that down to one acre per household to simplify the math. Besides, we all could eat a little less meat. My numbers are very conservative here, because some researchers claim the number is closer to one acre per person for meat eaters, so 2.54 acres per household.

But let's keep it simple at one acre per household as the goal for an agrihood.

If a developer is building 100 homes in an agrihood, he would need to set aside 100 acres of open land for farming and food production to feed each household and to be considered fully self-sustainable; that is, a community able to provide for its own needs. Again, this does not mean that the developer must farm all that land from the beginning, because residents will not look to the farm for all its food needs, but he could set that land aside as farm capacity and not develop it for any other non-farm purpose.

To make the project financially viable for the developer each household will be paying for an extra acre of farm land with the purchase of their home or lot. If the lot sizes average one acre, it doubles the cost of the land (and the retail prices). That I admit might be a stretch for the developer and the lot buyer / home buyer. But is there a minimum we can set for an agrihood that might be more reasonable and achievable for the developer and the home buyer? One-quarter acre of growing space could come close to providing households most of the food required for a vegan diet using the best, most intensive growing methods under the best conditions, so can we all agree that a minimum of one-quarter acre per home is the minimum, and one acre is the target or goal? At least we've set the bar somewhere for an agrihood. And under that minimum expectation, 100 homes would require 25 acres in farming and pasture. If those 100 homes are condensed housing on one-quarter acre lots, they'd all fit on 25 acres, so half the land in the project is saved for food production. That's not bad.

There is a premium that many people will pay to achieve this agrarian lifestyle, much like the premium people pay for homes and lots adjacent to a park, nature preserve or golf course. It can be explained, and they can understand, that land has been set aside that can grow your food needs in this sustainable agricultural community. It's really not unlike the premium people pay for living on or near a golf course. While some golf courses take up about 150 acres of land, the average golf course is about 74 acres of maintained turf, and lot buyers around a golf course usually end up paying a premium to help offset the development costs. The green space surrounding a working farm has as much appeal to some people as a golf course does to others, and people should be willing to pay a premium to live next to it. But the farm represents more than just a pretty view.

As it happened, our 55-acre farm was located adjacent to a newer golf and wellness community called The Cliffs at Walnut Cove. Started in 2006, The Cliffs is a planned community for up to 600 homes, and 270 of them have been built and there are another 47 under construction as I write this. Homes are built on the mountaintops and around the hillsides of Walnut Cove, and the golf course takes up much of the flat valley at the bottom of the cove.

The Cliffs at Walnut Cove is the only high-end gated golf community in Asheville, and homes can run from a low of around nine-hundred thousand dollars upwards to five million and more. Most Walnut Cove residents are retired and moved here from other parts of the country for the climate and the mountainous beauty of the region, and most residents are financially well-off, like retired doctors, lawyers and the CEO's of companies.

The Cliffs community borders my farm on two sides, and the northern edge of my farm butts up against the number 3 and number 6 holes of a Jack Nicklaus Signature golf course. If you slice your tee shot on the third hole, you'd end up in my corn field, and good luck finding your ball.

The developers of the Cliffs tried hard to buy the farm when they were first planning the community at Walnut Cove, but Gilbert wasn't interested in selling at the time. When he sold it to me several years later, I paid the going rate on land in a booming land market, and I paid more for farm land than any farmer in his right mind would pay, as noted, $30,000 per acre. And also, as noted, most farmers will tell you that you can't make a living when land costs you that much, no matter how good of a farmer you are. And I'm not a very good farmer.

But we scrambled and got up the cash to purchase the farm anyway knowing that there might be a way to sell off part of it, the part along the golf course, to help pay for it if we had to. We decided that if we just sold 10 or 11 acres, from the 55 acres, subdivided into lots of approximately one acre, we could recover some of the costs.

The 11 acres that I would develop look out on wonderful views of the farm and the pasture and the surrounding Blue Ridge Mountains, with an old barn right smack in the middle. As my wife and I sat there looking out over the farm pasture and the old barn one afternoon, the thought first occurred to us that this farm view could be a major selling point to some types of people. Some people might want to live here because of the farm. This view of the farm could really mean something to some people.

From that humble beginning, the whole concept of the agricultural neighborhood began to take on a life of its own.

We started restoring the old barn and set aside two acres of the land for a community supported agriculture program, and hired our farm manager, Melissa, and there was no turning back. We've since cut out another four acres from the farm for vegetable production to support Melissa's growing CSA program, so she's farming six acres now in organic vegetables with her assistant, Anna. To those who know organic gardening, that's a huge garden and a lot of work.

Some of the lots would likely sell for more money because they look out at the golf course as well as the farm, but you couldn't play the course. It was a private course for residents of the Cliffs only. The lots would certainly be worth more if they were part of The Cliffs, so I decided to have a meeting with The Cliffs management to talk about it. On the day of that meeting, just to break the ice, I was going to tell them that I was thinking about turning part of the farm, the part that butts up against their golf course, into a pig farm. I would say that I love pigs and I wanted to get a lot of them, and I hoped they wouldn't mind the noise and smell too much.

As funny as that idea was, I didn't have the heart to say that. After a brief conversation about the farm, I simply asked the team assembled if they'd be interested in bringing a small piece of my farm into their community – just the part along the golf course. Richard Hubble, who runs the land development side of the business for the Cliffs, loved the idea right away. Richard is a very smart guy and could quickly see the benefit of protecting the south side of the golf course, from pig farmers, to noisy neighbors on 4-wheelers without a muffler, to anything else that might end up there. But he also understood the agricultural neighborhood that I envisioned and didn't object to the idea of my promoting this agrihood concept for the lots that I would develop and sell within the larger Cliffs community.

One key to making all the numbers work for our little agrihood would be the premium prices that we could charge for lots inside an existing gated golf and wellness community. The high price we paid for raw farm land in Asheville could be offset by the higher prices we might charge for lots inside the Cliffs. It looked like a win-win. Except that we'd have to purchase another five acres to gain access to the Cliffs road system and utilities. It was a gated community and we needed access to the road that came through the security gates. For that five acres, we'd get into this a little deeper. Half a million deeper.

The numbers for an agrihood would probably be a lot easier to work out in an area that is not growing as rapidly as Asheville and in places where raw farm land prices have remained relatively stable. Further away from town, where land prices might drop to $9,000 or $10,000 per acre, it becomes more financially feasible to pay for and set aside undeveloped land for farming. However, the market for home buyers drops as you get further away from town and dwindles as you get 45 minutes or an hour away by car.

I say all this as a tiny fish in a big pond. In the larger world of big money developers with access to investors and finance tools outside of my reach, it would be possible for a big development firm to build a golf and wellness community and add the agricultural feature that could be offset by a much larger community of homes. It also would allow the developer to keep the community relatively close to a town or city.

Aside from Richard Hubble, I don't think the rest of Cliffs management was so sure about this "agrihood" idea, but they were just as happy to protect the south side of their golf course. They were glad to know that any homes built adjacent to the golf course would now be Cliff's style homes and fall under their building guidelines. We also agreed to pay a percentage of the lot sales back to the Cliffs as an access fee, which I thought was fair.

But for our part, we gained access to a readymade wellness community, with all the wellness features anyone might expect, including miles of walking trails through wooded hills; a state-of-the-art 20,000 square foot wellness facility with weights and cardio equipment; yoga classrooms, indoor and outdoor pools, hot tubs and steam rooms. They already had everything in place that made for a true, top-notch wellness community. This was important because the agrihood concept is really an extension of both the local food movement and the wellness trend in real estate. Total wellness is about diet and exercise, and you can't have one without the other.

And we had the other half of the wellness equation to complete the Cliffs wellness offering: we brought the food. No other wellness community could offer the whole picture like this. By luck or providence, it became a great partnership.

Just a few weeks after we closed on the deal, the Cliffs sent out an email to all residents on our behalf asking if anyone wanted to join a new CSA that we were starting up. Within two days we had enough members and had to stop accepting any more membership requests. Melissa wanted to limit the number of shares the first year to make sure she could grow more than enough food, but we instantly knew that there was a big demand for organic food produced in the community.

We had the farm, and we had Melissa and a CSA program up and running, now we had to develop the lots that we would sell. The development process never goes as quickly as you think it should. The next two years went by as I navigated my way through the twists and turns of the county permitting and approval process, worked with contractors on the construction and installation of roads and utilities, and storm water and erosion control measures. I was getting up to my eyeballs in debt. In addition to the development costs of infrastructure, like power, gas, water and roads, we had to purchase the five acres of land that would gain us access to the Cliffs road system and utilities, and that didn't come cheap.

I was finding out that it takes deep pockets, an abundance of creativity, and a lot of risk to create a combined wellness and agricultural community. And while I'm just describing my experience and the way things worked out for me in my situation, every developer and urban planner's situation and environment will be different and have its own unique circumstances to deal with. I fumbled my way through zoning and planning and the whole process as best I could.

For most agrihood projects, homes can and should be condensed on much smaller lots, perhaps just quarter-acre lots, maximizing available farm land and reducing the overall cost of the project. In an agrihood model, there will be plenty of open land around the community for residents to look out on and enjoy from a smaller, condensed lot, and many homes can be directly adjacent to the growing fields. In more rural areas outside of town where there are no sewer lines, home lots will need to be bigger to accommodate septic fields and so cannot be condensed as closely, but land is also cheaper as you get further out from the city center where those sewer lines don't exist.

In our situation, the main sewer line that ran down Avery Creek Road went to a pump station that was, we were told by the county, maxed out. If we wanted sewer lines, we'd have to pay the cost to replace the pumping station with a larger system, in addition to tearing up the road and replacing some pipe. It became cost prohibitive for just 12 lots, so we decided the lots would have their own septic fields. In Buncombe County, homes with septic require a minimum of .72 acres of land.

Theoretically, if we had sewer access, we could have placed 44 homes on the 11 acres that we developed and had enough land left open and in farming (45 acres) to feed everyone. But we developed just 12 home sites in a less condensed project, and so would have only needed 12 acres of farm land to feed everyone under the agrihood model proposed earlier. We had 45 acres in farming, so a lot of excess capacity to feed more people than those that lived in this little neighborhood. In 2016 we opened up the CSA to 65 households within the Cliffs (about 150 people) and still had excess capacity. We were to discover ways to use this excess farm capacity to feed some food insecure households in Asheville, which is described a little later on. But I can say now that a developer should be considering the good that can be done with excess farm capacity in the broader region from a project like this.

There are now five times as many farmer's markets in the United States as there were just 20 years ago.[13] Farmers markets are third places for people to meet and shop and feel good about it. They have become tourist destinations for many cities and towns and a big economic boost for downtowns everywhere. And they provide vital income for local farmer-entrepreneurs.

Freshness matters, and not just to the taste. Vegetables lose vitamins as they travel the 1500 miles and wait for you at the supermarket. But the grow local movement is about a lot more than just fresh veggies. Most shoppers at the local farmer's market can tell you that the real costs of conventional farming are related to petroleum and CO_2 emissions for transportation, and chemical fertilizers and pesticides in the environment. Those shoppers will also tell you that it's all about protecting local farm land and giving local farmers a chance to make a living. And knowing where your food comes from and who grew it is important to a lot of these people. They want to know their farmer by name. It's a radical idea, this grow local movement across America, and it's changing the way people think about food, and now influencing decisions on where they might live.

On another front, backyard and community gardens have increased dramatically in the last decade, and 1/3 of the U.S. population now does some form of gardening. There's no question now that people are into fresh, healthy food. As the developer of an agrihood, this is all I really had to hang my hat on. We were creating a new lifestyle choice and a new food web at the same time and basing it all on a food movement that keeps growing.

With this dramatic rise in local food interest, there can be a positive loop between farms and the real estate industry that never existed before. It can be a synergistic relationship that helps and supports each other in new ways never dreamed of. Where it used to be adversarial, and one industry supplanted another, farms were the losers. Now it's completely different. Real estate developers and farmers need each other. It was an unlikely pair just ten years ago.

Under the agrihood model, a developer can actually help a farmer, rather than just take his land. He can provide the land, equipment, facilities and customer base to ensure that a farmer is successful and profitable. It's a different world out there now.

Developers, planners, government officials, real estate sales agents, brokers, and investors need to learn about this new potential interaction between food and development that will create spaces which add value and hopefully increase economic, health and environmental benefits for an entire region. It's a new concept, and it's why I wrote this book in your hands. Hopefully this is just the start. Others will continue to find newer and better ways to build communities around food. We must, in fact. We can't continue to depend on far-away places and other countries for 98% of the food that we consume. Just two percent of the food Americans eat is local food. That can't continue.

Food plays an important role in social interaction and building community, and the real estate industry is discovering ways to help people come together to experience and share food. Around the world people have a growing interest in healthy and sustainable food, and it's up to the real estate professionals to just give them what they already want- access to it. Not only can the growing, cooking and sharing of food spur the local farming economy and help the planet, it can produce dividends and profits for the developer. The agrihood is a creative and innovative real estate concept that generates returns for the growers and the builders.

The bottom line is that an investment in food-centric communities can go to the developer's bottom line. If better community health and improved environmental quality comes from it, all the better. But it must be profitable, or it won't get built. I'll throw some more numbers out there for costs of infrastructure below to give you a better idea about how relatively inexpensive it is to add the agricultural feature to a community after the land has been accounted for. Numbers can be scaled up or down depending on the size of an agricultural community and the size and quality of the facilities that are built. You could easily spend a few hundred thousand dollars on a very nice, architecturally designed stone barn, but the chickens won't really care. The clients you want to attract might.

The first question for the developer of an agrihood is this: "If you build it, will they come?"

The answer is a resounding "Probably." Maybe.

The second question for the developer is: "Will I ever get my money back out of this harebrained idea?"

The answer: It depends.

Every regional and local environment is different, so it's tough to generalize on costs to build this more sustainable and resilient community, but the cost of farm land is critical. You're giving up land that you could otherwise develop as homesites, so the question is, can you recover that lost potential revenue by charging a premium on the lots that you do develop and sell.

To simplify the math, let's say that you paid $1 million for 50 acres, which is $20,000 per acre (cheap by today's standards near any city of a decent size.) And for simplicity, let's just say you'll develop 10 one-acre home sites on one fifth of the land (10 acres), leaving four-fifths open for agriculture (as we did in our project). You'd have to charge $100,000 for each of your 10 lots to cover the cost and just break even on the land, and that's before any development costs. In our area, that cost usually averages about $50,000 per lot to develop with roads, power, and water, so now you've got $150,000 cost into each lot. No profit built in, just the break-even point on the land. What can you charge for a home lot in your area? Good question to ask before you go any further. What is the cost of raw land and what premium will people pay to live in an agrihood.

We had roughly $1.8 million in land costs, plus $240,000 in building costs for the old school house next door (now the education center). The total infrastructure costs for our project came in at about $750,000. We were getting in deep now with raw land and infrastructure costs totaling over $2.8 million, all on a gamble over the value of carrots and tomatoes.

Here's the good news. The capital expenses for an organic farm operation, which includes equipment and facilities to grow and process food, is really not that much in the overall scheme of things. It isn't large-scale conventional farming, so you don't need a huge tractor, or a million dollar combine. The tractor is pretty easy – get yourself the new John Deere 5085 M series. The 3038 will do, and is easier to handle, but you'll want to move up soon enough (guy talk). With the necessary attachments, including a front bucket loader, roto-tiller, disc tiller, and back blade, we spent about $50,000. I planned to can get the potato ripper later with the other cool attachments my wife didn't know about.

Water of course is critical to agriculture, and you can't use a city water line because of the amount of water used and the cost of city water. We drilled a well for about $5,000 and ran electric to the well and a garden shed for a couple thousand dollars.

We knew that we couldn't just pull the carrots out of the ground and hand them to someone. We needed a facility to wash, prep and box the vegetables. We accomplished that in a simple garden shed the first year, which cost under $10,000. We ran water from the well to the shed and purchased large stainless-steel sinks which drained out onto the ground (because we were just rinsing the dirt off the vegetables). The shed also stored tools and supplies.

Keeping the vegetables cool after you pull them from the ground is critical to keep them fresh. Our farm manager needed time to pull and prep the veggies every week for all our CSA members, so some would be stored while she's picking others, and people may not be picking them up until the next day. On a hot summer day, vegetables can start to wilt after an hour which will degrade the quality of the product, so having a place to cool and store them was important to the operation, and it needed to be close to the garden fields.

There're a couple ways to do that which we learned from other small farm growers in our area. In our first year, we dedicated half the garden shed to cool storage. We walled off half the structure and insulated it to the extreme. That included thick foam insulation board in the walls, ceiling and floor. A normal window air conditioning unit will cool the space if you purchase a secret weapon that many small growers know about, called the Cool Bot. All window AC units come with a preset temperature sensor that only allows you to cool a room down to 60 degrees. A Cool Bot over-rides the temperature sensor on an AC unit and will allow it to cool down to as low as 38 degrees, or lower, depending on the unit you buy, how big your cooler is, and how well you insulated it.

If you've got the money, you can buy a professional outdoor cooler unit that restaurants sometimes use when they run out of room in their walk-in coolers. Or you can modify a trailer unit, as described above, so you can move it around if you need to. Some organic raspberry farms I know of in our area pull an insulated trailer with a store-bought AC unit and a generator to run it right out into the field where it follows the pickers. They can get the fruit into the cooler within minutes of harvesting.

After the first year, we built a separate cooler unit, a free standing 12 x 16 building that could house enough vegetables and packed boxes for over 100 CSA members. It's tucked away near the main garden for easy access and close to parking where people pick up their vegetables and eggs every week. We also added a 20 x 30 greenhouse at a cost of around $10,000 that gives our farm manager an early start with her seeds and extends the growing season in both spring and fall.

We're not done yet with capital investments, and here's an important one. For reasons I'll discuss at length in a later chapter, we needed a building for community events, and preferably one with a commercial kitchen. An agrihood needs spaces and places for people to gather and celebrate food. We needed a shared space to offer cooking and canning classes, farm to table meals and events, and facilities for formal and informal education. It's the community space that pulls the entire community together around the growing and celebration of food, and I think it is critical infrastructure for an agrihood.

Here we lucked out again. We were able to purchase a three-room 1920s schoolhouse that sat directly adjacent to our farm and gardens. It was a very cool, old wood building built in 1924 when Avery Creek Road was still a dirt road, painted red, with a cupola and even an old school bell. In its many lives since it was first constructed it became a church occupied by different denominations and congregations over the years. And to our great luck, it already had a commercial kitchen that was installed 10 years before we purchased it. We invested $240,000 in the building, and it gave us a ready-made community space with a lot of character; a very quant, old red schoolhouse that had been well-kept by church members for almost a hundred years. Depending on the size, style, quality and design of your community center, some cost must be planned and budgeted for a community building and meeting space. If it turns out to be a big barn, make it a nice barn with a commercial kitchen and bathrooms.

Once the capital expenditures for the farming operation are paid for, the farm should eventually become self-sustaining, with labor and operational costs offset by products sold. Operational costs for the farm and CSA program will vary depending on the size and who's running it. We lost about $50,000 in our first year of operating the CSA with just 35 members. Our farm manager wanted to limit the membership the first year to make sure she under-promised and over-delivered, which limited revenue that year. There were a lot of questions related to soil quality because the field had been in corn for so many years in a row, and Melissa couldn't be sure how productive it would be in that first year.

Our costs for seeds and transplants came in at about $7000 each year over the first two years of operation, which isn't a significant cost in the overall project. Labor costs are the largest operating expense in an agrihood or just about any small-scale farming operation. Our CSA employed a full-time year-round farm manager, and an assistant farmer who worked during the eight-month growing and harvest season, and our labor costs averaged about $50,000 per year. To have a self-sustaining CSA program, we determined after the first year of operation that we would need 80 CSA members to hit break-even and cover the costs of labor, seeds, transplants, amendments and other supplies. All the necessary capital expenses were already paid for, including the tractor and attachments, a cold storage building, a garden shed, a 30 x 50 greenhouse, two caterpillar tunnels seven feet high by 15 feet wide, several smaller tunnels (all to keep the bugs out and protect against early frost), and most of the hoses, driplines and assorted hand tools. Eighty CSA shareholders would cover the supplies and labor costs for the year and hit breakeven.

Melissa is a full-time, year-round employee. To get the right person and keep a good farmer, we believed that we needed to offer that person a job that will support her throughout the year, and not just the summer months, and we didn't want to risk losing her. Melissa keeps busy in the winter months with planning and ordering supplies for the next year, treating the soil, and taking care of the chickens. Besides, after a long hard summer growing all that food, she needs a little break. Her assistant, Anna is summer help, working from March through late October. Anna gains the knowledge and experience of working with an experienced organic gardener like Melissa in addition to her salary. And that's all that Anna really wanted right out of college anyway, a summer position to get a feel for this kind of work and lifestyle. In any case, labor costs are the biggest budget item for the farm in an agrihood.

The agrihood concept can be added to an existing community, as we did, or planned and built into a new, much larger development. The costs described above will vary for every project, of course, and a budget can be adjusted to accommodate a much larger or smaller operation. But the capital investments and costs to set up an agricultural feature in any community are not significant compared to the rest of the infrastructure costs. The bottom line is that it's not that difficult or expensive to build and maintain the farming infrastructure for an agrihood, and certainly much less expensive than a golf course. The average golf course maintenance budget in the United States was about $750,000 in 2016. Some municipal courses are maintained at a lower cost of around $500,000 or less depending on the quality of the course. The cost to build a new golf course again depends on the quality of the course and the designer, but they average from a low end of about $2 to 3 million to a high of about $6 to 7 million. Aside from the old school house, our capital expenditures just amounted to the tractor, cooler and shed buildings, greenhouse, hoop houses and other supplies like hoses, easily purchased for $100,000.

The only significant build out cost or capital expense for our farming operation was the community building, which could be considered optional. And for the same price that we paid for the old school house ($240,000), we could have built a very nice wood barn with bathrooms, a kitchen, washout stations and a walk-in cooler. And for that money, maybe even some nice stone work along the outside. But the point is that for not a lot of money you can create a great gathering place for meals and other events.

We didn't have any of the "build out" expenses for the CSA garden like you would for a golf course, like moving and sculpting tons of dirt and planting trees and building ponds and sand traps and all the wonderful things that go into a golf course. Our 2017 and 2018 operating budget including labor and supplies were both surprisingly just over $71,000. From that it's easy to calculate that one hundred members at $750 a share hits breakeven. Since we have most of the supplies now, like irrigation drip lines, and we're becoming more efficient in our operation, and the soil is improving, our 2019 operating budget is for $60,000 which means we hit break even at about 80 CSA members.

I should point out that it's possible to just lease the farm land to a third party, a farmer or organic gardener, at little or no cost, and let them take on the management, costs and risks of the farm operations, so that they're not even on the company payroll. But you would lose some control and really must trust the farmer. An HOA, community association or board of CSA members can hire the farmer or execute the yearly land lease agreement for the next growing season. The farmer might be able to supplement her income by selling food at a local farmers markets, but the business of growing food for residents and CSA members is all hers. The community can still feel good about giving a young farmer the land, equipment and infrastructure, and an existing customer base, which gives her a start in this important occupation.

In the end, the agrihood is a food-based development strategy that can create marketing opportunities and a competitive edge for the developer. But it can also improve the vitality and vibrancy of a community and increase the sustainability, food safety and resilience of the surrounding region. It also improves public health and can, depending on your reach, provide some social equity and food for the food insecure.

FARMING THE FAIRWAYS

The first time that I tried to explain the concepts behind the agrihood to a group of people was in the spring of 2016. I called an informative meeting at the education center for our original 35 CSA member households and about half of them showed up. The meeting was about building sustainable and resilient communities, and it covered some of the material in this book. Because I knew many of the people that attended the meeting would be avid golfers, I included a couple slides in the power-point presentation that I knew would freak them out.

I talked about community resilience and asked, "What happens if you flip the switch and the lights don't come on? What happens if groceries suddenly stop showing up at the supermarket because of an attack on the power grid or a couple consecutive hurricanes knocked out oil refineries in the Gulf of Mexico and along the eastern seaboard?"

"Don't worry," I said, "we can grow enough food to feed everyone in Walnut Cove, and then some. All we have to do is just plow under the golf course."

I looked up for a response. I saw that one guy's left eye started to quiver. Shock and dismay covered several other faces. I proceeded,

"We already have the pond and irrigation system which can run on a generator." I flipped to a slide that showed the fairway on the number three hole and continued. "I think we should plant corn and beans on number three, and number eight would be great for squash, tomatoes and onions."

I looked again for a reaction. One guy in the back started convulsing, and another guy was shaking violently. He's going to WHAT! Plow under the g-g-g golf course!

What fun. Their reaction wasn't quite as overwhelming as I just described, but I was having fun with this and so I continued a little longer.

"The golf course includes 160 acres of flat, fertile land which could feed close to 960 people a plant-based diet if we used organic and intensive methods." I showed a map of the golf course.

I said, "Really, we'd just be putting the land back to what it was before the golf course was built."

I sensed now that people were wondering what kind of maniac was running this meeting and some were about to walk out, so I threw them a bone.

"But the good news is," I told them, "just because we have food growing on the golf course doesn't mean you can't play golf on it. We can leave the putting greens. Of course, if you're a golfer like me, then you'll be looking for your ball somewhere in an onion patch, or shank one into the cucumbers."

That got a laugh out of some, and most were realizing

that I wasn't seriously thinking about tilling the fairways. Not right now anyway. But it was a good exercise to let them know that resilient communities have a backup plan, and they plan for everything.

The truth is, if we plowed under the backyards facing the golf course, the fairways, greens and rough, we'd feed well over 1,000 people. Walking distance from the farm is a company called Eden Brothers Seeds, a giant mail order seed company with a warehouse full of vegetable seeds. That'd be my first stop if all hell ever broke loose. We keep lots of heirloom seeds, but not enough to feed 1,000. I didn't say anything about this to the group. But I know it's there.

BUILDING COMMUNITY AROUND FOOD

My wife Kara and I have always been conscious of the mounting threats posed by climate change and the contribution that fossil fuels have had on that. We knew that we needed to be less dependent on fossil fuels in our operations and minimize food waste. Allowing people to take what they really needed, and leaving the rest for others less fortunate, where we knew it would be put to good use, was just another part of the equation and our community plan.

The environment – the farm – had been stressed for decades with feed corn. We knew that we needed to mend and heal the soil, and that meant that the food that we could grow at the beginning had to be limited to those plants which could help add minerals and nutrients back into the soil. People wanted corn, and we wanted to grow it, but we couldn't. The soil needed a rest from that crop. No corn this year, or for at least three more years. There were other organic growers in the region that we could just buy corn from or work something out in trade for our CSA program. We had to plant crops and cover crops in the winter that would help build the nutrients and organic matter back up in the soil. A good crop rotation plan was critical, and our farm manager Melissa was all about that. A comprehensive composting program is also essential to building up organic matter in the soil. There are so many good books out there on organic farming and gardening that I don't really need to go into that detail here. But we read a lot and reached out to other organic farmers and did whatever we could to build up the health of the soil.

A big part of building a new community food system is providing access to a commercial kitchen for other local growers and producers. To really help the local and artisan growers in our area, we decided that we could create a kind of "culinary incubator" using our commercial kitchen space. Most small growers and producers don't have access to a qualified and inspected commercial kitchen for food processing for products that are cooked or prepared to be resold at retail stores, and it's not currently legal to do that for most products in a home kitchen. Our kitchen now helps several food entrepreneurs by allowing them space to prepare and package their products, from jams to salsa to hot pepper sauce. The kitchen can help these small producers while it supports the overall objective of building food resilient communities. And packaged and labeled local food like the apple butter and hot sauce that came out of our kitchen can become a hot commodity at local stores and the farmers markets that provides value-added income to a local grower.

A community kitchen is also important to an agricultural community because it offers numerous opportunities for classes in cooking, canning, nutrition and meal planning skills. It's not enough to just offer the fresh vegetables. To be community health conscious and a more vital part of the larger community health story, we tried to build the skills that will really impact health and serve a larger region. As one example, we started offering cooking classes on how to prepare simple, fast, healthy meals for parents in low-income households. Many young, low income parents don't know how to prepare vegetables so that they taste great and so the kids will eat it. This simple thing, it seems to me, is one of the most important things that we could do with this commercial kitchen for the broader community around us – teach at risk homes how to make quick, simple, healthy meals at home.

The education center now offers many programs for rich engagement and learning experiences, including both formal and informal learning opportunities. It's the hub to organize and develop partnerships with other supporting and like-minded groups and organizations. It can build upon the strengths of existing organizations and nonprofits in the region, and it can create opportunities for local growers and provide land and equipment for those opportunities. It all ties in together in a new kind of food web that reaches out to the broader region.

ADDING STAKEHOLDERS

I knew we had to get a little creative in this agrarian business model and find the right partners and stakeholders to increase awareness and support of the project from the larger community around us. The whole concept was about adding value and building community and social ties around food. Building strong ties between residents and farmers and chefs and nonprofits and educational sources helps everyone learn and share the farm experience and gain some benefit from it.

We didn't have to reinvent the wheel here; just find those already existing local groups, organizations and institutions that have a common goal around healthy food and partner with them to create something new but authentic. Getting outside stakeholders behind our project, and doing some good for the broader region, can add an army of support and recognition. When you can do that effectively, people suddenly begin to feel a sense of attachment to a project because it is culturally relevant to them. It supports what they already believe is important.

Early on at Creekside Farm we started looking for those ties and partnerships with like-minded people who shared our goals. We started looking for partnerships with other farmers and chefs, local colleges and universities, nonprofit groups like MANNA FoodBank, Appalachian Sustainable Agriculture Program (ASAP), the Organic Growers School, the local farm extension office, and even local health providers. Each one of them could help us in a unique way to create this more food centric community that might benefit a lot more people than just those residents living here. The benefits we were looking for included a list of health, environmental, social and economic benefits. Food security and a little more self-reliance were part of it also. A return on our investment would be nice, but we understood quickly that the reach of this agricultural neighborhood could go well outside the gates of this little community and benefit a lot more people.

Urban planners and developers need to have vision and look at things from a broader scope. For us, it was all about wellness and good nutrition, and educating others about growing, processing and cooking healthy food locally, and we could do that even more effectively outside the gates of the community. We also felt it was our mission to try to feed everyone that we could, within reason, and not just those who can afford to live here at Walnut

Cove. We knew early on that the right partnerships could help us do that. And as most developers know, what's good for the community is good for business. It can help build trust and a brand, and it can attract more partners and stakeholders and get them behind and supporting your project. When the self-interest of a developer aligns with the broader interests of a community and region, and some good or public benefit is the result, it can surprise a lot of people and generate a great deal of support.

Partnering with other, larger and better-known food groups can also help build recognition. This type of reaching out can create an identity for a farm and a neighborhood, and people start talking and saying things like "they help young farmers get started" and "they grow veggies for MANNA". By associating our farm and community with larger, better known organizations in our area, we grow in recognition and prestige. It's gorilla marketing on the farm.

Early on we started forming partnerships to help build awareness and access to healthy food within a much broader region. Our vision was to help create jobs for farmers and a lot more people in the food chain downstream. It all became part of the initial plan for the community we were building. The Organic Growers School and the Appalachian Sustainable Agriculture Project were two early key partners and worth mentioning here.

ORGANIC GROWERS SCHOOL

We started working with Organic Growers School and the Appalachian Sustainable Agriculture Project (ASAP) looking for ways that we might get involved and help these two organizations with the important work that they do. If nothing else,

I thought, we could provide meeting space and a kitchen for some of their events and programs.

Organic Growers School celebrated its 25th anniversary in 2018 as an organization that has a mission to inspire, educate and support people interested in farming, gardening and living organically. They have educational programs to teach people who dream about living and working on an organic farm the realities of this difficult and challenging business. They offer several educational courses and programs to farmers and gardeners throughout the year, and they are, I believe, vital infrastructure in the local food movement.

Lee Warren, the director of the Organic Growers School (OGS) told me that while there are plenty of people who want to get into farming these days, "People think it's easy. But it's not. We try to teach them the business side, like sales, marketing and promotion, as well as the organic farming side." It's a yearlong program, and a life-long learning process. Lee is a very intelligent lady in her late 30's with jet black hair, and a realist in the business of dreamers. She also isn't the type of person to sugar coat anything.

"We also tell them 'don't quit your day job' because it's going to take a while for you to grow this farm business.'" OGS takes dreamers and teaches them the hard reality of organic farming and how to be successful at it for the long term. Lee told me, "We teach them how to become smart farmers so that they don't burn out or quit in frustration. We teach them the commitment and dedication that it takes for long term success, as well as the technical know-how to grow food organically."

Organic Growers School (OGS) is a nonprofit organization that started in 1993 as a way for a group of farmers to gather and discuss the serious need for 'nuts and bolts' training and education in growing food in the unique environment and climate of Western North Carolina. Since that time OGS has become the premier provider of practical and affordable education in organic farming in the Southern Appalachians and beyond, helping to build vibrant food and farming communities across several states. Their goal is to boost the success rate of organic home growers and new farming businesses in the region through hands-on training, workshops, conferences and partnerships. "We want to educate and support people with a desire to farm, garden and live organically," Lee said.

The OGS web site states the problem, as they see it, pretty clearly: "Big agriculture and globalization results in a loss of biodiversity, environmental crises, reduced food and community resilience, increased world hunger, and an over-reliance on industrial food systems. Our food and farming heritage and culture are fragmented by the agribusiness agenda and our communities have little cohesion with regards to interdependence, skill-sharing, or celebration of food and growing." My guess is Lee wrote this—nothing sugar coated about it.

But they're right, and I agree. Traditional methods of farming and knowledge transfer have been lost, and the barriers to entry in the business are large and difficult, including access to land, capital, training and support. But what's worse, says OGS, is that "misinformation and manipulation by our current food system is leaving people sick and ill-informed."

Their solution is to create and support small-scale organic food systems made up of farmers and growers, and food conscious consumers and eaters, that can lead to "a thriving food shed that is diverse and resilient." Organic growing and eating leads to "a robust, vibrant, secure, viable, and resilient food region." The ultimate goal is to increase the number of viable organic farms in the region and increase the number of community leaders and advocates for resilient food systems.

OGS believes that farmers should be a celebrated central component of a vibrant and healthy community, and that home growers are another integral part of our food sovereignty and security. To support these farmers and growers, the OGS plays another role, and that is to increase the number of people who shop and eat locally and organically through community education and outreach programs.

I attended the annual OGS Spring Conference in 2018 held on the University of North Carolina Asheville campus and took several helpful classes over the weekend-long event. So did hundreds of other people. The Spring Conference is a one-of-a-kind event that offers regionally specific workshops on organic growing and sustainable living. Presenters give lectures on a wide variety of subjects; everything from permaculture to bee- keeping to hog raising to homesteading. A dozen classrooms throughout campus have presentations going on at the same time over the entire weekend. For 25 years, the Spring Conference has brought together environmentally minded folks from 17 eastern states and Canada, and it's a weekend celebration of learning, networking, and growing.

The mission and goals of Organic Growers School aligned perfectly with our own goals of building a support network for young or new farmers. We initially offered the education center to Organic Growers School for their board meetings and some of the classes that they run, and they liked the building so much that they considered moving their offices into the second floor. They love its proximity to the gardens and the farm, right outside the front door, and I loved the idea that some smart and dedicated people would be so close by. Lee knows that the space is open to her whenever she wants or needs it.

ASAP

The Appalachian Sustainable Agriculture Project (ASAP) is the organization in our region that connects local growers and farmers with restaurants, grocers, institutions and the greater community. They help growers build their business by connecting them with buyers. ASAP organizes an annual CSA fair, a Business of Farming Conference, and farm tours to help people build connections and a better understanding about how important it is to support local farmers and healthy, local food. ASAP's Appalachian Grown certification program works with over 800 farms and over 500 businesses and provides practical supplies such as waxed boxes, twist ties and bags that benefit the farmers by saving them money and lets their customers know the product is Appalachian Grown.

ASAP's mission is to help farms thrive by linking farmers to markets and the food industry, and to build healthy communities through the connections to locally grown food. They have a vision of strong farms, thriving local food economies, and healthy communities where farming is valued as central to our heritage and our future. The ASAP Local Food Guide is a critical tool that connects growers with buyers, including restaurants and institutional buyers.

ASAP is all about helping farmers find markets for their produce and encouraging farm tours and farm visits to increase awareness and build connections. Among the many services that this nonprofit provides is a program called "Growing Minds" that provides support and resources to preschools and schools so that they can create and sustain successful farm to school programs. The Growing Minds team does this through various training programs and by providing free seeds and mini-grants. It also offers lesson plans, a searchable database of children's literature, weekly activity sheets, a lending library and cooking kits to make it as easy as possible for an educator to incorporate farm to school activities and lessons into their curriculums. They also work with School Nutrition Directors to procure local food for meals and snacks.

A Program Director of this nonprofit, Emily Jackson, is a regular, invited guest at our functions at the farm and education center, where she often gives a talk about the valuable work that they do. The Creekside Farm Education Center is always open to ASAP for some of the many programs and classes that they offer, like a "teach the teacher" program that brings teachers out for farm and classroom instruction on the best lessons and curriculum to teach young kids about healthy food and where it comes from. One lesson is called "Garden Plot", where kids take a piece of bread, spread it with peanut butter or humus as the "soil" and "plant" whatever vegetables they want in their garden like carrots or celery. Then they eat it. Just about everything goes good with peanut butter or humus, and you can't make a bad garden or a bad sandwich.

For groups like ASAP and Organic Growers School, the Creekside Farm Education Center is a place to bring people together to share ideas and discuss solutions to the healthy food challenges that we face today. Our food events and farm to table meals scheduled throughout the year are designed to celebrate food and those who grow it. The events also add to the quality of life and a sense of community as we share and celebrate food together. But these events also give us the opportunity to invite various groups to speak at them to increase awareness in the broader community, and groups like OGS, ASAP and MANNA Food Bank (another partner) welcome any opportunity to stand up on the soap box and tell people what they do and ask for support. And as we partner with groups like this, we expand our network and increase our impact in our own community.

A BROADER MISSION

Some of the farm to table meals and cooking classes that we hosted at the Education Center were part of a "Guest Chef Series" that we started at the education center. We wanted to help young chefs to create a name for themselves around healthy local food, and so we invited them to come prepare and cook some of the meals for our members and we gave them as much promotion and recognition as we could. At the same time, we wanted to make local farmers famous, and raise them up to the same status as celebrity chefs, so whenever we sourced produce like corn or blueberries from another farm, we made sure to promote that farmer and farm by name with all our CSA members. We wanted food-entrepreneurs to sky-rocket to fame and fortune.

Great community food systems don't happen by accident. You must plan for it, and it involves educating people about health and nutrition and cooking. We weren't just educating the residents in Walnut Cove, but trying to educate the surrounding community and region, and the farm and the education center and the kitchen was our opportunity, our venue, to do that. And with the help from some local chefs that shared our passion for teaching, we created community outreach programs that became events for the whole family. We developed budget cooking classes, and classes for teaching working moms and dads how to prepare healthy meals fast. It's still a work in progress, and we need to expand it significantly, because it's critical to building the healthy eating habits of lower income people. We can teach people about the importance of healthy whole foods, but if it sits there and rots in the fridge because they don't really know how to prepare it, it does no good.

And from the education center it's a short hop into the garden, where we show visitors where the ingredients came from. We always encourage visitors to create their own gardens at home, which would promote healthy exercise and more connections to food. Perhaps they'd even start a community garden in their own neighborhood. Studies have shown that a community garden can reduce chronic disease and depression, particularly if residents are out their getting exercise in the garden on a regular basis.

The bottom line is that one food-based community actively promoting healthy food can reach much further out and do some real good to a larger region. The goal at Creekside Farm is to increase access to healthy food, preserve and conserve farmland and open space, reduce the environmental impact of food and food waste, provide jobs for farmers, and provide a space for education to teach about nutrition and how to grow, prepare and cook healthy food. By seeking out partnerships with other nonprofits and working with other farmers and growers, chefs and food entrepreneurs, we can increase our impact to a much larger region. With regular food-based events and programs, we grow our circle of influence with shared priorities focused on health. And as we found out, many people want to become a part of this larger story.

The community center, like our Education Center, is critical infrastructure in the agrihood because it becomes the hub in a new community food system, the center of a new food web, where teaching and education are as important as sharing food in farm to table meals.

When we choose what to eat, we probably should be considering the consequences to the natural environment. We're both contributing to and threatened by greenhouse gas emissions in our food that we eat. We're affecting climate change with every bite.

At Creekside Farm, hopefully we'll be increasing interest in sustainability while we selfishly promote our real estate project. Hopefully we'll be making people a little more aware about the importance of protecting farm land, and why it's important to encourage young farmers to take up the trade, as we callously market our real estate product. We're growing food, but it saves on the lawn maintenance bill. We're helping protect the environment a little, and for that, we're making a profit. It all seems so strange. But the universe sometimes aligns in curious ways, and developers can do some good in the world, if they want to.

It's now coming down to developers, in some measure, to help reduce the high levels of greenhouse gas affecting climate change that is generated by our current industrial food web. They can leverage market interest in sustainability to do something about it, to create change. They can help the planet by simply telling the guy on the bulldozer to stay inside this line and leave the rest to a couple young farmers. The developer simply must learn some of the principles of sustainable agriculture and promote the heck out of it.

Picture this in your mind for a moment. A big-time developer, with the sparkly gold chains around his neck, learns that he can help the environment and help feed people, both of which are good for marketing and his brand and will help him turn a healthy profit. Condense the housing onto a smaller footprint, keep the rest of the land open and untouched, which adds an amenity at no real development cost, and keep the money rolling in. He stands up and says "Ba-da-boom, Ba-da-bing!"

Like I said, the universe aligns in curious ways sometimes. Most developers of course don't wear big gold chains around their neck, I just said that because it was funny to picture it. The developer will be, however, running an organic farm from his yacht in Miami.

That was another joke, but the truth is, unless there's profit in it, it 'aint happening. People investing money expect a return. Leveraging current trends in sustainability and healthy food can lead to real estate success. Conserving farmland can bring you customers. It might also help you when you go down to the county office for your permits. Some public offices might help streamline the process because of the public good expressed within the project.

The developer is in a particularly powerful position to affect change because of his access to capital (and therefore land), which puts him in a position to help young farmers access land to grow food for the community.

The beauty is that maintaining food production can cost about the same as your typical landscaping. A developer pays an average of about $30 per square foot to create traditional landscaping garden areas.[14] Melissa can plant a lot of food for about the same cost, including labor and supplies. The value of the food amenity that she has created is very desirable to potential residents and should generate more property sales.

It's a small investment with a potentially big impact on sales, maybe even more so than a tastefully planted bed of annuals or banks of azaleas and rhododendron.

The interest and appeal of organic food continues to grow. Sales of organic food rose to over $43 billion in 2015, up 11 percent over the previous year, while the overall food industry saw just a 3 percent growth rate.[15] Organic is growing at a much higher rate than the overall food market. It's part of the reason large food corporations are buying up organic farms in California. They see the trend, and they're not dummies. Neither are developers.

CHAPTER FOUR

BUILDING FOR WELLNESS

As we sat overlooking the farm and gardens one day, my wife said, "You're not really a farmer." I was a little unsettled by that, and she could tell.

"You don't really want to be an organic farmer. You're not out there pulling weeds or feeding chickens. You're not digging up potatoes or harvesting beans. You don't want to do that work."

"I don't?"

"Other people like Melissa may want to do that work, but you're not one of them."

"I'm not?"

"No, you're not. You like the big-picture stuff, but you always pass the details on to someone else."

"No I don't," I proclaimed.

"Yes, you do. You like the *idea* of being a farmer," she continued, "or going 'back to the farm' or 'living off the land', but you don't really want to do all the work that comes with being an organic farmer. It's a dream for you, but when the hard reality sets in, the hot sun, and the bugs and gnats are buzzing around in your face, and you're bent over pulling weeds, well, let's just say you're not the first guy in line to do that job. You'd rather hire someone else to do it."

She was right. She kept a large garden for years, and she knew what went into it, what it takes to pull food out of the ground. I didn't.

"Well," I said, "I'm farm management, anyway." I liked the sound of that.

"Can't I just be the handsome figurehead, for the farm I mean? Like the CEO or president?" I don't know if farms ever have CEO's but it sounded more like a job that I could handle.

Kara smiled but her point was made. She gave me the reality check that I needed. So, OK, I'm not a real farmer. I was a pretender. I didn't do the hard work. And I wouldn't be ruined by the weather. I would still make it through the next year, and the year after that. I didn't put it all on the line, every growing season, like most farmers do. I was resourceful perhaps, and I had the resources to cause the land to be farmed, but I was no farmer. I didn't risk everything, and I certainly wasn't out there sweating in the fields every day. I haven't earned the title of farmer, and to call myself that would be misleading at the least. Yes, I've purchased farm land, some equipment and bought some animals and seed, and hired people to do all the work, but to call myself a farmer would be a misnomer. My wife always has the uncanny ability to see things as they really are. I loved the idea of farming but couldn't handle the work. Now whenever someone asks me what I do for a living, in front of my wife, I say that I'm just a simple goat-herder and leave it at that.

But in truth, I guess I would have to say that I'm a small farm investor and advocate. I find myself often touting a message about what might be considered ethical economic behavior. I tell people to step out of the Industrial Ag Machine, pay a little more for local food once in a while, and in doing so you're no longer just a cog in that industrial wheel. You become an integral part of a community where the local farm and farmer become the new hub in a new wheel. But that requires a longer conversation, so usually I just say, "Goat-herder. What do you do?" I kind of like the sound of it also. We only have four goats, so it's not a full-time job, and the job title implies a certain lack of commitment on my part that appeals to me.

SELLING THE IDEA

To get a better feel for the sales and marketing side of this project, and really, to find out if I was just crazy for making this huge investment in a new concept like an agrihood, I met with a group of real estate professionals in the fall of 2017. The project was getting to a point where we were finishing the land development process at Creekside Farm, the water and power were in, and the asphalt had just been laid down on the newly graded road.

And now, finally, we were about ready to release lots in the new community, so I wanted to get some feedback on the whole agrihood concept from a group of real estate sales people. I needed to know, after investing just about every penny I had, and borrowed a lot more, if I was completely off my rocker about this whole thing. I needed to know if this idea had some legs and if they could sell it.

Would people actually care? And more importantly, would they buy into it?

At this first sales meeting in a nicely decorated conference room with a dozen real estate agents in attendance, I went through a long and detailed Power Point presentation about the agrihood concept. It was new to all of them, and most of them had never heard of the idea or the term 'agrihood'.

I went through recent media attention about various agri-hoods around the country in the New York Times and Forbes Magazine, and TV coverage on NBC Nightly News and CBS Sunday Morning programs. I said this trend is happening. They didn't recognize any of it.

The Power Point presentation included 70 slides with images of the site plan, home lots, the farm, the old barn and the education center. I had pictures of cows, chickens, open pasture and our farm manager Melissa on a tractor. I went through all the benefits of an agricultural community; that it protects our pastoral viewscapes from over-development; that it preserves farming knowledge and the local farming capacity for future generations; that it provides food safety and security against some unforeseen crisis like oil shortages or solar flares that could knock out the power grid; that it promotes healthier lifestyles and connects people to the land while building community around food.

I rushed to get through all 70 slides in 45 minutes, leaving 15 minutes at the end for questions and open discussion. I knew Josh Smith, the sales manager and he got it. He lived on a small farm, grew some vegetables and hops for beer, had some cattle and horses, and he was the kind of guy that could just sit on the porch and drink beer and watch the corn grow. I'd done it with him in fact. But I wasn't sure anyone else was getting it.

My whole presentation was based on what I thought were good reasons for building the agricultural community, but I didn't necessarily tell them how to sell it, which is really what they wanted. This became evident with the first question from the group.

"Can I get a cheat sheet or something?" said one of the agents, "I don't have that much time with my clients to go through all of this."

I realized right then and there that so much more is involved with marketing and selling a project like this that you can't really create a cheat sheet for it. You can't even come up with a one-minute elevator pitch, like "it's got a pool, tennis courts, a golf course, and cows." The decision we were asking someone to make involved the client's deepest values, perceptions and principles. There was no short answer, and that's probably why I decided to write this book.

I panicked. Then I remembered Andres Duany. I needed to tell this group the how to sell more than the why. No matter how creative, intelligent or responsible that I believed this life-style that we were offering was, some people just won't care.

I told the sales group that we should first try to qualify the customer and be prepared to drop those who know or care nothing about food, the environment or community. But I said that there are enough people out there already, right now, who do care. The farm to table movement at top restaurants, and the grow local movement at farmers markets and CSA programs everywhere give evidence to that. "It's very real," I said.

The other agri-hood communities under construction around the country gave me a great deal of confidence. I told this crew that there are enough people out there who would be interested in the agrihood concept, but many of them may have vastly different reasons, and that's what they must figure out quickly in a conversation with their client.

Remembering Duany, who had been down this road before as a land planner, I told the sales group this; "The customer can be grouped into four different types of customers, and your sales pitch will vary depending on who you're talking to. You've already eliminated the non-environmentalist."[16]

"Based on a fairly brief conversation, a few questions and the client's responses you should be able to tell if this person is an 'environmentalist', a 'trendsetter', an 'opportunist', or a 'survivalist.' Gear your pitch to one of those four types of people."

"A sales pitch to the environmentalist is a no brainer" I said, and I could tell this group was starting to sit up and listen a bit closer. "They already get it, just show them around." Duany says these are the leaders in the green living movement, probably drive fuel efficient cars and own a smoothie machine. Pretty straight forward, I said, just show them the garden and the farm, the animals, the old barn and the education center. "They'll be way ahead of you," I continued, "and they'll see it as the right thing to do. It'll be in line with things they already value."

"The trendsetter goes to all the new, hip restaurants where chefs are serving local food, and promoting it as much as they can, even going so far as to tell you the name of the farm and perhaps the name of the farmer that grew the food on the menu," I told them.

"Healthy is trendy. Just as smoking has become so passé these days, eating bad food is going that way now also. These trendsetters might drive a Prius now that they aren't so ugly and look kind of cool." They are also young and have big social networks that can move an idea like the agrihood to the forefront of our collective consciousness.[17]

"They'll buy in if it's cool and trendy" I said, "and they already know that eating processed junk food, like smoking, is not cool." I continued with another joke that I stole from Duany, "Tell them that the chicken coop was designed by Ikea. Sold." That got a laugh from my audience, and I had them now. They were mine. I sensed the enthusiasm building.

"The opportunist wants in on the ground floor" I told them. "If he can save money or turn a profit to go green, he's all in. Stress the media attention and the growth of the whole agrihood trend and thus the growth in resale value with these people."

"The survivalist wants first and foremost to protect his family from impending doom." They see decline and trouble ahead, and they will see the agrihood as social security against a future energy shortage, food scarcity and social unrest.[18] I continued, "The ability to produce your own food within a small community is the sales focus. Tell them we've got their protein needs covered with chicken eggs until the power comes back on."

I felt a little dirty after the meeting. But I think it satisfied most of my audience. I gave them a few short sound bites that they might be able to remember and use. But the experience brought home something in my own mind. The whole project that I'd been working on for two years can't really be broken down into a sound bite or even a 45-minute presentation.

I had just pigeon-holed everyone into four different groups, and their motivations I had been describing doesn't even scratch the surface in the real world. The difference really relates to values and what each group might feel as most important. I pigeon-holed everybody in order to give these sales agents something quick and easy. I know the reasons people might choose to live here are much deeper, and touched on deeper values and principles, even at a spiritual level, that would take some time for me to sort out.

Is there a future for this agrihood community? The answer is that it's all about the future. Duany writes that "sustainability to the point of self-sufficiency is where the market is going, especially if it becomes apparent that the campaign to mitigate climate change is being lost."[19]

Duany wrote this in 2011, long before Donald Trump became president of the United States, and before his climate change nay-sayers took charge. Duany couldn't see the political backlash against Trump policy that is coming, and in fact is here already, but he was right anyway. Environmentalism is now top of mind with many people who are also adamantly opposed to what they see as Trump's crass, destructive stand on the environment.

There are many signs of the environmental problems we face, from rising CO_2 levels, more frequent and severe weather events, the infertility of our soils in the Midwest (so that massive amounts of chemical fertilizers are now required to grow anything), the drop in underground water levels in the aquifers that water the breadbasket of the nation, deforestation to the extent that half the trees on the planet in 1950 are now gone, the serious loss of biodiversity in our oceans and rain forests. The list goes on.

I might have added another category to the pigeon-holed groups I described for the sales agents. That would be the spiritualist. As perhaps a subgroup of the environmentalists, this group has a more spiritual connection to mother earth. They see the earth as a living organism, sacred and holy. A sense of awe and wonder in the beauty of nature awakens this spiritual sense, and they feel respect and veneration for it. This sense of a spiritual connection to nature is one of man's earliest philosophical and psychological constructs.

Alberto and I traveled to a small farm in the Umbria region of Italy, about 80 kilometers southeast of Florence. We went to visit a friend of Alberto's on a small farm owned by Francesco Romiti and we sat with Francesco on a large patio one hot afternoon sipping a cool chianti and talking about his farm and growing up in this incredibly beautiful agricultural region of Italy.

Francesco lived at the outer edge of a small village tucked into an agricultural landscape, with rolling acres of farm land as far as the eye could see. He was a farmer, so was his father, on this same beautiful 80-acre farm in the rolling hills of Umbria that looked like a "Go to Italy" poster. His son who everyone called Kekko opened a small B&B with his wife on the farm to supplement the family income. Alberto and I were planning to spend the evening there at the farm.

Francesco told me that the oldest building on the farm, a tiny house made from stone up near the road, was at one time a toll house. It was located there on the outskirts of his small village to collect tolls on the road that still runs in front of the old building, which up until just 30 years ago was still a dirt road. The road linked this small village to other towns in the region, and before there was any federal or regional government authority to maintain the road, the townspeople collected tolls from every traveler and passing cart filled with produce coming into or passing through the village.

Its primary purpose was to collect funds to upkeep the road, which was prone to erosion and large ruts when the heavy rains came in winter. But Francesco let me in on a little secret, "It was also an unspoken way to extract tariffs, tariffs from people bringing goods or produce in from another town or region that might compete with local farmers and local artisans."

Francesco joked, "Oh, you're not from here? What's in the cart? That'll be five lira." His Italian accent made it seem funnier. This practice probably went on for hundreds of years, and perhaps even when people paid the tariff with coins that had Caesar's head stamped on them.

Francesco was in his late sixties but still strong as an ox.

Short and barrel-chested, with big hands and forearms that came from years of throwing hay and working a rake. After a couple glasses of chianti, he began to tell me a story about how he met and courted his wife back in the '50s. She lived in another small village about 30 kilometers away, and when he would ride his motorcycle to her village to visit her, the other boys from that village did not appreciate or approve of it. They didn't like the idea of a boy coming from another village to take one of their girls out on a date. "Especially the prettiest girl," Francesco said.

"Almost every time I got into a fight with one of the boys from that village, so that it became a regular and expected event on Saturday night, a sort of 'toll' I had to pay," he said with a big grin.

It was his way, he said, to show his dedication and love for this pretty girl from that village. He said, "I had to earn her love in this way, and fortunately for me, most of the time I won the fight, until finally, when the other boys from that village learned that I wasn't giving up, they stopped confronting me altogether."

He told me how difficult it was making a decent living on this small farm in central Italy. He worked hard and long all his life, and what I saw now was all he had to show for it. It was a beautiful farm, with several out buildings including the large stone barn that had been converted into a B&B where Alberto and I would be spending the night. The stone terrace where we sat overlooked the golden fields of wheat, and what looked like soybeans, some olive trees, and a large vegetable garden that his son and daughter in law maintained for the farm to table meals for their guests at the B&B. A vineyard lay on a hillside in the distance.

I asked him why he chose this way of life. Why not move to a larger town and get a job that was less physically demanding and paid a much higher wage then what he could earn on this small farm.

"This little farm," he said, "and this small community of neighbors around me, it's very important to me. Food is important. Community is important."

I didn't quite understand at the time what he was saying. Was he talking about a cultural choice that flies in the face of industrialization and mass consumerism. Or was he just saying that he likes to eat. Then he added something else.

"My son has a shirt that he wears. It says, 'Eat Your View.' I eat my view every day. Con mucho gusto!" He tipped his glass towards us and took a deep gulp.

Ok, he likes to eat his view. From what I could tell, most of what Francesco ate came from the hills around him, as did the wine he drank, and a lot of it right from his own farm. He supported his neighboring farmers, and they supported him.

After about an hour and a half of drinking wine, admiring the beautiful landscape around us, and chatting with Francesco about his farm, and now starting to really feel the wine, Alberto and I decided to take a little walk through the countryside to work up an appetite for dinner, and really to keep ourselves from getting too drunk with Francesco. This was his local wine, and he was used to drinking it, so that I'm quite sure we were feeling it's affects more than he was. We walked down the dirt road that ran along Francesco's farm and up into the neighboring hills. It was an old farming road used to access fields; the occasional dilapidated farm house spotted the landscape. It was lovely, and it felt like home, like this was how we should all be living.

As we walked down this dusty country road, I asked Alberto what he thought about the "eat your view" movement in Italy.

"People are concerned about what they put into their bodies now, that's for sure. But more than that, they understand that you have to support farmers and farms. Most of Italy's farms are small, only about seven acres on average, and most are still family owned. You have to support them, or they might go away."

"That's why the organic movement in Italy is so important," he said. "Did you know that Italy has the largest area of land in organic farming and the greatest number of organic farms in Europe?"

I said I didn't know that. He continued on a roll.

"It is. In the past 20 years, the number of organic farms went from about 600 to now over 50,000 farms. The number of hectares under organic cultivation grew by 200 times and is now over 1 million hectares under organic production. That's a lot for little Italy."

"It's a big success story in Italy," said Alberto. "The European Union encouraged organic farming, and financial support for organic farms helped it to grow. You know Italians care about quality ingredients in their food. It was only natural for us to take the lead on this. And we have a good climate with long growing seasons in some regions for organic fruits and vegetables."

"How did the EU encourage organic farms?" I asked.

"The EU established subsidies for organic farms over 25 years ago as a way to help protect the environment with better agricultural production methods. That helped to get it started. But as people became more aware of the harmful effects of chemicals, that really made it take off. The demand was there."

"But it's still mostly the younger farmers who farm organically and take advantage of the subsidies. The older guys don't want to fill out all the paperwork," Alberto told me.

He continued, "I've talked to a lot of older farmers, mostly in very rural areas, and asked why they don't switch over and farm organically in order to get the subsidies. Especially if they are in a marginal area for production, where farming is already difficult on that land because of the climate or soil conditions. Mostly they are just set in their ways and don't like the paperwork and the bureaucracy. Younger people don't have a problem with filling out the forms."

"As many farmers have expressed to me," Alberto said, "it is strange that the organic farmers are the ones who must fill out all the forms and prove that they don't use any harmful chemicals, but the people who dump a bunch of toxic pesticides and other chemicals on the land don't have to fill out any forms. They can use potentially dangerous chemicals without asking for any authorization or filling out any single form. It should be the other way around, don't you think?" I didn't even have a chance to agree before he was talking again.

"The Italian government recently put a tax on pesticides, and the revenue is supposed to go toward supporting organic produce in some way. So that's another step in the right direction," Alberto told me.

I said that I wished the United States had more programs like this to support organic farms. Even a small percentage of the massive subsidies that we give to farms using millions of tons of chemicals would go a long way to help small organic farmers, like it does here in Italy.

"Everyone knows about Italian olives and wine. But we are now a big country for organic food production. I'm very proud of that," he said with a big, satisfied smile.

After about a 30-minute walk, we came upon a group of pigs hanging out in a small field adjacent to the road, and we stopped to admire them. The group made their way over to greet us and to see if we had anything to offer in the way of food.

There was a big one who must have weighed over 450 pounds, and he was obviously the leader, and he was first to reach the old rusted gate where we stood.

"What a wonderful pig" Alberto said, "he's huge." He continued to praise the pigs, "They're beautiful, and look how big that guy is." The big guy, the leader, poked his head through the gate and made a couple grunting noises. We stood there watching as he dug his snout under the lowest rung of the gate and lifted it slightly. Alberto said, "He's pretty smart. Do you know how smart pigs are? He's trying to lift that gate up. Pigs are very smart."

After standing there and admiring the pigs for a little while, we turned to continue our walk and hadn't gotten very far when we heard a loud noise from back at the gate, and I turned just in time to see that pig lift the entire gate with his snout and huge neck more than a foot off the ground. He lifted it right off the hinges and pushed it open in one impressive display of strength. Alberto exclaimed, "Mamma Mia!" – he didn't really say that, he said something very loud in Italian, but you get the idea. It could have been the wine, but confusion and panic quickly set in on both of us.

We walked very quickly back to the gate, and the leader was already trotting down the road making his escape. A trot for a large pig like that is not really very fast, and Alberto took off after him yelling in Italian. I stayed by the gate and corralled the other smaller and more timid pigs back into the field, yelling in English, so they obviously must have been bilingual. Very smart pigs indeed.

I was able to stand up the gate and turned to see Alberto using some of his childhood soccer skills on the big pig, shuffling his feet left and right to stop the pig. He'd go left, the pig would go right. Alberto had a yellow sweater tied around his neck and was wearing $300 Italian leather shoes of course. Like most Italian men, Alberto was fashion conscious and always dressed nicely. It made the whole spectacle look more amusing.

Somehow, he was able to convince that pig to turn around,

and as he made his way back toward me I dragged the gate open, still not on its hinges so that the chain on the other end became the hinge, and I opened it wide enough to partially block half the road. Fortunately for us the pig trotted right back into the field. We struggled to get the gate back on its hinges while Alberto continued to curse at the pig in Italian. For my benefit, he said "Stupid Pig" in English.

Beads of sweat had formed on Alberto's forehead, but after a moment, with the pigs secured back in their pen, the adrenalin started wearing off and the warm calm of the wine took its place again. I looked at Alberto and said, "Shall we go eat?" He said, "Yes, let's go eat" and we turned to head back down the road from where we came. "Stupid pig," he said again.

Kirkpatrick Sale defines and describes a Spanish word, querencia, which implies not just a "love of home" but a word that means much more than that to the Spanish people. "A deep, quiet sense of inner well-being that comes from knowing a particular place of the earth," writes Sale, "its diurnal and seasonal patterns, its fruits and scents, its history and its part in your history." He continues, "whenever you return to it, your soul releases an inner sigh of recognition and relaxation."

I think Francesco and Alberto both felt that sense of place where they lived. I felt it too when I finally returned to my home and little farm in the mountains outside of Asheville, North Carolina. The rolling hills and mountains around Asheville remind me a little of Tuscany and it's a beautiful landscape. I think the views are comparable. But it's that deep, quiet sense of peace and inner well-being which comes over me whenever I return to Asheville and my farm that reminds me why I chose to live here.

Asheville has a lot to offer. It's a big draw for art lovers also and has more artist studios and galleries than most cities of its size. It's a free-spirited place. Hippies, young and old, gather on a main square Friday night to bang on drums, or bang on cans or anything else that makes an interesting sound when you hit it with a stick, in non-stop rhythms that usually get other hippies who didn't bring a drum to get up and dance like they're at a Grateful Dead concert. Meanwhile 50 to 100 other townsfolk and tourists stand around and watch the spectacle. Every Friday night in the summer- don't miss it.

Asheville is a tourist destination because of the wonderful Blue Ridge Mountains that surround the town, and it keeps an interesting mix of free-spirited young people and wealthy retirees in its population. It's a Mecca for outdoor lovers and has become known nationally as a "Beer City" for all the microbreweries in town. More microbreweries exist in Asheville per capita than any other city.

Asheville won the title "Beer City" several years in a row and brands itself as "Foodtopia". Asheville's efforts to brand itself as a "Foodtopia" started years ago and focused on promoting local foods, local beer, Asheville-only restaurants, and the true bounty of the region. City officials continue to promote it—and have for a decade—as a local food city. Encouraging and promoting chefs and restaurants that serve local food, and raising farmers up to celebrity status, like chefs, are very good initiatives to building the necessary infrastructure for the 'eat your view' local food movement. Eating local food (and drinking local beer and wine) is a big part of the travel experience and adds greatly to the pleasure and memories of traveling.

I was becoming part of this local food movement, but I didn't start off my career as a land developer and building agricultural communities for a living. This was all new to me. I started other businesses and sold different products for about 25 years. I often traveled around the world looking for product ideas and places to make them. I imported leather goods from Italy, plush goods from China, and tote bags from India. I've sold books to college students, teddy bears to the United States Navy, coffee mugs to the CIA, and backpacks to Wal-Mart. My companies were in such diverse industries as manufacturing, importing, licensing, and publishing, and I'm happy to report that none of them failed, even though employees would often lose sight of me for weeks, so I can't really take any credit for it. In truth, my wife and business partner, Kara, deserves most of the credit. I always liked to see myself as the handsome figurehead of the company, and as Kara pointed out to me, was inclined to pass on the details to her and everyone else.

We eventually sold the companies and used most of that money to start buying and developing commercial real estate. That's when I started reading books on urban planning and the modern history of urban development. At about the same time we also purchased a small 10-acre farm in the mountains of Western North Carolina, and in the middle of my life I decided to try to learn how to farm. I learned about a lot more than farming.

Here's what I learned about modern urban planning.

Our industrial society made some mistakes in the 20th century. We plowed under farm land to create sprawling suburbia. We built massive shopping malls that urban planners believed would be the place everyone would go for social interaction in the new suburbs; a place to meet and catch up with your neighbors. That never really happened, and people are realizing now that mass consumption is not sustainable or all that fulfilling. CNN recently reported that 20 to 25% of the malls in America will be closing in the next five years.

The rush to the suburbs after World War II made us totally dependent on the car and petroleum. Suburbanites are literally trapped at home without these things. Unlike cities where everything is condensed, and things are more walkable and there's better public transportation, you're stuck in the suburbs without a car and it's not very sustainable living. It's certainly not good for the environment, and not just because of the gas it takes everyone to get anywhere. We paved over usable farm land to create miles of asphalt and rooftops spread out as far as the eye can see.

At the same time in this short history of the past 70 years, people became separated from their food and where it comes from. The closest most people get to a farm these days is the vegetable aisle in their local grocery store.

NEW URBAN DESIGN

When we incorporated our agricultural neighborhood, Creekside Farm, into the larger Cliffs community, we brought healthy food production to the community, but what did the Cliffs bring to the table in the deal? In terms of life expectancy and longevity for residents, they brought a lot into the equation. We had the healthy food aspect covered, and people could get some exercise in the garden, but the Cliffs really completed a package that could really add to a resident's vitality and longevity. True wellness and longevity is about both; a healthy diet and exercise. You can't do one without the other if you really want to improve your health and possibly extend your lifespan. The Cliffs offered plenty of ways to get the exercise in enjoyable ways, whether that is golf, tennis, swimming, a yoga class or a hike through the woods. We need to dig in a little deeper to this side of the health equation.

While the agricultural community is related to the healthy food and grow local movement at restaurants and farmers markets, it might also be considered an offshoot of an already booming "wellness community" trend in real estate planning and development. And there's good reason for that.

The World Health Organization reported recently that three quarters of all premature deaths worldwide by the year 2020 will be directly related to the environment and a person's behavior or lifestyle within that environment. The report shows that our health problems are mostly related to unhealthy food and a sedentary lifestyle. The WHO found that 80-90% of our health problems can be directly linked to where we live and how we live. The report suggests many different contributors impact health, but pollution (air, water and land), unhealthy food, and a sedentary lifestyle are the three key factors for premature death. Genes play a role, but how people live has a significantly higher impact on overall life expectancy.

Long before that report, most Americans already understood that our sedentary lifestyles and a poor diet are the major contributors to our health problems. It wasn't really anything we didn't already know. The healthy, organic food trend is already well under way, and more recently urban planners got into the game and decided to do something about creating healthier, more active environments and smarter spaces for us to live in.

Our rush to the suburbs since the 1950s has contributed greatly to our current health crisis. Nothing is walkable in the suburbs, and we've become more isolated as we've become totally dependent on the car, and the rates of psychological depression have continued to rise along with rates of diabetes and heart disease. Some urban planners want to change all that by designing healthier communities that are more walkable and that create spaces and opportunities for social connection.

There are few market squares or town centers that you can walk or bike to in the suburbs, and less chance of social intercourse and connection with other human beings. Stress, isolation and pollution have been built into our communities over the past 70 years. Long commutes from the suburbs to work in the city only adds stress and pollution, and the commute home leads us to isolated cul-de-sacs without much chance for social interaction there. The car is king, and in many suburban areas a bike path or sidewalk doesn't even exist.

This realization is creating a big change in the way developers and urban planners think and plan new communities in the 21st century. And they're starting to redesign spaces in existing urban communities to make them healthier and allow for more connections to nature and to other human beings. This trend is usually referred to as "New Urban" planning. New Urbanism is an urban design movement which promotes healthier, environmentally friendly practices. They do that through more sustainable building and home design and creating neighborhoods that are condensed and walkable and that consider nature and natural elements. They reduce traffic and carbon emissions by creating walkable neighborhoods containing a wide range of "mixed use" spaces (mixing housing, retail and work spaces closer together).

There is also a thoughtful focus among urban planners now on building what are called wellness communities, and the market is quickly growing for that type of community. Recent research from the Global Wellness Institute shows that there is a rising movement in healthy living, with people making lifestyle changes and choices that improve health and longevity, from the growth in organic food to yoga studios and other forms of exercise, to meditation and mindfulness classes, to the significant rise in sales of athletic shoes and apparel.[20]

It all points to a more health conscious society, and Millennials again are leading the way. People are beginning to understand the current health crisis in America and what causes it, and many people are making decisions based on that understanding and now choosing to live in a wellness community. Wellness communities are sprouting up everywhere around the world because they provide the amenities that make it easy for people to pursue healthy activities, like swimming pools, exercise studios, and walking trails.

Planned wellness communities, or new developments that feature wellness amenities and activities as a major selling point, are now a booming business in real estate, and developers are finding that they can charge a premium on the price for building these wellness features into their communities. Some estimates put the market value of the wellness community worldwide in the hundreds of billions of dollars.

Nature is often featured as a wellness amenity by incorporating walking and biking trails through natural settings. Protection of natural resources, like wetlands, and the sustainability of the environment, are important in this type of development, and the developer should stress the steps that were taken to protect and preserve those resources in his marketing literature. People will want to know that.

Green homes are often featured in wellness communities. Wellness communities can also be located in urban or city settings, where buildings or neighborhoods are transformed to offer healthier activities, amenities and natural landscaping that invite social and physical interaction. Just offering a few nicely landscaped places for people to sit and chat is a good start.

Wellness communities are sometimes developed to look and feel like spa resorts in the mountains or at the beach. They can be located near national parks to attract active, outdoor lovers while taking advantage of the already existing opportunities for healthy outdoor activities. They can incorporate anything from the latest wellness exercise equipment and technology to meditation gardens to aromatherapy rooms to classes and instruction in eastern philosophy, you name it. Just about any wellness activity that you can think of can be brought into the menu of wellness amenities offered by a developer of a wellness community.[21]

The wellness feature in residential developments is not entirely new, but it has grown exponentially over the past 20 years to become a major movement in real estate development. The real estate market has changed so that wellness has become an expected feature within many cities and regions of the country. Middle and upper income buyers are asking "Where's the pool?" "Where's the gym?" And "Where's the bike path?" It's a trend that is transforming the business, and by most estimates it will continue to grow.

A home is the most expensive purchase and biggest asset for most people, so it's only natural that people will look at health and wellness as an important part of an investment in their future. If the surrounding neighborhood or environment offers activities and opportunities for healthy choices and lifestyles, then most people now will choose it. They may not always use it or take advantage of it, but they want to know it's there. They might see their "future self" taking advantage of it someday.

The wellness features in any community can lead to healthier choices simply because these activities are close by and easily accessible. The heart of these communities is usually the wellness center with pools and yoga or Pilates studios, weight rooms and cardio vascular equipment. The best communities also tie into nature with walking trails through wooded areas and near ponds or water features because that's good for our psychological health as well as physical.

Processed foods and a sedentary lifestyle are contributing to the trillions of dollars that we currently spend on health care. The industrial food complex and the built environment since the 1950s has had a direct impact on these healthcare costs. It's time we take a closer look at how to fix the problem rather than treat the symptoms. The way communities are planned has a key role.

Thierry Malleret, a well-known economist with the World Economic Forum, was a keynote speaker at the 2013 Global Wellness Summit in India, and there he said, "In the future, in some countries, wellness will become mandatory."[22]

When you look at the skyrocketing costs of health care that governments across the world are trying to control, he may be right. I'm sure he's just talking about 'mandatory' from the developer's perspective, like the developer must include some wellness feature for the residents or consider wellness in the overall plan. I hope he's not talking about the 'wellness police' who make you drop and do 50 sit-ups when they catch you eating a donut. For now at least, wellness is optional.

The point is communities need to be walkable and offer opportunities for physical exercise. They need connection points to nature, including parks, green spaces and access to woodlands or waterways. We, as a society, need to spend more of our resources on prevention by transforming our communities into more livable, walkable and socially interactive spaces.

The savings in health care costs in the long run will far exceed any costs of building these healthier environments.

So the solution to many of our chronic diseases now lies to a good measure on the shoulders of urban planners, developers and real estate investors as much as it does with the medical profession. The good news is that there is plenty of demand for a new wellness lifestyle, and that demand with its corresponding opportunity is a strong incentive to the development and construction industry.

Just as the 'green building' trend has changed the construction industry, so too can the wellness trend. With some help and guidelines from the government- but not much- there are industry standards and certifications now for green homes. And just as that trend has moved from niche to mainstream, so too will the concepts of building communities around wellness. If there's a customer and demand, businesses will try to fill that demand.

Wellness is a concept that goes way beyond housing developments. Here's a few more facts from the Global Wellness Institute report. Wellness tourism, where healthy activities, like hiking and bicycling are a primary or important part of a tourists travel agenda, is a $563 billion-dollar business. And while wellness tourism accounts for over $500 billion in economic benefit to the tourism industry, the category defined as eco-sustainable tourism adds up to another $325-480 billion. Culinary tourism (food being the primary reason for travel) amounts to an estimated $350-550 billion. Agricultural tourism, like the agritoursimo in Italy, would likely fall under all three of these categories, because it encompasses healthy activity on or around a farm, eco-sustainability in food production, and fresh, healthy farm-to-table food. People are spending money and going places because of what they believe is important, and they believe healthy activity while traveling is important.[23]

Placemaking is another term used by urban planners which refers to using design strategy to create public spaces that are inviting, lively and vibrant with activity. It involves architecture and landscape design to create places for people to connect and interact and enjoy the environment. Planners and developers can also use placemaking theory to create a rich experience around food and agriculture. Many developments and communities are now being planned with "food hubs" at the center, where restaurants and small artisan food shops are focal points, and with plenty of outdoor seating. It's not an entirely new idea, this placemaking around food. The best part of going to Italy, in my view, is sitting at an outdoor café and people watching. Large public squares at the center of many Italian towns are often closed to vehicle traffic and surrounded by restaurants and cafés with outdoor seating and colorful umbrellas. That's placemaking around food.

Ancient streets in London were often named by what you could find and buy on them, and roads in or near the old historic food market have names like Pudding Lane, Fish Street Hill, Pie Corner, Bread Street, Poultry Lane, Lamb Street, and Milk Street. How do you create food hubs? It couldn't be clearer than that. Gather food producers and retailers together into one area, call it Main Street, and make sure there's some outdoor seating. People will come.

Until the mid-20th century, towns and cities generally consisted of mixed-use buildings with business and living spaces close together or above each other. Businesses and shops usually occupied the first floor, with living space above. For most of history, cities and towns were generally walkable, and with the advent of public transportation like the street car, cities extended further out in connected communities and neighborhoods.

When the automobile became affordable, particularly after

World War II, urban planners, builders and developers focused construction toward low-density single-family detached houses as a product for the growing middle class and suburbia was born. The interstate highway system started by Eisenhower in the early 1960's had a lot to do with it also because people could get from the new suburbs to work in the cities quickly. Local and regional governments began to focus on municipal zoning ordinances that would segregate and separate residential development from commercial or industrial areas, and they began to physically separate people and where they lived from where they worked, shopped and spent their free time. This made the population and our culture completely dependent on the automobile.

The concepts of New Urban design are starting to influence many areas of real estate planning and development across the United States, and developers are starting to build communities with town centers or market squares that are in reach of most of the homes by a short walk, less than a half mile, reducing dependency on the car and enabling some exercise by foot or bike.

Mixed use means work is not separated from living spaces like in our suburbs or work is located within a small proximity, and businesses and homes or apartments are mixed in or located close to each other. It means condos or apartments are located above shops, and single-family housing is condensed on smaller lots and within walking distance from the town center or market square. Someone lives above the bicycle shop, it just might not be the owner of the bicycle shop like 100 years ago. Just imagine walking to work, and not having to get in the car for that hour commute through rush hour traffic. That means less stress and better mental health, while reducing carbon emissions into the environment, and getting a little exercise to boot.

Just four miles from Creekside Farm is one of the best recent examples of New Urban Design, a mixed-use planned community called Biltmore Park Town Square. Biltmore Park mixes living spaces with work spaces in a walkable market square design and where most of the homes are within a half mile walk from the town center. Apartments and condos occupy the upper floors of 4 story buildings in the town center, with retail and office space taking up the ground floor. Several cafés and restaurants line the main street and offer outdoor seating, with a large YMCA as anchor at one end of the main street, and a large movie theater complex at the other end.

The Biltmore name comes from The Biltmore Estate, still the largest private home in America with over 250 rooms and now the biggest tourist destination in Asheville. The heirs to the Vanderbilt estate developed Biltmore Park Town Square over the last decade on a small portion of the remaining 8,000-acre estate.

The Biltmore home was built at the end of the 19th century, and surprisingly, it was purpose-built for health and wellness. The fresh, clean, mountain air of Western North Carolina was a draw to the Vanderbilt family, as was the thousands of acres of natural beauty of the Blue Ridge Mountains nearby. The estate was originally 125,000 acres, a huge chunk of land. The home includes an indoor pool (highly unusual for the time) and a large exercise room including medicine balls and other interesting 19th century exercise equipment. The estate includes a large working farm and pastures for livestock.

The new urban project could have been the perfect agrihood if the estates farm and pasture land were closer to the Biltmore Park development, and not located five miles away like it is now. If people living in this condensed, mixed use community could walk to the farm and pick up fresh vegetables, it would truly be the perfect sustainable and resilient community, but the food grown on the estate now goes to support the restaurants that feed the tourists who visit the estate. Biltmore Park does have a weekly farmers market on the main street and invites farmers from all over the region to sell their products there every Wednesday afternoon in the summer, so it does support the local food movement in a big way.

The Biltmore Park community is food-centric and offers outdoor seating at several restaurants which brings the celebration of food outdoors and into the public spaces. Several non-chain food related businesses and restaurants line the Main Street including a bakery for your dog (but it could use a bakery for humans). It has the weekly farmers market, but a large permanent indoor market would be even better, with meats, cheeses and other specialty food items that spill out onto the street on tables and carts. A large, permanent market like this would be walkable for most residents to pick up something to prepare for dinner and likely become a tourist draw and destination by itself, if it were large enough. Many large indoor markets are major draws in cities like Seattle and contribute to the quality of life there.

The Biltmore farm and gardens grow only a small portion of the food that is used in the restaurants on the Biltmore Estate; there are too many tourists for the farm to supply all the needs of the estate. I met with the farm manager Eli and Director of Horticulture, Parker Andes one sunny day in March of 2017. Eli took Melissa, Kara and I on a tour of the farm and pastures where they grow vegetables, cattle, sheep, a few pigs and about 50 laying hens for eggs. The biggest cash crop for the farm now is microgreens grown in hydroponic trays in one of the greenhouses. Two more greenhouses for microgreen production were under construction on the day of our visit. Because microgreens grow quickly and can be produced year-round in the greenhouses they're something that the farm can supply to the restaurants on a regular basis throughout the year. People clearly enjoy the idea of eating something grown right on the estate because it adds to the overall experience, so it's good for business.

The Vanderbilts first came to the area because of the fresh mountain air and healthy natural environment, and they could walk or horseback through miles of pristine woods and mountains. It was a lifestyle choice based on healthy living away from cities and pollution, and more in tune with peaceful nature. George Vanderbilt couldn't have gotten much further away from the city life here when he built the home at the turn of the 20th century. Just thousands of acres of woods and mountains.

So the question is, was George right, and will choosing where to live really affect your health and longevity? He invested millions in current dollars in the idea of providing his family with a healthier place to live, but was he right?

In his book Blue Zones, Dan Buettner travels to locations around the world that have the largest populations of people living into their 100's. Blue Zones are communities that somehow seem to increase longevity, and although separated by thousands of miles, have common elements of lifestyle that include healthy diets, regular physical activity, and a positive, low-stress outlook on life. They eat little or no processed foods, lots of vegetables and natural foods, and get regular exercise in diverse ways: from climbing hills to herd sheep from one pasture to another, to tending a small garden in the backyard. Another common element is close social ties and interaction with neighbors and family.

Because there are these well-defined concentrations of centenarians in certain towns and villages around the world, Buettner shows us that where these people live has some impact on health and longevity. But where they live can vary greatly from rocky island hillsides in Italy to lush tropical regions on Okinawa.

Where they live has affected the critical elements of a wellness lifestyle- what they ate (a plant-based diet) and what exercise they got (sheep herding or gardening.) The book shows readers how they might live a longer life by simply practicing what many of these centenarians' practice: a healthy plant-based diet and regular exercise, however you might get it. Family and social ties are important because a close-knit community helps reduce stress. It's good to have friends to lean on because they can help get you through stressful, challenging times.

The book would suggest than that creating a wellness community that encourages a healthy diet and enables some physical exercise, along with building a sense of community and ties to others, might help someone add a few years to his or her lifespan. Urban planners and developers are now working to design and create physical spaces and communities that support this idea. So was I in my little neck of the woods, out in the mountains of Appalachia.

CHAPTER FIVE

———

FARMING AND CULTURE

"It is a grand mistake to think of being great without goodness and I pronounce it as certain that there was never a truly great man that was not at the same time truly virtuous."

-Ben Franklin

As Alberto and I walked through Greve in Chianti after dinner one evening, Alberto said to me, "You know, two thousand years ago, the farmer, when he came to town with his produce, he could grab a bite to eat while he was in town at one of many bakeries and food shops that lined the street just like this one."

I had never heard or thought about that and I wondered where he got that information.

I said, "Were there any drive-thru's?".

I don't think he realized that I was joking and replied, "There weren't any drive-thru's, so he'd have to stop and get off the cart, which you Americans consider a hassle. But people would 'eat out' quite often even back then."

I asked him, "How do you know this?"

He replied, "I'll show you. We'll go to Pompeii."

Pompeii, the ruined Roman village swallowed by volcanic ash in 79 AD is not exactly a short drive from where we were in

Tuscany, but over dinner one evening a week before I had told Alberto that if I had time, I wanted to see the Amalfi Coast in the south. Pompeii happens to be on the way, and it would prove his point about ancient diners, so he drove me there.

A few days later Alberto and I walked around the ancient ruins at Pompeii where he showed me how many little café's and food shops lined the streets of the town that could still be recognized, with fragmented pictures of food items and remnants of painted menus still visible on the walls.

There were also food storage warehouses and food preparation facilities scattered throughout town. Pompeii, like all ancient towns, had other shops to be sure, shoe shops, fabric stores and the like, but its primary function, Alberto suggested, was geared to the processes related to food production, storage, preparation and distribution. It was an agricultural community, like all towns and villages in the ancient world.

In fact, even today, because food is so essential to life, you might say that we all live in one enormous agricultural community. Yet with today's industrial food complex, much of food production is now hidden from our eyes in faraway places. We don't know where that chicken came from or how it got here, but everything in society and in our culture, all cultures, relates back to food.

OBESITY IN AMERICA

Almost 40 percent of adults in the US are obese.[24] Obesity has quadrupled in adolescents over the past three short decades, since the '80s.[25] But while we continue to see obesity rates increase, the USDA says that 14 percent of our population is classified as food-insecure, and the rates of food insecurity rise as you get closer to the poverty line.[26] Poverty is the main cause for hunger and food security issues. But it's not just hunger, it brings with it illness, stress and psychological suffering.[27] Hunger also affects learning ability and test scores in children.[28]

Obesity is medically defined as having a body-mass index of more than 30. The recent CDC findings on obese children in the U.S. (20%) comes on top of a recent World Health Organization report that childhood obesity is soaring around the world, increasing more than tenfold over the past four decades.

The CDC report further says that a full 70% of American adults are now overweight, which is directly related to the rapid rise in diabetes and heart disease over the past few decades. This serious health crisis is closely linked to our relationship with food.

The CDC says that almost 40% of American adults are obese — the highest rates ever recorded for the U.S. The continued weight increase in the youngest Americans is especially worrisome for the long-term health of our nation. One in five adolescents, ages 12–19; one in five kids, ages 6–11, and one in ten preschoolers, ages 2–5 are considered clinically obese, not just overweight.

Overall, 70.7% of Americans are either overweight or obese, meaning that an unhealthy weight has become the norm in this country. The Americans living at a healthy weight, with a body-mass index of less than 25, are now the minority, and less than a third of the population. This has major health care cost implications for our future.

What the CDC report doesn't reveal is why the obesity crisis continues to worsen. Public health experts say that an unhealthy diet and the lack of exercise are the two biggest culprits in our obesity crisis. The fact that there's a huge amount of cheap, accessible, highly processed food available everywhere you go, and at almost all hours of the day or night, has something to do with it. And while many people are doing more recreational activity these days, the overall activity level, household activity and occupational activity, has decreased in recent years. As we've become more of an information economy and stopped manufacturing so many products over the past few decades, we're doing more work on computers and leading more sedentary lives sitting in front of computers while at work.

The consequences of the obesity epidemic are devastating to our national health and our health insurance system. High blood pressure, diabetes, heart disease and stroke are not only killing millions of Americans annually — the obesity epidemic is also a terrible burden on the American health care system, making up over $190 billion a year in weight-related medical bills. The health crisis will eventually become a national debt crisis as we look for ways to pay these rising health costs, which will continue to rise for the foreseeable future. Everyone, in every industry, needs to step up here, including the real estate industry, to solve the problem. We can't just leave the problem to the medical industry to treat the symptoms. We need to look at the root causes, which keep coming back to diet and exercise.

It comes down to what we're eating and where we're eating it. Fast food, soft drinks, sugary cereals, chips, candy bars and other high calorie snack foods, all made from corn derivatives, are helping us pile on the pounds in this 21st century. The sad thing is that kids are pretty helpless to the onslaught of corporate advertising and the tasty snack foods placed at kid level in every gas station. It's not a fair fight for them. Kid's don't understand all the future ramifications that will come from eating unhealthy foods. What can we do about it? It's a difficult problem, and where you live plays a role in it.

WHERE YOU LIVE CAN BE DEADLY

Depending on what neighborhood in New Orleans that you live in can cut 25 years off your life expectancy. According to research by the Robert Wood Johnson Foundation from 2013, the life expectancy at birth varied by as much as 25 years based on which neighborhood you lived in. People living in the Lakeview neighborhood could expect to reach the ripe old age of 80 years old. But in the Treme neighborhood, you can expect to live to just 55.[29]

Similar results have been found in other cities. A small distance, perhaps even a short walk, can make a big difference in life expectancy in the United States. There's probably a lot of reasons, but poverty, stress, fast food, liquor stores, convenience stores, and no grocery stores selling fresh food had something to do with it.

It's been estimated that about 9 percent of the population live in what has been called 'food deserts' with little or no access to grocery stores selling healthy food.[30] Convenience stores don't qualify for that. It's hard to find an apple, broccoli or even rice in many neighborhoods, much less in inner city neighborhoods.

The other problem in inner cities is that if residents can find healthy food, like vegetables, they're going to pay a lot more for it than the suburbanites at large chain supermarkets.[31] They'll pay more for quality food at the smaller grocery stores that might sell meat and produce in their neighborhood. Access and cost of healthy food can be directly correlated to health. And education about the importance of eating right is just as important as access.

Easy access to fast food is the rest of the story. When you're working two jobs to support a family and you don't have time to prepare a decent meal at home, and you know the kids will eat fast food and like it, what are you supposed to do? The problem of course, is that this high calorie junk food causes weight gain and other health effects, and obesity rates soar.

Hungry households often chose quantity over quality, and that often means inexpensive, high fat, high sugar processed foods. It may not have much nutritional value, but if it fills up the kid's bellies, that's what they'll choose if that's what they can afford. It's always going to be quantity over quality, and you can have a full belly and still be under-nourished.

Chips, candy and soda, all smartly placed at kid level in convenience stores throughout the city, and everywhere else, contribute to poor nutrition and weight gain in a big way. One study in Philadelphia showed that kids on average purchased more than 350 calories at convenience stores on every visit, and almost 30 percent of those kids went into these stores at least twice per day, five days a week.[32] Not a good way to get your daily intake.

Poor diets and high rates of obesity occur in low-income rural areas just as they do in cities. But how do we get more healthy food into the hands of low-income people? There are some ways that agricultural communities can help to feed the hungry and food insecure. There will be excess food grown in an agrihood, or an excess of some types of vegetables, because you can't always predict how well a crop will do or if something might fail, so you must plant more than you think you'll need. That extra food can go to some very needy places, and a plan should be in place to account for it, even grow for it, in a socially responsible agrihood. An important part of a sustainable food system is making sure all the food produced gets eaten and isn't wasted. Collecting over-production with a plan to distribute it to the poor or food-insecure should be part of the strategy and community plan. Unused food needs to be diverted to people and not landfills or compost piles.

We used to be a nation of farmers, but a lot of our food comes from other countries now, including Central and South America, and far away China. China, by the way, is by far the largest producer of agricultural products in the world. The United States is not really the bread basket of the world like many people think. We actually rank #3 in total agricultural production, behind China and India. We're the top producer of corn, but China produces twice as much wheat as the US, and leads in several other commodities like rice, potatoes and other vegetables. It only stands to reason since both China and India have a lot of mouths to feed. Indonesia and Brazil follow in the #4 and #5 spots for total agricultural production based on GDP.

While one-fifth or 20 percent of the total food that Americans eat comes from a foreign country, the rate is even higher for fruits and vegetables.

Most of our meat and carbs (corn, rice, wheat) still come from US producers, but more than 50 percent of the fresh fruits and 30 percent of the vegetables Americans consume come from other countries, predominantly Mexico and Canada, but also Central and South America, and even far away New Zealand (apples). Meanwhile, we use more land to grow food for export than we do to grow what we eat in the United States. Roughly 83 million acres are used to grow wheat, grain and feed for export versus 77 million acres to grow food to be consumed here in the U.S.[33]

The United States currently imports 60 percent of the oil it uses from a foreign nation; just 40 percent is produced in this country. Much of that imported oil is used to produce fertilizers and harmful chemicals that we spray on our fields to grow crops that we then export back out of the country. When you start tracking all the inputs and outputs, the circular nature of our global food web is enough to make your head spin; but I just don't like the idea of importing oil so that we can dump it on our fields so that we can export feed corn to cows in another country. It just feels like we've become a chemical dumping ground.

The total acreage in crop land is roughly 391 million acres in the United States. Yet the actual land area used to grow the food Americans eat is much smaller at 77.3 million acres, or roughly one-fifth of the crop land, and only about the size of Indiana, Illinois and half of Iowa combined. About 127.4 million acres are devoted to feed crops (mostly corn), so significantly more crop land goes toward feeding cows than humans. More than a third of the entire corn crop is devoted to ethanol production, which equates to roughly the state of Michigan. More land is used to grow corn for sweeteners than corn (as a grain) for humans to eat. It's in processed foods, but we drink a lot of it as high fructose corn syrup.

So most U.S. cropland is used for livestock feed and exports, or is left fallow. When it comes to pasture land, cows take up a huge chunk of the total U.S. landmass. More than one-third of the lower 48 U.S. landmass is used for pasture—by far the largest land-use type in the contiguous 48 states. Nearly 25 percent of that land is administered by the federal government and is open to grazing for a fee, with most of it out West. The primary residents on this vast stretch of land, of course, are cows. Between pasture land and cropland used to produce feed for cows, 41 percent of the U.S. landmass in the contiguous lower 48 states revolves around feeding cows.

Food drives the world. Aside from clean water, food production is the most important concern for countries and people on earth and it's by far the largest industry. It's critical to the health and security of every country. The rapid rise of the "grow local" movement in this country is indicative of a newer, positive trend in our society, but certainly not driven by food scarcity or the need to grow more food. People are starting to understand how important it is to try to eat healthy, fresh produce, and at the same time eat less processed foods that come to us from the industrial food complex.

It's part of a shift in values in America. And anyone who's read Michael Pollan's book The Omnivore's Dilemma understands how the global industrial food system, and our corn-based society, is problematic and not sustainable. Government subsidized corn derivatives, like high fructose corn syrup, are not nature's way of feeding animals like us humans, and we're seeing the results in our rapidly growing obesity rates.

High fructose corn syrup and other high calorie sugars are contributing to this massive obesity problem that is affecting all age groups. We're a fast food nation caught in a food web that's been designed by food scientists and marketers, and Michael Pollan explains how it all started. All life on this planet is the result of the solar energy captured and stored by green plants in the form of complex carbon molecules. Those plants in turn feed the animals, who don't happen to have the ability to synthesize energy and calories from the sun like plants do. As Pollan points out, the industrial revolution in our food chain started right after World War II, and it changed the fundamental rules of the whole system.

Fossil fuels are now turned into fertilizers, giving us a short-term burst of the sun's energy. "Industrial agriculture has supplanted a complete reliance on the sun for our calories with something new under the sun," says Pollan, "a food chain that draws much of its energy from fossil fuels instead." The energy originally came from the sun, but fossil fuels are a finite resource, and will result in a temporary boom in the amount of food we can produce. Given a limited supply of fossil fuels, our industrialized food system is not sustainable for the long term.

Factories that were designed and built for creating bombs as part of the war machine during WWII were quickly converted to produce new fertilizers that used many of the same raw materials that were used for making explosives. This resulted in a huge increase in food production but came at a big cost to the environment. We're pumping these chemicals into our soils and streams at an alarming rate. Because of mono-cropping and not rotating in other crops, we've depleted our soils to such an extent that the only way we can grow anything now is by using larger quantities of chemical fertilizers derived from fossil fuels.

The damage we've created in the last century from agri-business has been just as devastating to the environment as it has been to our health. There is now a massive dead zone in the Gulf of Mexico directly related to the vast amounts of chemical fertilizers and pesticides running down the Mississippi and into the gulf from the huge corporate farms in the Midwest. How are the fisheries in the gulf going to get repaid for the damage to their lives and livelihoods? Much of the damage like this won't be paid by us, and unfortunately it will have to be paid for by our sons and daughters and the future generations after we're long gone.

Pollan adds that "at various points our technologies come into conflict with nature's way of doing things, as when we seek to maximize efficiency by planting crops or raising animals in vast monocultures." Anyone who has driven past the endless miles of corn in Iowa or Illinois, or who has seen images of a massive Confined Animal Feed Operation (CAFO), understands what Pollan is talking about. It's not nature's way, and it's creating serious environmental problems.

By raising millions of animals in unnaturally close confinement and feeding them foods that they did not evolve to eat (corn), it creates problems and health risks for the animals and for us that we are just now beginning to recognize. The overuse of antibiotics in these CAFOs is rapidly causing a decrease in the number of antibiotics still viable for human use because disease causing viruses are gaining resistance to them.

Wendell Berry is a writer and was an early outspoken critic of the industrial farming machine in the seventies, and often spoke up about what he saw as the destruction of the American farmer and the decimation of rural, small town America. He was one of the early voices speaking up about the environmental damage that was taking place from heavy chemicals and large monocropping producers. Berry once suggested that the environmental crisis we've created is ultimately a crisis of the American character. In his book *The Unsettling of America*, Berry tells us that there is a profound split between what we think and what we do. He gives us an example from the mid-1970's when conservation groups like The Sierra Club were investing in stocks and bonds from some of the companies with the worst pollution records in industry, such as Exxon, steel companies, strip mining companies and pulp mill operators. The investments were deeply embarrassing once they were made public, but Berry wasn't really surprised by it. It was to be expected, and the absurdity of it all is the moral crisis of our time. Berry says, "Once our personal connection to what is wrong becomes clear, then we have to choose: we can go on as before, recognizing our dishonesty and living with it the best we can, or we can begin the effort to change the way we think and live."[34]

Berry suggests that our values have been corrupted and we're shucking the responsibility for our actions. If that's true, then we're all welfare queens, passing on the debt and burden of our environmental destruction to others, our children and their children, while we live high on the hog at their future expense. The same could be said of our massive government debt that we seem all too eager to pass on to our grandchildren. We're taking out loans now under the names of unborn millions, which we're quite certain they'll be happy to pay back for us later.

We need to face up to the facts – our extractive worldview and fossil-fuel based form of agriculture is not sustainable for the long term. Fossil fuels will eventually run out. And the industrial agricultural system led by global corporations is proving to be terribly unhealthy for humans and the environment. Something has to change.

Over the past few years, like a lot of people, I've been asking myself questions like "What are the most important things a person can do to create a healthier, more sustainable world and have less impact upon it." These are moral questions, and as I learned more about farming, I began to see how so many of our environmental problems are directly related to moral questions and our connections to nature itself.

I sensed that Wendell Berry was right – our social and environmental problems are closely related to our values and national character. The concepts of "values" and "character" are deep notions, but I think we as a nation need to take a closer look at our values from time to time. It might help us to determine where and what we shop for, and what we put into our bodies. Local food is not harmful to the environment, and understanding that, gives you a choice based on your values and what you believe is important.

Some people, like many farmers that I know, have certain traits and values within their character that will determine how they understand and interact with the environment. I hope and believe that there is a great shift in values coming from the grow local and farm to table movement, and the larger environmental movement, that will help us to make the right choices in the future.

Connecting with local food is a way to get to know a place, and the long agricultural history of a place, and that connection helps determine our values and what we think is important. To get rooted in a place is a human need, and it's good for the soul, and it's better for the environment.

When we really begin to investigate it, we might discover that we don't need to look to far-off places to supply all our needs and that we can become a little more self-reliant. We might find that instead of sending our money and wealth to far-off banks and far-away corporate offices and huge mono-cropping farms, we can just water the garden at home. We should look to the bounty around us first.

Knowing a place, and doing what you can right there, is all we really need to do. Most people don't know how they can really impact larger global problems, like the deforestation of the Amazon rain forest, or how to stop over-fishing the oceans, or how to save the beluga whale, but they can join a CSA or go to the farmers market. These are values-based decisions that when done collectively can have a big impact on the local environment and economy, and anyone can do it.

BUILDING A NEW FOOD CULTURE

As noted previously, it appears now that we made some mistakes in the 20th century. Urban planners in the United States during the 1950s, '60s and '70s believed that shopping malls would become the social hub for all the new suburbanites that were moving out of the city in droves. They believed that people would meet at the mall for social interaction, and they believed that social interaction would be based on shopping as a leisure activity.

Planners believed that retail was enough of a magnet to draw people to the mall, and we didn't need a main street or market square in suburbia. This was the grand mistake of the late 20th century. Shopping as entertainment is waning because it's just not that enjoyable or fulfilling of an activity, in fact many people don't enjoy it at all.

So suburbia was not destined to become Utopia. Nothing is walkable, and people suddenly became totally dependent on the car and on petroleum; as a result, they've become much more isolated. By contrast, the agricultural community can provide social interaction and activity grounded in a culture of food in all its many aspects – growing, gathering, preparing, and celebrating it at the table with others.

The agricultural community is designed to support useful and productive activities that at the same time improve community health and well-being. It's all based on a more compelling vision and values than consumerism and commercialization. With the decline of the consumer age, the agricultural community provides 'other places' to gather outside of the home or workplace for social interaction without any pressure to buy something. The farm becomes a place to simply enjoy and interact with nature and with others.

The barn, the garden, the community kitchen where people can come together to cook or can goods, the meeting or dining hall; all these things can be incorporated into the agricultural community as spaces for interaction and community hubs for socialization. They're places to just stop to say hello and chat for a while with a farmer or a neighbor. There's never a shortage of topics to discuss, with different things coming up in the garden all the time, and different pests causing problems, so it becomes a learning opportunity at the same time. There is of course the old stand-by icebreaker, the weather, which to a farmer is a very important topic of conversation.

The purposeful processing of food from the garden, such as canning beans, making preserves, or preparing meals, creates many more opportunities that extend social networks. Picking up your CSA box of fresh vegetables on a Wednesday afternoon offers a great opportunity to check out what's coming up in the garden and check in with your farmer and neighbors. Community farm to table meals and events such as the Fall Harvest Festival are organized activities that intentionally bring people together to celebrate food. The fall harvest festival is a recurring theme and ritual that goes back thousands of years as a way to communally come together to celebrate the harvest. And it's a darn good reason to throw a party. Food is abundant, and we celebrate it with much gratitude and thanksgiving.

The agricultural community offers many opportunities for exercise to those who choose it, from simple egg gathering, to getting your hands dirty in the garden, to feeding animals. The biggest health benefit of course is truly fresh, healthy vegetables, free of the chemical fertilizers, pesticides and herbicides, and the waxes and preservatives used to keep them looking fresh and colorful at the supermarket. Because most produce in your grocery store traveled the average 1500 miles to get there, it was likely picked a couple weeks ago, and not this morning, so it's already lost much of its vitamin impact and health benefit.

The biggest regional benefit of an agricultural community is that it protects open farmland and the pastoral views that we all enjoy looking at, which also contributes to our health. Some studies have shown that just 20 to 45 minutes in nature, even just viewing it, dramatically reduces stress levels, which is good for the heart and cardiovascular system as well as your psychological well-being.

In a conventional development, open land is lost, and when it's gone, it's probably gone forever. Whether that land becomes a housing development, a shopping center or a parking lot, there are costs to others in the region, including more traffic and pollution, in addition to the loss of beautiful green spaces. This is clearly why most people oppose any kind of development. As noted previously, you can't really stop growth, but you can try to set aside and save some of the open space, and the agrihood is one model that might help in that regard.

The pastoral viewscapes are what brought a lot of people to the Asheville area, and sadly, it's quickly disappearing. According to Buncombe County population statistics, more people die here than are born here, so the population would shrink a little each year if it weren't for so many people moving here from other parts of the country.

The agricultural community allows for some growth, and

people moving here for the climate and beautiful scenery need a place to live. But it is an attempt at a more ethical development model that preserves as much of the pastoral beauty and food production as possible. It's an attempt at mindful development. In my agricultural project, Creekside Farm is developing just 12 home sites on roughly 11 acres of land but leaving 45 acres in animal pasture and food production. We developed one-fifth of the land, but at the same time our goal from the beginning was increasing farm production overall yield by five times, along with the economic value associated with that higher yield. It's another trade off.

The increase in production yield and value comes from more intensive farming practices using organic methods and hand tools while improving the overall health of the soil for better future crops. This type of farming is more labor intensive and costly, but the residents of the community and CSA members are willing to pay for that. It's a fair trade. And it's certainly more environmentally friendly than bulldozing the entire farm for a couple hundred tract homes. We placed the 45-acre farm into the Buncombe County Voluntary Agriculture District to show our commitment to keep the farm in agriculture and not develop it for any other non-farm purpose. It was a way to connect what we think and what we do.

Organic farmers are a good example of people who have connected these two things. And thank goodness I found our young farm manager, Melissa, who cares deeply about the environment and wants to be a farmer. Melissa is a pretty blond 26-year-old who was raised over by the North Carolina coast. She came to the mountains to attend college and ended up sticking around. She received a degree in sustainable agriculture from Appalachian State University in the mountain town of Boone, North Carolina, a couple hours north of Asheville.

I'll get into why she chose farming for a career later, but the fact is she didn't grow up on a farm, which is where most farmers come from, and her father is an insurance salesman. But I'm very grateful that she chose this career path because she became the critical link in our little farming community.

An American farmer on a conventional farm feeds an average of 129 people (120 years ago the number was 10), and I wanted to see if our little farm could compete with that using organic farming methods. We could certainly feed the 12 households in our little neighborhood, but could Melissa feed all the residents of Walnut Cove? And could she at least feed the same 129 people that the average conventional farmer feeds without using the chemicals and sprays?

Before we even broke ground on the new agrihood project, we set aside a couple acres of good bottom land and started the Community Supported Agriculture program. Melissa was able to feed 35 families the bulk of their produce needs in her first summer running the program, and in 2018 she opened the CSA program to 65 families (about 150 people) and was growing food on 6 acres. If Melissa was able to increase production by building healthier soils and growing on more land, which was available, and if we increased calorie output by growing some grains, we might be able to provide the necessary calories to feed 129 people through-out the year. I'll get into more detail on this little experiment in community self-reliance later, but we had cattle that could supplement the protein needs of our community, and along with 75 laying hens and their eggs, Melissa would be able to provide much of the community's protein needs as well.

Melissa has a movable chicken house on wheels that she calls the "egg-mobile", which she loves, and she pulls it around with the tractor to the different gardens and pastures every week. This allows the chickens to do what they do best: scratch up bugs and fertilize the garden (with a seemingly endless supply of high-quality, organic fertilizer).

Melissa, like most small-scale farmers, always finds better, smarter crop rotation patterns to increase the fertility of the soil every year. Knowing exactly what type of vegetable has been grown in one plot of land and following it with another crop ideally suited for that soil condition improves the soil and future yields. An intense composting program also adds greatly to the health of the soil. Healthy soil can radically improve the yields from the garden, even double it. Better organic pasture maintenance increases the minerals and nutrients in the grasses for our livestock, and makes for happy, healthy cows.

As Joel Saladin says, "We look at a pasture and all we see is grass. A cow looks at a pasture and sees a salad bar, with lots of different types of grasses and clover to choose from." And Joel says that the cow will end up choosing what her body wants and needs at that moment. Melissa does most of the hard stuff around the farm, but I'm starting to become a decent grass farmer, thanks to Joel and his many books on sustainable agriculture. Joel's a rock star in the sustainable farming world.

Melissa works very hard and is often in the vegetable gardens just as the sun rises in the summer. Organic farming is much more physically demanding than commercial farming, and you really need to keep a close eye on every vegetable plant. She squats close to the earth, and looks very intently at plants, turning over the leaves to see the backside and who or what might be hiding there. She spends much of her time on the internet in the evenings trying to find creative, organic methods to solve the next problem that inevitably pops up, whether that's a new fungus or a new bug that has taken a particular liking to some of her plants. Fortunately, it's a labor of love for her, and she has more patience than I do when it comes to fighting these battles. I'd start freaking out and pull out the machete or a torch.

When my two sons were younger, my wife and I would always pack them up in the car every summer to go visit famous historic sites from the American Revolution. As a lay historian, it was Dad's interest, and I was driving, so that's where we were going.

One summer I packed them all in an RV and followed the Lewis and Clark Trail from the Mandan village in eastern North Dakota to Oregon and the Pacific Ocean. Thomas Jefferson purchased a vast tract of land under the Louisiana Purchase from Napoleon, who needed the cash to finance his ongoing wars in Europe, and Jefferson bought it for about four cents an acre. Jefferson sent Lewis and Clark out to explore this new land, it's soils and climates, and to see if they could find an easy route to the Pacific Ocean. I wanted to see if he got a good deal or not.

I had a copy of Steven Ambrose's brilliant book *Undaunted Courage* that describes the Corps of Discovery's journey as our guide. We often tried to place ourselves into the same scenery the corps had first witnessed. We stopped everywhere we could find in the book and on the map, in remote places that kept much of the natural beauty the Corps of Discovery would have seen, and other places where towns and cities sprouted up.

Along the Lewis and Clark trail there are commemorative signposts that follow the Missouri River and the old Indian trail across the Rocky Mountains as it picks up the Snake and

Columbia rivers on the other side. It was a long trip with little kids, lasting about 4 weeks, but we camped out most nights and read Ambrose's stories together about men getting chased by grizzly bears.

Ambrose describes in some detail the Mandan Indian village where the Corps of Discovery spent their first winter. We stopped at a recreated Mandan village run by the National Park Service and let our little wild Indians out of the RV so they could run around for a while.

The Mandan people lived historically in North and South Dakota along the banks of the Missouri river and its tributaries, the Heart and Knife Rivers. Unlike many plains Indians that lived in portable tepees and practiced a nomadic lifestyle following the buffalo heard, the Mandan developed a settled, agrarian culture in permanent, established villages. We walked around and into some of the earthen homes that were recreated for visitors and tourists.

My boys of course suggested that we build a mud home in the backyard that they could sleep in when we get home. My wife said, "Not happening." I don't know why she was looking at me when she said that. I didn't want a mud home. Igloos made from snow, and snow forts, are much easier to build, and there's always ready ammunition nearby. I grew up in the Chicago area so I'm an expert at building those.

The Mandan were a settled group that lived in agrihoods and farmed the Three Sisters: corn, beans and squash, and foraged for berries and other foodstuffs, and hunted buffalo and deer. They often farmed near river banks which would flood and add fertility to the soil from upstream, and sometimes gardens could be located miles from their home. Crops would be planned so that they would grow enough food to last an entire year, including the harsh, cold and snowy winter months.

Buffalo were also important, and the Mandan would perform spiritual rituals, like the Buffalo Dance ceremony, to call the buffalo to come to their village. Every part of the buffalo was used, from the skin to the meat to the bones. The Mandan were deeply and spiritually connected to the land around them, as were all Native Americans. To the Native Americans, everything was alive and everything had a spirit. And the Grizzly Bear had a big spirit.

It wasn't long after the Corps of Discovery returned with stories about the vastness and beauty of the American West that people started heading out that way. The open fields and boundless prairies were just waiting to be settled, farmed and grazed. The Corps opened the door to the breadbasket of the continent, and it had one of the greatest early impacts on this nation of farmers. Leaving aside the discussion of the devastating affect that it had on the indigenous peoples living there, the early settlers that followed had tremendous courage and a true sense of independence and self-reliance. The lifestyles that these early settlers were choosing, like that of the Mandan, was defined by farming and agriculture.

FARMING TODAY

Approximately 1 billion people, or over 1/3 of the available world-wide work force, are employed in the global agricultural sector. In different countries and regions, the number of people employed in agriculture varies widely and can range from less than 2% in countries like the US and Canada, where production farms constitute the bulk of farming practices, to over 80% in many African nations, where there's a lot of sustenance farming still going on.

Agriculture is the number two producer of greenhouse gasses worldwide, just behind the energy sector. In 2011 it was responsible for emitting about 6 billion tons of greenhouse gas. The word billion is actually a very difficult concept to get your mind around. If you tried to count to a billion, continuously in perfect rhythm, one number per second, it would take 31 years, 251 days to get there. Times that by the word "tons," that's 2,000 pounds. The numbers are staggering when you think about it. Anyway, agriculture accounts for 13% of all global emissions. Deforestation to make more room for more agriculture adds another 4% to global emissions. Global emissions lead to rising sea levels and extreme weather events, say most scientists, which in turn can lead to catastrophic damage to infrastructure.

The average American prepared meal contains ingredients from at least five different foreign nations.[35] California, what many consider now the vegetable basket of the United States, released over 70,000 tons of carbon dioxide into the atmosphere in one year just flying in nuts, fruits and vegetables to feed their population in that state.[36]

Why California flies in so many nuts and vegetables in the first place is a very good question. According to a December 31, 2016 article in the New Republic, California's often drought-stricken Central Valley grows 80% of the world's almonds, and that growing trend continues as more people are starting to drink almond milk as an alternative to dairy milk (not a good idea- you're about to see why). California now has over 1 million acres in almond production and has been plowing under other crops to plant more almond trees because it's a high value crop. Since each nut takes a gallon of water to produce, almonds account for close to 10% of the state's annual agricultural water use—or more water than what the entire populations of Los Angeles and San Francisco use in a year. It takes 920 gallons of water to produce one gallon of almond milk (yikes!). But most of those almonds actually end up going to markets overseas. About two-thirds of California's almond and pistachio crops are sent to foreign nations while using up our own over-tapped water resources in the process. Call me nuts, but somethings wrong here.

And this issue is more serious than just the startling amount of water that goes into California crops, it's beginning to have an impact on the watershed itself. Back in 2013, a team led by US Geological Survey hydrologist Michelle Sneed discovered that a 1,200-square-mile area of the southern Central Valley, a landmass more than twice the size of Los Angeles, had been sinking by as much as 11 inches per year in some parts because the water table had fallen from pumping massive quantities of water out of the underground aquifer, with a large portion of that to feed almond trees.

With their growing overseas sales and profits, almonds and pistachios have attracted large financial investors hungry for a piece of the action. As Mother Jones magazine reported recently, Hancock Agricultural Investment Group, an investment company owned by the Canadian insurance and financial services giant Manulife Financial, owns at least 24,000 acres of almonds, pistachios, and walnuts, making it California's second-largest nut grower. So all that water and profit ends up going to a foreign insurance company. TIAA-CREF, a large retirement and investment fund that owns 37,000 acres of California farmland, is also one of the globe's top five almond producers. From a strictly financial standpoint, the investment may make sense and is probably a good investment for the short term. The company management are probably doing right by the people they answer to, the investors and shareholders. But the investment has other serious ramifications.

Given the unsustainability of the production based on limited water resources that are used to feed foreign nations a luxury item like almonds and pistachios, the investment seems a little short-sighted. You might notice some similarities here with the investors of the Far Distance Company in the early spice trade (from the introduction). They didn't see the cultural and ecological damage that their investment was causing either.[37]

Raising livestock accounts for about 18 percent of greenhouse gasses emitted around the world, which accounts for more than all forms of transportation combined- truck, train and plane.[38] Cows already emit more greenhouse gasses than all the cars on the road. Most worldwide agriculture land, in fact, goes to cattle grazing and growing feed crops like corn for them, estimated now at 80 percent of agricultural land around the world.[39] The methane gas from cows is mostly emitted as a belch from the cows' stomach in the digestion process. Methane is a much more serious heat-trapping greenhouse gas than carbon dioxide, and as China and the developing world begins to eat more meat, the problem will get worse.

As recently as 2010, more than 30% of Earth's ice-free and water-free land area was used for producing livestock. For all of history the amount of land used for cattle has grown every year with the most significant increases in livestock production over the last 50 years. Chicken production increased by nearly a factor of 10 in the last 50 years.

At the same time over the past 50 years producers started using more intensive selective breeding practices that focused on creating livestock breeds and crossbreeds that increased production (faster weight gain) while reducing genetic diversity. This practice has led to a significant decrease in genetic diversity among livestock breeds, including chickens, which is leading to a corresponding decrease in disease resistance.

The rapid spread of industrial agriculture in America has created a system of chemically intensive single crop farm production (corn, wheat and soybeans), and massive livestock CAFO operations that look and run more like the modern industrial operations or auto plants, and not living, breathing systems. The harsh impacts of industrial agriculture on the environment, public health, and rural communities would suggest that it's an unsustainable way to grow our food over the long term. Better, science-based methods are available, and while they may be more expensive and labor intensive, they greatly reduce the long-term costs associated with the environment and human health. As Wendell Berry says, now that we know what we know, we have a choice in how we think and how we live. Or we can just forget about the whole thing and keep going down the path that we're on. But the problems will continue to get worse.

The reason that monoculture farming relies so heavily on chemical inputs such as synthetic fertilizers and pesticides is because growing the same plant (and nothing else) in the same place year after year quickly depletes the nutrients that the plant relies on, and these nutrients must be replenished somehow. The pesticides are needed because monoculture fields are highly attractive to certain weeds and insect pests. Our farm manager Melissa learned that hard lesson.

In the old days, a farmer wouldn't think of planting corn again in the same field for at least three years. Now it's planted every year, for 20 years straight, making it the perfect ground for pests to grow and gain resistance to the chemicals used. The unhealthy soil without the microbes and other beneficial organisms becomes a dead breeding ground for these resistant pests, weeds and bacteria. The chemicals we use slowly become less useful and the pests more resistant and widespread. The over-use of Roundup has created superweeds that are now creating serious problems for growers in the Midwest and the South.

Healthy animals in the United States consume more antibiotics than sick human beings, creating a systemic problem of antibiotic resistance that is having a serious impact on the treatment of human infectious diseases. Animals in CAFO's are given regular doses of antibiotics as a preventative measure, not because they're necessarily sick at the time.

WASTED

The amount of food we waste in the US would feed another country; a very large country. The greenhouse gasses that we emit to grow all that wasted food using our fossil fuel intensive system is enough to rank third in the world behind the US and China for emissions.[40] Just the water we use to grow that wasted food is more water than is used by any other country.[41]

Farmers will often leave a crop out in the field if prices are so low that it doesn't cover his labor and fuel costs to bring it in. Waste comes from grocery stores and distributors as food loses freshness or because it has a slight blemish or is misshaped in some way and just doesn't look perfect. At home, we throw out about 25 percent of the food that we buy.[42]

With about 40 percent of our food going to waste in America (and some estimate 50 percent), that represents about 20 pounds of food per person per week. It comes to about $165 billion per year in wasted food. And it comes from points all along the food chain.[43] I'll say it again, the amount of food we waste in the US would feed another country; a very large country. Organizations like MANNA Food Bank reclaim a lot of the food that would otherwise be wasted and uses it to feed low-income households, an important first step in resolving our food waste problems.

Food waste emits more greenhouse gasses in the form of methane gas as it decomposes in our landfills. When it comes to global warming, methane gas is about 21 times harder on the atmosphere than carbon dioxide. Food waste makes up a big, gooey chunk of the municipal solid waste in landfills and it's the number two item that goes in there, behind paper.

Reducing waste through composting on organic farms helps return nutrients and build healthier soil. Melissa not only composts all the scraps from cleaning and the vegetables that are inedible but takes a big portion of waste from the Tavern Restaurant at the Cliffs to complete the food-to-waste-to-food cycle there. Many of our CSA members bring their food scraps back to the farm composting station. And many communities like Walnut Cove have a good recycling program for plastics, glass, paper and other recyclables, but if we could figure out a way to recycle more organic matter from food waste at home and put those valuable minerals and nutrients back in the growing soil and not into landfills, we'd take a huge leap forward in the food-to-waste-to-food cycle. That's the next challenge to our younger generations. Some companies are starting food recycling programs in some communities, but we need to find economically viable and efficient ways to dramatically increase the scale. If we could put the 40% of the food we waste back into the soil, we'd need far fewer chemical fertilizers and use far less fossil fuels to make them.

All our food problems can be improved, but it's going to take a cultural shift. We all need to understand that our society and culture is on an unsustainable path, and we need to change the way we look at food and how we grow it for the long term; what we think and what we do. Simply considering the possibility and opportunities for sustainable agriculture within a local community is a good first step. But there will be resistance from some seriously entrenched players in the food industry.

While there are only just a handful of large multi-national corporations that provide most of the food we eat, Michael Pollan points out a disturbing truth for anyone who understands how big business works. The fact is that CEO's and board members are judged in their performance by growth. Shareholders expect it; they demand it. And they expect a better return than they can get in a CD or other financial investment instrument. But how do you achieve a desired corporate growth rate of, say 4 or 5%, when your population is growing at less than 3%? The answer, says Pollan, is that you sell people more food (and calories) than they really need. Add some more sugar and salt, and they'll eat more of it. Tasty, high-calorie snacks are one way to get more people to eat more calories. Getting people to eat more food than they really need is a key objective and growth strategy for our current industrial food complex. Corporate growth is adding to the growth of our waistline, and American investors should hold up their investment portfolio and ask, "does this make me look fat?"

Farming is a defining human activity. Farming is what led us to civilization and culture. Fast food will perhaps lead to our decline. It seems more and more evident that we need to change our perceptions of farming in order to reconnect to the land and our food in a more symbiotic and sustainable way.

The separation and distance from our food and from nature that we have witnessed over the past 70 years is causing a great disconnect in our national psyche. It's becoming more evident that we as a nation need to change the way we live and interact with nature. We need to reconnect to the land, live closer to it, and begin to really appreciate it, if we're going to solve some of our food problems in the 21st century. We need to begin by enabling smaller farm producers to make a living in a more sustainable manner. Local communities need closer connections to food again, like the old days.

Some psychologists argue that growing your own food is good for the psyche and feelings of self-esteem and self-worth. By learning to produce some of our own food, not all of it, just some of it, we increase our self-reliance and gain freedom from total dependence on others, and that can be quite liberating. Some studies have shown that just being able to feed yourself, by your own hard work and effort, and just taking some personal responsibility for supplying some of our own everyday needs like food and sustenance, brings feelings of accomplishment and satisfaction that you didn't know existed or was possible. A small meal of homegrown food becomes a feast, and your level of appreciation and satisfaction grows exponentially when you've pulled this food out of the ground yourself. You also tend to waste less food because you know how hard it is to grow it, and how hard someone worked to produce it.

But even more satisfaction comes from living up to our values and the vision we have for ourselves. If you sometimes feel like a babe in the woods, and you believe that it's important to try to become more self-reliant, growing some of your own food is a good way to live up to those values and that image you have of yourself. I think this is what underlies the grow-local movement, farmers markets and CSA programs around the world. It's a way to assert your independence and self-reliance as a person and a community, which improves your own self-confidence and self-esteem.

Farming first brought us together to live in settled groups. Then we had to learn how to live together in a larger society and culture, and human belief systems, values and virtues were developed over time and in different societies to help people live in harmony with each other and the environment. We may need to relearn some of these values in order to keep living in harmony with nature. CAFO's are a good example. Most people believe it isn't right to keep an animal like a pig in a terribly confined space for its entire life, especially when they learn that pigs are proven to be just as intelligent and sensitive as dogs. When we see the mistreatment of animals, we feel an empathy for fellow creatures on this planet, a slight twinge in our moral conscience, and that comes from thousands of years of human evolution as we developed and passed on our moral reasoning skills. The innate sense of justice, what is right and what is wrong, runs deep in human beings.

But that's how most pigs live their lives now, squashed against each other in confined spaces that hardly give them enough room to even turn around. Large scale pig farmers often cut off the tails of pigs which makes them more sensitive, so the tightly confined pigs don't allow their neighbors to chew on their tails, which can cause infections. It's a short and stressful life, about eight months long. The same goes for chickens and cows: short lives in confined spaces. Many people now believe that a cow should be a cow, and roam freely on open pasture grazing away to her heart's content, as God designed her and intended. Our values are telling us that maybe there's another way to raise a pig, a cow, and a chicken.

People are starting to make choices that relate directly to

their values, such as free-range chicken eggs and organic, pasture raised beef. They're gaining a better understanding of the harmful chemicals that go into our food and into our streams and rivers, and so are choosing organic produce when they can find it. And they can find it now at a lot of grocery stores, not just Whole Foods. People are also seeing the value of growing food locally because it reduces pollution from transporting all that food across the country and around the world. There is also value in knowing where your food comes from, and even knowing your farmer by name. These are values-based choices that we're making right now in our food culture.

The fix to so many of our problems, including our food and obesity problem, and the environmental damage resulting from how we grow food and livestock in this country, requires a shift in values, and we're beginning to see that shift in the grow local movement. The local organic farmer is really selling an idea and a lifestyle. She's selling a principle, beliefs and values, and not just food.

The grow local and farm to table movement is changing our food choices and is now affecting our food culture and how we live (and I might add, how long we live). Organic farmers have recognized the health and environmental risks of corporate agri-business and are beginning to establish new forms of food webs and lifestyles based on very different values and connections. They are defining a values-based and principle-centered approach to food that can restore our health and create a more resilient food system for future generations.

So how exactly do our values influence patterns of behavior, and ultimately, a movement? After meeting so many local growers and organic farmers I started to believe that it came down to certain character traits and strengths that people develop over time, and how these people express them through their values. And to get a better understanding of what really drives so many people in the local, healthy food movement, I went right to the textbook on the subject, *Character Strengths and Virtues* (Oxford University Press). Yes, I actually read an 800-page (small print, no pictures) textbook on the subject of human virtue. It took me over a month to get through it. But if Wendell Berry was right, and our farming and environmental problems are related to "character", I needed to go there.

The textbook (and brother, it's a big one) is used in the psychology departments at the most prestigious universities across the United States, including Harvard, Yale and the University of Michigan. Whereas most of the research in psychology and psychiatry is focused on mental illness and what is wrong in people, like psychosis and neurosis, this book is based on modern research in the field of Positive Psychology and describes in great detail the character strengths (or virtues) found in human beings, or what is good and right in people. A course in positive psychology, in fact, has become the most popular undergrad course at Harvard and Yale. It's a new field in psychology and a lot of young people are interested in it. I'll refer back to this research a few more times as we try to understand the underlying motives for so many people in the healthy food movement and discover what's really driving the whole thing, because I think that Wendell Berry was right, and the fix has to do with what's good and right in people.

Modern research in the field of Positive Psychology tells us that some people have signature strengths in their character that motivate them toward certain beliefs and actions, such as a strong sense of justice; a belief in fairness and doing what they think is right. This human virtue goes beyond personal interest, cost savings or profit, and can express itself in a person's belief in protecting the environment for future generations and the unborn millions of Americans who will inherit the earth from us. I believe that many environmentalists have this strong sense of justice as a character trait. The fair treatment of animals, the desire for less chemicals in food and in the environment and a more sustainable food supply goes back again to a sense of justice and doing what is perceived as right and fair. The research in positive psychology shows that character traits and strengths in people are learned, and they are developed and strengthened, like a muscle in your arm, with practice and exercise. The research tells us that anyone can build and strengthen their own character at any point in their life, but it takes practice and effort. The key seems to be pushing past your own comfort level, like performing a brave act, which will develop the muscle (or trait) of courage.

The character strengths of independence and self-reliance are expressed in many ways, and not just in the actions of local growers and farmers, but also in the actions that help local farmers, or more broadly in a person's desire to preserve farm land and the knowledge of growing our own food. Some people would rather not completely trust their food supply to a few large corporations like Cargill and Monsanto, and many people have a real concern about the health and quality of the food they eat and the food they give to their children. These again are values-based beliefs and choices based on certain character traits that people have learned and developed within themselves, like self-reliance. Values and a belief system are key motivators that are influencing the new food trends in our society. In fact, they're at the root of it.

People in the environmental movement also seem to have the character traits closely related to spirituality, or deep spiritual connections to nature and an appreciation of beauty. The ability to truly appreciate beauty is a character trait, say psychologists, and it means a deep, positive emotional experience; a sense of awe and elevation in the presence of nature and beautiful surroundings, and it comes with an innate desire to protect it. [44]

Another important trait or character strength for the environmentalist (and the farmer) is the ability to have hope. These people seem to have optimism and expect the best future, and they work toward achieving it. They often believe that the best way to predict the future is to create it. They're involved and have a voice, and often use it, because they have hope for a better and brighter future and believe that they can do something about it.

Audrey Hepburn once said, "To plant a garden is to believe in the future." Farmers, by necessity, must keep hope as a key character strength, otherwise they'd just give up. They risk it all every growing season and are often at the mercy of armies of pests and disease that can destroy them financially. Yet they put it all on the line and let it ride every year. All the hard work and investment in machinery and seeds could get wiped out in a moment of bad weather, a hail storm or drought, but farmers have hope and press on. Farmers are also brave, so that courage, independence and self-reliance are key character strengths found in just about all of them.

We'll discuss how other character strengths and values in America are influencing the food movement in the coming chapters. The person that can provide for some of her own food is not helplessly dependent on the food industry, and influences the food industry because she is not helplessly dependent on it. As Wendell Berry says, "the responsible consumer must also be in some way a producer. Out of his own resources and skills, he must be equal to his own needs…He influences the market by his freedom…By making himself responsibly free, a person changes both his life and his surroundings…He is a responsible consumer because he leads a responsible life." Berry concludes that some organizations (and people) "have no clear perception of, and therefore fail to be responsible for, the connections between what they say and what they do, what they desire and how they live." Ultimately, the failure of the American character that Berry describes relates to the break between what we know to be right and what we end up doing anyway out of ignorance or self-interest. The character trait of Justice, and doing what we believe is right and fair, is at the root of our democracy, and the root of a new food movement. The character trait of justice helps us connect these two things— what we know or believe to be right and what we do.

CHAPTER SIX

FOOD JUSTICE

"Earth is a goddess and teaches justice to those who can learn. The better she is served, the more good things she gives in return."
-Greek historian Xenophon, 4th Century B.C.

A tightly woven network of massive petroleum, chemical, agri-business and corn producers control our food system and supply. Alternative food systems grew in response to all that, particularly all the chemicals that were being used, and organic produce went from fringe to mainstream rapidly over the past ten to twenty years.

But savvy marketers at large multinational food companies discovered the trend and that 'organic' sells and could be a terrific branding opportunity for their companies. Large food processors and distributors started buying up all the organic companies and labels they could find, so that a map of organic brands and their corporate owners started looking like another food tree with names like Kraft and General Mills becoming the trunk or largest branches. While that may have negative connotations to many people, the truth is that the availability of more healthy, organic food is a good thing, even if some small, organic food company did sell out to the man. But the problem remains, if some people, particularly poor people, still can't get access to healthy food, it's not socially just or fair. Many people and some terrific organizations are trying to right this wrong, and they are driven by a sense of justice, one of the many human virtues.

On page 758 (OMG), our psychology textbook says, "Justice is the human virtue that underlies a healthy nation."[45] It involves moral reasoning which leads to the right and fair treatment of others in a society. Justice includes the trait of fairness which means treating others in similar ways and means treating people equally and without bias. Giving everyone a fair voice and a chance in society is at the heart of justice.[46]

When it comes to food, a core requirement for survival, I think that everyone will agree that every human being has the right to eat something. No child should grow up hungry anywhere in America, but one in five children in the United States still struggles with hunger. Food justice also means the right to healthy food. What have been called "food deserts" in our inner cities does not necessarily represent fair and equal treatment of all citizens. When inner city people in poor neighborhoods don't have access to grocery stores and fresh produce, like people in the suburbs do, it can contribute to health problems and shorter lives for these city dwellers, and that's not exactly fair or just treatment.

Many farmers markets now accept SNAP benefits, the Supplemental Nutrition Assistance Program formerly known as food stamps. This greatly helps low income people gain access to fresh vegetables. Over 19 million in SNAP benefits were redeemed at farmers markets across the US in 2015.[47] Community outreach and education efforts contributed in no small way to this. However, there just aren't enough farmers markets or easy access to fresh vegetables for many city dwellers.

There are some people who are trying to do something about that, and they seem to be driven by an innate sense of justice. A new urban agrihood in inner city Detroit is now feeding a lot of people fresh vegetables for free. On what was vacant land in a depressed neighborhood, a 3-acre farm has sprouted up to feed the people. It includes 2 acres of vegetable gardens that are managed by farmers working for the Michigan Urban Farming Initiative (MUFI), a nonprofit organization dedicated to doing something about providing healthy food choices to inner city residents.

The term 'urban agriculture' is related to very small-scale farming and vegetable gardens within existing cities and suburban neighborhoods. In cities it often utilizes vacant lots, repurposed by people who have regular jobs and work as a community of neighbors part time to keep up the vegetable garden. The people at MUFI have taken this concept to a whole new level.

The Detroit project also includes fruit trees and a sensory garden for children, so children learn about what good food looks like in the ground and where it all comes from. MUFI co-founder and president Tyson Gersh said in a statement, "Over the last four years, we've grown from an urban garden that provides fresh produce for our residents to a diverse, agricultural campus that has helped sustain the neighborhood, attracted new residents and area investment." The project is about teaching a healthier way of eating as much as about providing the food. It attacks nutritional illiteracy and food scarcity at the same time.

MUFI is also working on a community resource and education center to be housed in an adjacent vacant building. The workers are all volunteers, and the nonprofit receives most of its funding from donations from a few larger businesses like Sustainable Brands and the chemical company BASF.

Scientists studying in the field of positive psychology say that the human virtue of justice includes such ideas as teamwork, equality, citizenship, leadership, social responsibility and loyalty to a group. All these concepts are identifiable in this group of volunteers working for the greater good of the community in this Detroit neighborhood. This is what good citizenship is all about. Good citizenship means identification with, and a sense of obligation to, a group and a common good. It includes the need for leadership, which means getting a group to do what they need to do and keeping up good relationships and morale among the group to get the job done.[48] And they're all working toward some sense of community food justice in this inner-city neighborhood.

Farming is hard work, especially small-scale farming with hand tools, and I've often questioned why people choose to do it. Many will say they enjoy the connection to the soil and the satisfaction of growing something with their own hands and hard work. But if you ask this group of urban farmers and gardeners why they're doing what they're doing, I think many would tell you that there is something more going on here. Many are simply trying to live their lives with some integrity by doing what they see is the right thing, filling a need, not because of potential reward and recognition, but simply because there must be a consistency between your inner values and your actions, between what you believe and what you do. This project helps them to connect those two things, and they get satisfaction from that. In some ways it satisfies an innate need for justice while it builds feelings of self-esteem. It's a gift that goes both ways.

It's hard work, no doubt, but it has its own rewards. The

psychological benefits go deeper. This consistency between what these growers believe and what they do reinforces a sense of integrity and self-esteem and promotes a feeling of self-worth. It seems to be based on the value that you place on yourself. It can be the greatest source of confidence and strength, and many people have discovered that inner strength through the service of others.

The people tilling the earth in this bright green field located in the middle of urban decay are dreamers. They saw a problem in this food desert and decided to do something about it. At some point in our lives, we all need to know that we have done some good for our fellow man that is beyond our own self-interest. It is an internal, self-determined act based on a soul-searching process that helps us discover who we really are. The standards that these growers live up to are the ones they created for themselves. I think many have discovered that happiness is encouraged by living up to a standard you envision for yourself, the person that you imagine and want to be.

These workers are unpaid, but happiness does not always come with money and wealth, and we humans seem to need something more than that. We need to have a positive self-image, we need to feel self-worth, and that has more value than money or property.

Virtue and values are closely related concepts. Virtue (or character strengths) help determine our values and what we believe is important. Values can provide a source of inspiration and meaning and connect you to a deeper purpose beyond your own personal self-interest. Values are a guide, a road map, and an anchor. Values can be the source of strength which will help you to endure the hardships of sacrifice and strife, including the back-breaking work of harvesting potatoes on the corner of Custer and Brush Streets in the city of Detroit.

The food system in place here in the United States was first developed in the 1950s. It's based on industrial production methods that are now considered by many scientists and conservationists as harmful to the environment and not sustainable for the long term. Many scientists, nutritionists and environmentalists believe that this system is not good for the long-term health of the soil, the environment, animals or people. If the current food system is unjust because it's harmful to the health of our young people and the future health of the planet, are we morally obligated to do something about it? Will empathy and compassion for our younger generations, even for millions of yet unborn Americans, drive us to act in a fair and just manner for all?

The question then arises- is this the only way to produce food and can we find a healthier and more sustainable way to do it. Clearly there are other ways to produce much of our food, and the rising grow local movement and the rapid spread of farmers markets across the US has proved this. Justice is a core value in America, and it is more powerful in the hands of the people than corporations.

FOOD MILES

In our industrial food system, we expend more energy in the form of petroleum than we gain in the form of calories. In our fossil fuel-based food system it takes 10 units of energy to produce one unit of food energy (in the form of calories). The energy that it takes to bring us our dinner, in the form of solar energy captured in fossil fuels, to fertilize, grow, process, store, package and distribute our food is far greater than the energy we get from it. In other words, we expend 10 times the energy to get the food to our table than we get from the food in the form of calories. Our food system is absolutely dependent on fossil fuels, and in turn our nation is now dependent on other nations for that oil. We need oil as much as we need food, must have it in fact even before we can even eat.

Using energy from the sun through organic farming means we're not using tons of fossil fuel energy to produce the chemicals and fertilizer. From the fertilizers to the long-distance transportation to the packaging, the main ingredient in dinner is oil. And eventually, at some point, it's going to run out.

Somewhere between 80 and 90 percent of the food consumed in the big farming state of Iowa comes from outside of the state or a foreign nation. It's surprising because almost the entire state is made up of interconnecting farms and the deep, black, rich soil in that region.[49] They're shipping most of what they grow (corn and soybeans) to places and processors outside of the state, only to import most of what they eat.

Research from Iowa State University showed that the modern, conventional food system uses up to 17 times more fuel for transportation than locally sourced food. That's 17 gallons of diesel used to produce and transport food in our national and global system versus one gallon for locally grown food. We look for energy efficiency in our homes, cars, and appliances, but fail to recognize or consider the big energy savings in food sourcing.[50] We need a more energy efficient means of producing and delivering food to where it's consumed, whenever possible, and it's certainly possible in the summer time. Locally grown food is the "road less traveled".

The current food system uses approximately 16% of the total energy used in the United States. If everyone ate more local food, just in the summer time, it would represent a huge reduction in fossil fuel usage and oil dependency. It would also reduce the costs associated with transportation, since 6 to 12% of food cost is related to transportation.

A Swedish study of food miles used the ingredients from a typical Swedish breakfast (apple, bread, butter, cheese, coffee, cream, orange juice, and sugar) to get a total of the distance that food traveled to get to the breakfast table. They added up the distances that each food traveled from the producers to consumer. The mileage estimated for that one morning meal was equivalent to the circumference of the earth, or 25,000 miles. The apples from New Zealand and the coffee from South America really piled on the miles. So did the orange juice.[51]

In another study in the United States, the distances traveled for locally and regionally grown foods were compared with the distances traveled if those foods came from conventional sources normally supplied from outside of the state. The average total distance for the three locally sourced meals in one day was calculated at 1,198 miles. The average total distance for the meals using the same meal ingredients obtained from conventional sources was 12,558 miles, more than 10 times the distance. That's also half the circumference of the earth, in just 3 meals. Most of the food in the locally sourced meals were from relatively short distances, 50 miles or less, but the morning coffee still packed on the miles. What are you going to do, not have coffee? That's crazy talk.

The local food traveled an average distance of 44.6 miles across all food used in the three meals, while that same food would likely travel an average of 1,546 miles if it came from conventional sources. When considering produce only, the local food traveled an average distance of 37.9 miles, while the produce would likely travel an average of 1,638 miles if it came from the modern food web.[52]

The infrastructure and decision-making in the current food system is based on cost and profitability, and it does not consider external environmental costs, but there is clearly a connection between food choices, fossil fuel use, and greenhouse gas emissions. Making others more aware of this connection might get them to buy more local produce and support local farmers. 'Eat Your View' is a major campaign and new initiative at Creekside Farm that includes everything from handing out bumper stickers and distributing t-shirts to a web site (www.eatyourview.com) and social media accounts on Facebook and Instagram page (follow them also at Eat Your View). We're doing whatever we can to spread this simple message- Eat Your View- because getting people to buy and eat more local food is the key to supporting local farmers and building the necessary infrastructure for a new food web while we reduce food miles and dependency on oil.

We need a dependable, long term food supply, but we've delivered American agriculture into the hands of multinational corporations and based it completely on fossil fuel consumption. At the same time, the current food system has deprived Americans of any independent access to the staples of life. Our food has become the domain of speculators and the stock market, OPEC and big oil. Why don't we all try to be a little more self-reliant and independent. Why not go to a farmer's market next weekend and buy some radishes. Our web site has some other ideas, and can help you find a local farmers market or CSA program. www.eatyourview.com.

Are we willing to accept total dependence on others and faraway places for all our food? And can we produce enough food for everyone locally in a sustainable manner? Is it possible today that one small, local, organic farmer can feed an average 129 people, the same number that farmers do now in the industrial system, but using more sustainable techniques?

We can't give up completely on the current conventional food system, nor would most people want to. Food has become so accessible and inexpensive that we won't be radically changing the entire system any day soon. But we can try to grow and eat more local food – at least some portion of our diet. And we can try to practice more sustainable methods of conventional farming, like better crop rotation and crop selection (remember almonds). More farms growing organically in California is another step in the right direction, but growing more food locally for local consumption can be accomplished without overhauling the entire system.

Labor costs are certainly going to be higher because we're using hand tools and more labor-intensive ways of controlling pests and weeds, and not using massive amounts of chemicals to do that job. There will be a higher cost for the food produced, but if you break it down, that may be offset when you add the long-term costs to the environment and the government subsidies to farmers that everyone currently pays through taxes in the industrial system. Certainly, simple steps like better crop rotation can be achieved without significant costs. Reducing subsidies on corn and letting soft drink companies pay the real cost for high fructose corn syrup might be another step in the right direction.

Even if you did pay a little more for locally grown food, it's fresher, has less chemicals and retains more vitamins, and as with most things you buy, you get what you pay for. You'd still be paying much less for food than your grandfather did. He ate organic food by the way, at least while he was a young man before the 1950s, and before all the chemicals. It was all organic food back then. Your grandfather also ate pasture raised beef and chicken, and without all the growth hormones and antibiotics. Organic is nothing new, it's been the food we've eaten for all human history.

The argument that we need industrialized, chemically intensive production methods to feed our growing population loses some of its validity when you talk to your grandfather. He remembers the family meals his mother made. We begin to understand that we can feed more people organic and sustainably grown food, more often. It doesn't have to be everything we eat, but we can and should try to eat more local and organic food. Just adding a little of it to your diet now and then will go a long way to supporting the necessary infrastructure.

The growing of more organic food, even if from a large corporate conglomerate like Kraft Foods, is a very positive thing. The big change in the industrial food supply towards more organic foods is driven by consumer demand (or consumer values), and the success of stores like Whole Foods prove that. Whole Foods has made it much easier to find and buy organic food, which means a lot less chemicals going into the soil and making their way into streams and eventually the oceans.

Many large farms in California grow organic food close to the fields where the same company and growers still grow vegetables using the old chemically intensive industrial methods, and the rows of crops look pretty much the same. These large growers and producers are simply reacting to market demand, but the organic food is often grown using some of the same old mono-cropping techniques and still heavily dependent on fossil fuels as it travels long distances to get to the grocery store in refrigerated trucks.

While the grow local movement reduces the use of fossil fuels because it greatly reduces transportation, the movement isn't going to completely take over the industrial food system any time soon. And it's not for everyone. It's really just another option for people to choose from related to what food products they purchase. But clearly there is a movement going on, and everyone from farmers to consumers, to urban planners, to developers, to real estate professionals, to those involved in local, state and federal governments should be aware of it by now. Local food is huge.

Farmers who grow the food, and the people who attend a farmer's market, and the chefs who choose to seek out local produce for their restaurants, are driving this 'eat your view' movement based on a common set of principles and values and a desire for a healthier food chain and a healthier environment. These people are moral trendsetters showing us the way to a more ethical economy where food dollars stay closer to home. That's food justice at work in the supply chain.

SUSTAINABILITY

Farmland is a scarce resource now in many regions of the country, and it should be a resource that is protected for the future. I believe that Creekside Farm is choosing a course of action that will limit the loss of farmland and improve the quality and quantity of food produced here locally while allowing for some social and economic growth in the region today. The goal of sustainable development is satisfying the needs of the present without compromising the ability of future generations to meet their own needs. It means treating current and future generations in a fair, equal and just manner.

Sustainable development can meet human development goals while at the same time sustaining the ability of natural systems to provide the resources which the economy and society ultimately depend on. The desired result is a state of society where human needs are met without undermining the integrity and stability of the natural systems. This is sustainability.

Sustainable development should focus on economic development, social development and environmental protection with a goal of balance and equilibrium. Biologists call it human-ecosystem equilibrium (homeostasis), and sustainable development should look to this more holistic approach and balance before a bulldozer hits the ground. We need to save some green space for future generations.

Sustainable development could also be viewed as a way of managing healthy growth in a region while at the same time maintaining or replacing resources used with resources of equal or greater value. In our project as an example, 8 acres of feed corn were lost to development which fed roughly 8 cows for a year, but 6 acres of vegetables were planted that feeds 80 families their vegetable needs for six months. We've also greatly reduced the cost or burden to the environment because Melissa has been able to increase the volume of produce from the land (food resource), while greatly improving the quality of the soil (another valuable resource), while reducing our carbon imprint from fossil fuels (no chemicals). A fair trade.

Sustainability on the farm means all biological systems need to remain diverse and productive for the long run, long into the future. This means healthy water, soils, plants and animals, and these things need to live and endure along with human development, economics, politics and culture. But the farm, even our farm, is highly dependent on fossil fuels to run our tractor. When it comes to the sustainable farm, the question naturally arises, what is to be sustained in sustainable farming if it still counts on a limited supply of a natural resource like petroleum? Can there be a sustainable use of a non-renewable resource, since any use will eventually lead to the exhaustion of the finite supply? Is an organic farm that is still dependent on the tractor and fossil fuels really sustainable long into the future?

Over the long term, 50 to 100 years from now, we need an answer as to how to power our tractors without petroleum because fossil fuels aren't going to last forever. We're eventually going to need another way to power our tractor or we can plan on going back to the draft horse and some really hard labor at some point in the future. Melissa could not do everything she does, or feed nearly as many people, without a tractor.

The answer might lie in bio-fuels that we could grow right on the farm, so I decided to take it upon myself to investigate this issue as an excuse to not do any real work on the farm for a couple days. Besides, I'm farm management, and I tinker around with stuff like this just to look busy and feel like I'm still important to the overall farm operation.

I met with the Vice President of Agriculture at the Biltmore Estate farm, Ted Katsigianis, to see what they were doing with bio-diesel. That was a nice title, I thought, VP of Agriculture, and Ted has held that position since 1983, over 35 years, and I wondered if there was a CEO of Farm Operations. If there was a VP of Agriculture, then there certainly could be a

President, so I ordered some new business cards the following week and made myself President of Creekside Farm. Now it was official, and I could work on projects like this and not feel guilty about not doing any real work on the farm. Problem solved, and I think it was an excellent executive decision.

Ted told me that the farm at Biltmore is growing about 75 acres of canola, a plant that buds in fields of beautiful yellow flowers in the summer and that tourists love to romp through. Farm workers have a hard time keeping all the tourists out of the fields in fact, and it drives them crazy; the beautiful rolling fields of little yellow flowers make for a wonderful backdrop to a family photo. But that's not all that canola is good for. The Biltmore farm has invested in equipment that will turn the seeds of the canola plant into canola oil, the same that you buy in the grocery store. The oil is used for cooking in the restaurants on the estate, primarily to fry foods in the deep fryers (and some for salad dressings), and then the oil is reclaimed from the fryers and sent back to the farm where it's turned into bio-diesel. The diesel is then used to power the tractors on the farm in a wonderful circle of plant to food to fuel, nothing wasted. The oil that is used to fry your French fries will soon go to power the tractor that plants and harvests the potatoes. How cool is that.

The process of turning canola oil (or corn oil for that matter) into bio-diesel is fairly simple and straight forward, and you don't need to be a chemist to do it. Ted showed me the old barn where all the magic happens, and the equipment used included just two machines and some storage containers in a small 20 by 30-foot room. He said that he purchased the oil extractor (to remove the oils from the canola seed) for about $20,000 and that they can supply the restaurants at the Biltmore Estate with over 100 gallons of cooking oil every week.

The extractor basically crushes the seed and squeezes the oil from it, and the solid matter left over goes to feed cattle and goats on the farm. Nothing wasted there.

The equipment necessary to turn the oil that they take back from the restaurant's deep fryers into bio-diesel costs about another $20,000., and that equipment is basically a mixer that blends the oil with methanol and lye (sodium hydroxide). After a few hours, the glycerin in the oil separates and settles to the bottom of the stainless-steel tank, and what's left is bio-diesel that will run a tractor. It looked like a fairly simple process and the equipment required was not really all that expensive (although I know some people can even make it in 5-gallon buckets in their garage). Ted said that he can get about 100 gallons of bio-diesel from an acre of canola. As the new President of Creekside Farm, with the advice and consent of my Chief Financial Officer, Kara, I decided we would plan on purchasing the equipment and start a bio-diesel operation at Creekside Farm as soon as we had the cash. We can grow the canola, supply the Tavern Restaurant and others with cooking oil for their deep fryers, and then reclaim it again for bio-diesel on the farm. We'd become a little more environmentally friendly and sustainable, and if we reclaimed cooking oil from other restaurants in the area, and sold bio-diesel, it might become a profit center. This is exactly the kind of thing, I thought, that farm presidents do – big picture stuff.

With a little more research, I discovered that there is a big difference in bio-fuels. Corn only produces 18 gallons of bio-fuel per acre, but palm oil can produce 625 gallons per acre. New research using a modified algae specially grown in seawater might one day produce an astounding 10,000 gallons per acre. That technology may be off in the future someday, and since I was hundreds of miles away from the ocean, and we couldn't grow palm trees in the mountains, I decided to stick with canola. But learning about some of the possibilities for bio-fuels was encouraging. Virgin Airlines is already using a bio-fuel that is made from coconut and babassu oil mixed with normal jet fuel in some of their 747's that fly around the world. If Virgin can use it to fly airplanes, then what else could we do with it, I thought. It would obviously run a diesel generator for electricity, and I started looking into using biofuels from canola to heat our greenhouse in the winter so that we might be able to produce food year-round. That equipment exists and is readily available. I started to think of other things I might do with this new title of Farm President, and I discovered a lot of easily identifiable problems that I could work on. So I did.

Experts say that our world population (currently at 7 billion) will approach 10 billion by 2050, and that's a lot of mouths to feed. About 1 billion people (or one out of seven of us) goes hungry right now and is mal-nourished, with a high percentage of them being children. The Food and Agriculture Organization of the United Nations estimates that agricultural production needs to double by 2050 to feed everyone. But 80% of the arable land in the world is already being used.

Some scientists who study the world's carrying capacity have suggested that the number of humans that the earth can support in a sustainable manner is somewhere between 300 million and 2 billion. They point to studies that show we currently use 30% more of the earth's natural resources then can be replaced through the earth's natural systems. They also suggest that if everyone on the planet wanted to live a lifestyle like a European, we'd need three planets worth of resources. For everyone to live like an American, we'd need five planets. This has a significant bearing on the future as billions of people rise out of poverty around the world.

Medical costs are going up 8% every year, and 16.5% of the US economy now goes to health care costs. We industrialized the farm and then processed the food and created this health care problem. These are obviously huge issues to tackle, so I decided to try to fix things in my own backyard first. Can we create a neighborhood, even a city, that can feed itself and that is more sustainable for the long term?

The solution is in reducing our dependence on petrochemical-backed agriculture and replacing it with something more sustainable. We need to work with the ecosystems rather than run roughshod over them. We need to optimize our food crops and food systems using some science tied into ecological solutions. And it needs to be profitable.

Feeding the world isn't just about the production side of the equation, it's also about distribution. Some argue that we already grow enough food to feed everyone with the incredible amount of food that is wasted. But the answer doesn't lie in finding novel ways to move this excess food around the world. The solution is moving the farm. The solution is giving everyone, including third world countries, the capacity to grow their own food. It means teaching people better ways to farm using new ideas and technologies to make it sustainable, and then giving them the tools to do it. As the saying goes, give a man a fish, and you feed him for a day. Teach a man to fish, and you feed him for life. All nations need to become more self-reliant when it comes to food, and that's the investment (or charitable donation) that pays the biggest dividends (and has the greatest impact). And from my experience, throw a little profit in there, and you get a lot more smart people interested in working on the solution.

Don't just teach a man a better way to fish, try to make a profit at it, and then plow those profits back into the company, hire 100 more people, and begin transforming the fishing industry, or any other industry. That kind of effort starts helping people at scale. [53] That's what I wanted to do. But what kind of new business model would make a profit producing food and be worth researching and investing in.

I was familiar with hydroponics, and using hydroponics to grow food was one area that seemed worth looking further into. I know that a great many more people, and some very smart people, are starting to use hydroponics to grow marijuana, given there's money to be made in it (and no jail sentence) so the science and knowledge in the field is probably growing exponentially and might be applied to growing food. The science of hydroponics has been around for a while, at least since the 1940's, but it has grown quickly in recent years because of changes in laws in this country, and there's money in it now.

Hydroponics is the growing of plants without soil in a nutrient rich water solution. During World War II scientists began researching ways to feed soldiers stationed on far flung and arid islands scattered across the oceans using hydroponics. More research in hydroponics was done to support soldiers in the Middle East that were stationed there to protect the oil supplies, and since World War II scientists have continued to perfect the chemical composition of the growth median.

Some existing hydroponic operations can harvest lettuce as much as 20 times in a year, instead of just one or two harvests in soil-based farming, and no pesticides or herbicides are used because of the closed loop, indoor system. And importantly, hydroponics uses 70% less water than soil-based farming. Newer technologies called aeroponics, where roots hang freely in the air and sprayers apply a mist solution directly to the root system, use much less water which makes it even better for arid third world countries. Add an aquaponics operation for some protein, where feces from fish grown in tanks is used to fertilize the plants, and you've closed the loop in a cycle that requires little if any fertilizers and you can harvest the fish. Aquaculture (fish farms) already account for 30% of the seafood that we consume, so tying that into an industrial scale hydroponics operation makes some sense and might be effective in feeding more people in developed and developing nations. I'd seen this kind of operation on display at a local hydroponics store in Asheville, with trout swimming around in a large plastic tank at the end of the line. Add a little fish food (the only real input) and pump the tank water back "up stream" to the plants, where it feeds the plants as it flows back down into that big tub again in a very cool closed system.

I knew that the Biltmore Farm was now growing micro-greens hydroponically in three greenhouses on the Biltmore Estate, and that it was the largest and most profitable crop that they could provide to the estate's restaurants throughout the year. There are several stores in Asheville that sell hydroponic supplies, including the trays, pumps, growing lights and chemical solutions. As a test and to learn more about the process, I purchased a small hydroponic system and set it up in the basement to grow micro-greens. I lined the plastic trays with long sheets of burlap on which to grow the seeds, and as I had learned at the Biltmore, when it came time to harvest just a couple weeks later, I hung the sheets of burlap from a hook and cut the microgreens with an electric carving knife in just a couple of minutes. The test was a success, but I also knew that I couldn't feed that many people from my basement. I needed to bring this up to scale, and I needed other social entrepreneurs with cash to do that. I put the topic up for discussion at the next meeting of our little Creekside Farm junto, our think tank. More on that group in a minute.

There were other food problems that I wanted to work on at Creekside Farm, and one of them was related to beef production on the farm. Nutritionists say that ten to twenty percent of our food calories must come from protein, but ranching, where most of our protein comes from in the form of meat, produces more greenhouse gasses than all the cars in the world. And as people rise out of poverty, the global demand for meat is expected to double by 2050. Meat consumption doubled in China between 1990 and 2002 (just twelve short years). Meat, by the way, is one of the thirstier food products we can grow, requiring about 2500 gallons of water to produce one pound of meat. China already has a water problem, with two of its largest underground aquafers already running dry. Many areas are turning into dustbowls like the US experienced in Oklahoma back in the 1930's. As the Chinese appetite for meat continues to grow, who do you think will be exporting it to them? The US beef industry has been pushing to increase exports to China. That means we'll be dumping more chemical pesticides, herbicides and fertilizers on our fields to raise more feed corn to ship more beef to China. Starting to notice a pattern here? Recall then also that we import 60% of our fossil fuels that go into producing the chemicals that we dump on our fields. Then add the food miles to ship it overseas. I sure hope someone over there appreciates that steak, but I'm quite certain that all the costs to our own ecological systems has not been fully accounted for in the cost of that steak.

The truth is we need to cut back on our own red meat consumption here in America, if only for the health benefits, and we don't need to be encouraging other cultures to eat more of it. If we can cut back to a healthier meat consumption, some portion of the 40% of the worlds cereal grains now fed to cattle can and should be repurposed for human consumption.

At Creekside Farm, we were growing feed corn on 8 acres, but it wasn't feeding my cows. It was going to the dairy farm down the road. My 20 cattle were eating grass and hay but taking up 30 acres to do that. Certainly, other crops could have been grown on that land. But I couldn't get over the fact that I really like meat, and I wasn't quite ready to give it up. So the only solution to the meat problem that I could come up with was to continue trying to use the best organic practices in the pasture and just try to cut back on my own personal meat consumption, and try to encourage others to do the same.

Fish can provide the necessary protein, but 90% of the oceans large fish stocks are now gone, including tuna, swordfish, cod, halibut and flounder. The truth is, we've already devastated our oceans. Bottom trawling destroys about 6 million square miles of the sea floor every year—an area the size of Russia. The United States has polluted our coastal waters with toxic herbicides, pesticides, and fertilizers that run off our farms to such an extent that 90% of the fish that Americans eat now must come from a foreign nation. Your fish could have been caught on a hook that was attached to a line that ran for 60 miles, and it didn't just catch the fish you ordered for dinner, it caught a lot of other species that weren't intended. We need to let the oceans rest and recover, so expanding protein production from wild caught fish is not a viable option.

GENETICALLY MODIFIED ORGANISMS

Melissa probably could have used some help on the farm harvesting tomatoes, but I spent that day researching GMO's instead. While I hate the idea of concentrating the ownership of food genes in the hands of a few people, I don't think we should discount genetic engineering and the technology out of hand. Melissa would not agree with me on this, but I think the subject requires more research and open-minded discussion before we completely discount it. Particularly with a changing climate and the threats that may bring, we need to look at all tools and options to deal with it. And I think that genie is already out of the bottle anyway, because much of our corn and soybeans are already grown in the US using GMO's (without any known harmful effects to humans yet being reported). Most of the genetic engineering is concentrated in three crops right now, cotton, corn and soybeans, and hasn't yet focused on other vegetables. But there have been some proven benefits coming from GMO's including higher yields using fewer chemical fertilizers (and fossil fuels to make them), and less herbicides and pesticides (so less poisons entering streams). We're running low on phosphorus, another key ingredient in chemical fertilizers, and mining phosphorus in central Florida and other locations presents its own environmental issues. With fossil fuels in limited supply, we need to develop other more sustainable ways to grow our food that are less dependent on chemicals and GMO's might offer some promise here, particularly when you realize that GMO's could be used with sustainable and organic growing techniques that improve the soil. The two things are not necessarily mutually exclusive. If we can increase yields with less chemicals and better soil managment, genetic engineering might prove better for the environment in the long run as the science gets better.

Many GMO seeds don't require plowing, and that means less soil erosion and better carbon sequestration, while they've also been designed for better resistance to pests and drought conditions. Genetically engineered rice is in the pipeline that is fortified with vitamin A, which could save lives in many in third world countries. Vitamin A deficiency is the leading cause of blindness in some countries. I'm not an advocate for genetic engineering yet by any means, but with a rapidly growing global population, it might contribute to a solution if used alongside organic and more sustainable farming techniques. But while many technologies may look promising, including hydroponics and GMO's, there is still a lot more to learn. For now, we should try to be a less wasteful, more sustainable, eat less meat and eat a little closer to home.

Two areas of study that are helping us grow more sustainably are closely related concepts called agroecology and permaculture, both related somewhat to organic. Both agroecology and permaculture are related to the study of ecological processes and bringing ecological principles to bear in agriculture. They can help us determine new management approaches that improve the soils and environmental diversity. Both terms are used fairly broadly and may be used to refer to a science, a movement, or a growing practice. Both study a wide variety of ecosystems including soil, water, forests, and wetlands to understand the interrelationship of all things, and both try to mimic processes in the natural world. The goal is to develop systems that produce more food on less land while simultaneously improving the soils, ecosystem and biodiversity. One simple example is mixing in crops of a certain plant species that might repel insects within rows of corn. The principles are centered around simulating or directly utilizing the patterns and processes observed in nature.

The purpose of both permaculture and agroecology is to try to figure out the best means of growing food that are less harmful to nature, and in fact helpful to nature, and so more sustainable for the future. The health of the soil, plant, animal and man is one great, interconnected problem. The problem is ecological, biological, medical, and I might add, moral. And to put it in economic terms, if we deplete our soils, we're living off the principle and not the interest. There are a ton of good books on agroecology and permaculture, and as Farm President I figured I should know something about the subject, so I bought a few.

But the subjects that all required work and research to bring them to our farm, including hydroponics, bio-fuels, and permaculture, were now starting to become overwhelming for a farm president. So, I made another management decision, created the new position of Executive Director at the Creekside Farm Education Center, and assumed that position. No more farm chores for me. I'm way too busy for that.

In addition to my diligent and important work, Melissa greatly reduces the amount of petroleum that we use currently on the farm by growing organically. She uses methods such as compost and chicken manure, and cover crops that can add nitrogen and other minerals and organic matter back into the soil, and not fossil fuel-based fertilizers and pesticides. Overall our carbon footprint on the farm is low I think, with the tractor needed occasionally, an old truck to haul vegetables a few hundred feet (and not 1000 miles), and the electricity we use to run the well to water the garden.

Because sustainability is the most important element of a new agrarian community, agriculture in the community must use environmentally friendly methods of farming. The production of crops or livestock must take place without damage to human or natural systems if there is to be a balance and fair trade-off for the development. It involves preventing adverse effects to soil, water and biodiversity in the surrounding and downstream resources. If a farm that is attached to an agricultural community uses the same old industrial agriculture process to grow food with massive amounts of petroleum-based chemicals and fertilizers, it defeats the whole purpose and principles behind the project and the justification for it.

To be sustainable the agricultural community must also be economically sound and pay a living wage to those working on the farm so that they can continue working there. And it must pass on a farm to future generations that is improved and not depleted or polluted, with improved and healthier soils. This involves smart organic methods of farming that do not undermine the environment but work to heal it and improve it. That's a fair deal to humans and the environment.

As noted, transportation is a large contributor to greenhouse gas emissions. Research shows that one-third of all greenhouse gasses emitted into the atmosphere are due to transportation. Diesel trucks also release exhaust fumes that contain particulate matter which is hazardous to human health and another contributor to climate change. The Agrihood does not attempt to feed people outside of its close proximity and so greatly reduces transportation costs and environmental damage, making it much more sustainable in that regard. The end game of our agrihood is to reach some kind of balance for humans and nature.

THE FARM MANAGER

One spring day in 2017 Melissa asked me if I could help her for an hour or so setting up caterpillar tunnels in the garden. Caterpillar tunnels are short hoop houses that are used by organic growers to keep the bugs off plants and for frost protection. They're about 3 feet high, semi-circular hoops that you stick in the ground and then drape netting over them. Before you drape the netting over them, it looks like a croquet set for giants. After you drape the netting on, it looks like its namesake: a huge white caterpillar attacking your garden.

While we were working together, I started asking Melissa some questions about why she took this job as farm manager. I was curious because she could find a job anywhere. She had a college degree but was only making $34,000 a year to work for us and run our CSA program.

She said she didn't always want to be a farmer. That didn't really occur to her until her second year in college when she took a class in sustainable living at Appalachian State University. "That opened my eyes" she told me. She went on to get a degree in sustainable development with a concentration in agriculture.

"I love food and I like to cook, and I love what I'm doing because of the connections to food and the sustainability of it all." She added, "I know we can't keep going the way that we have been."

Melissa is a Millennial, and like many of this younger generation, she cares a great deal about the environment and wants to do what she can to help protect some of our resources for the future.

"This was my little way of helping climate change," she said with a smile. Melissa said that she always loved animals, and her first inclination toward farming was possibly raising cattle.

"For one summer break from college I worked on a raspberry farm," Melissa said, "and I remember when it first occurred to me how little people know about food and where it comes from, and I remember thinking that the person who is going to buy these raspberries will never know that I, Melissa, picked them."

"I was kind of sad about that," she added. "Would they even care that I did this for them, that it was hot out when I picked them, would they ever wonder or even care where these raspberries came from?"

That's a pretty existential question, I thought, so I ducked it.

"But why run this CSA program, really?" I asked.

"I can't feed the world, or even Asheville" she replied, "but I can feed maybe 100 people, and that makes me happy. Even feeding 100 people their vegetables over the summer is a small thing, but at least I'm doing my small part, doing what I can do."

She went on to say, "I want to help this community, help feed the community, build the community around this food." Melissa knew that I was putting in a road and developing lots near the gardens and the farm, but she had no idea that I would be writing this book, and here she just described one of its central themes.

"I think we need to change the way we look at food, and take a more positive approach to it," she continued. "So many people think food is a hassle, like 'we have to eat', or 'man, what am I going to make for dinner', like it's a burden. People need to look at food as interesting and exciting. Celebrate it. Don't just open a box."

I asked her how she is doing financially. I said that we wished we could pay her more, but she knew that the CSA program would eventually have to be self-sufficient, and until she had enough members to support her and the expenses of the farm, like transplants and organic fertilizers and organic chicken feed, she would have to make do with that salary.

"Oh, I'm OK," she said. "I buy less shoes, no pop, and make a few sacrifices here and there. I can still buy organic food." Our crops hadn't come in yet, and she shopped often at Whole Foods in Asheville.

I asked her what she thought about Whole Foods, referring to it as "Whole Paycheck", the running joke among people who often shop there.

"Whole Foods is really convenient. If you need something and the CSA pick-up day is still a few days away, or you don't have time to stop by the farmers market, if it's even open, then Whole Foods makes it really quick and easy to get what you need."

"Well, it's not all grown local of course," she went on to say, "sometimes it will say local if it is. And the packaged foods have less preservatives, which is good, and they all have a pretty picture of a farm on the box, and it costs more." She was smiling as she said that.

I agreed that a lot of the packaging at Whole Foods sure was pretty, with beautiful images of farms and rolling hills, a barn and usually a sunrise.

"What about all the hard work, weeding and digging in the soil and dragging hoses around everywhere, is it what you expected?" I asked.

"There are some pretty hard days. Farming is pretty romanticized. Some young people around here want to try to homestead, until they discover how hard farming is and how hard it is to get something to come up out of the ground and live long enough so that you can eat it."

She went on, "I do get frustrated and tired sometimes. Some days I even question what the heck I'm doing and is this something I really want to do with my life. Everything I direct seeded last year failed," she said with another pretty smile.

I knew she had a hard year last year. The field she was working had been in feed corn for probably 20 years, nothing else, never rotated. That creates a situation just right for bugs and disease, and she got one, a corn seed maggot, and it wiped out a lot of her first plantings in the garden.

"Organic farming is hard, and sometimes it's like fighting with one arm tied behind your back, when you know there is a chemical out there that could take care of the problem quickly", she said. Not an option for the organic grower. They wouldn't even consider it.

"Even with all the frustration, all these little armies of bugs and fungus attacking me and everything I've done, I have moments when I realize that there is nothing else I'd rather be doing." Then Melissa added, "Like when I find three little perfect tomatoes, and think, I grew these! With my own hands and labor, I grew these little guys, and they're perfect."

"Sometimes I think it's a spiritual thing. I need to do it," she said.

Melissa told me that her generation grew up seeing environmental damage on TV and learning about it way back in elementary school. She grew up with it and grew up understanding it was out there. Many of her generation, the millennials, she told me, know that we can't keep going the way we are, and a lot of them want to do something about it.

"We are the new generation of farmers," she said, "and there's a lot of us out there if we can get a chance. Thank you again for the chance, by the way." She smiled again.

I reminded her that if she needs more help to just let me know. She said she has absolutely no problem finding helpers with the CSA program. So many of her friends and people she knows want to try working on a farm, and some have volunteered to help her for free, just to give it a try.

This is Asheville of course, and there are a lot of free-spirited young people coming here. I knew that she was right, there are a lot of young people interested in doing this work. When I ran the ad on Craigslist to find a farm manager, my email inbox got loaded up with replies. I interviewed a few people, but after meeting Melissa, I knew right off my search was over. She was perfect for the job, and she had a degree in sustainable agriculture and had worked at a CSA the previous year. We couldn't have found a better person to manage the program. I get lucky like that a lot. Throughout my career people have always seemed to show up at the right time, perfect for the job at hand. But there are a lot of people out there like Melissa who would love the opportunity to run a community garden as part of an agrihood, and communities, developers and regional planners can easily find them when the time comes.

A CAPITAL INVESTMENT

Having a large, productive garden and farm was critical infrastructure to the agrihood concept I was planning. Having solved that problem with Melissa, there were the other structural things that needed to be addressed and worked out. As discussed previously, a true agricultural community needs spaces and buildings and facilities that can provide storage for equipment, like tractors and attachments, and a food cleaning, processing and distribution center.

We fixed up the old barn on the property to store the John Deere tractor and other supplies like hoses and sprinklers and bug netting. After 80 years, the barn needed some work, both structurally and cosmetically. We hired a mason to work on the foundation, and a carpenter to replace any of the rotted wood with rough cut boards that matched the original. We put a decorative rock face on the block at the base of the barn that made it look much better. I think we may have added another 80 years to its lifespan.

We purchased the old school house, tractor, greenhouse,

garden shed, high-tunnels, hoses and other necessary supplies, and it all started to add up on top of the normal development costs of infrastructure. We were getting low on cash and went to the bank to refinance our home.

I was getting into uncharted waters here. I had never heard of another agrihood having a communal building like our education center. I'd been to visit a few agrihoods that were new or under development, and I had seen a barn or a shed or other outbuilding for tools and supplies, but I had never seen a communal building for processing, preparing and sharing the produce from the garden. I had seen an outdoor wash station to rinse off the vegetables next to a garden, but nothing I had seen was like what we were creating.

I had seen some plans for an agrihood in British Columbia that Andres Duany had created, and the drawings showed communal buildings for processing food, administrative offices and classrooms, even a farmer's market; but that development was a much larger project and after years of planning it still hasn't been built yet. It was becoming a scary new world in uncharted waters, and we were running out of cash.

Because the agrihood concept is still very new, everything related to farming or food gardens that I had seen or heard about generally included a garden and sheds to store tools; but no building designated for the purpose of education or building community ties, like farm to table meals or canning classes. Come to think of it, I'd never seen farm animals either. The old red schoolhouse looks down on the CSA garden and the animal pastures. The location couldn't have been more perfect, but could we draw people to it, including other stakeholders that might support a broader mission?

What it all came down to was this; I was counting on people believing in this idea and wanting to live in an agrihood. But would they really care about the local farming economy and supporting young farmers? Would they care about the local food supply in its stand against the massive corporate food complex? Do they really care that much about the environment and chemical pesticides? Would they really care about community and food? I had been thinking and talking about a values-based, principle centered approach to sustainable living, but I could have been full of it. What I was doing was very risky, and I was starting to get really nervous.

As we got deeper in debt, I was starting to question everything. I'd put about every dime we had into this project, and some of the banks money, and it went into the millions. Could I be way off here? Was I nuts? At the time panic was starting to set in, I jumped in the car and drove down to Whole Foods in Asheville. The parking lot was packed. I went into the store, and there were shoppers in all the aisles. The fear had started to subside a little. "Maybe I'm not crazy," I said out load to myself while standing dead still at the front of the store, just staring down the aisles with what I'm sure must have been an intense and worried look on my face. A lady pushing a cart past me heard me say that out loud and looked at me kind of funny. The way she looked at me I thought she might say, "Nope, you are crazy."

All I really had going for me at the time was knowing what a success Michael Pollan's book The Omnivore's Dilemma was, and the popularity of documentaries like Food, Inc., Al Gore, the growth of farmers markets and chefs at restaurants promoting local farms. There weren't a lot of really solid and encouraging signs out there to tell me this new urban planning idea was going to work. There were other agrihoods sprouting up around the country, but most of them were just getting off the ground. I didn't have a lot to go on.

I didn't start this agrihood movement. There were others that started down this path before I did. And this book isn't trying to start a movement. Books don't start movements anyway. Movements start books. But it was a risky venture to be sure, and there was a time when my wife and I we're really worried about the whole thing, and we started cutting way back on our personal expenses. I knew at least that we had plenty of chicken eggs and vegetables, so we probably weren't going to starve. And that's more than most industrial farmers in the Corn Belt can say. They've just got feed corn.

A NEW FOOD ECONOMY

After many years in business developing different products, I know that the economic value that we place on most products has no relationship to the environmental costs to produce it. The cost of a cheap plastic toy doesn't really account for the full, long-term cost over its lifecycle. Whether that is damage to the earth by the extraction of materials to make the product; or the energy used to make it (limited resources like gas and oil); or the disposal costs and half-life of the product in a landfill (and the damage a landfill can do to an environment). These things don't really come into the equation when the price of a product is determined.

The price of a product is merely a reflection of the costs to make it plus a profit. Environmental impact, and the real cost to future generations, is not considered. In the raw materials that men take from nature, the market makes no distinction between renewable and non-renewable resources. The market ignores the entire social and environmental costs and bases prices entirely on cost of goods sold or expenses. Pollution in the manufacturing or the half-life of a product in a landfill, and the costs associated with the disposal of the product (the garbage truck), has no real bearing on price.

So corn production in the US does not account for all its cost. The environmental impact on soils, streams and oceans has no bearing on price. And we subsidize corn production to such an extent that the price of corn in processed foods at the grocery store has no real bearing to its actual cost of production. The cost of soda pop with its subsidized corn syrup has no relation to the real costs of production, or the costs of health care for weight related illness like diabetes or heart disease.

The same lack of consideration is evident in most land development projects. We don't consider the costs such as the loss of available farm land and future food production. Developers don't reimburse neighbors for, sorry, covering up that beautiful pasture or ripping out those trees to put in a strip mall. But clearly there is a cost to the local community and the environment that is not considered in the costs or pricing of the new development.

In a way, the agrihood does account for those costs to a large measure. A substantial portion of the land is intentionally left open and undeveloped for a reason. And the residents of that agricultural community are paying, to some degree, for that open space, and to keep what is left undeveloped and open. It's a new product for a new age, and a new math that accounts for more of the costs. And the full costs of food production are paid by the people who consume the food, without any subsidies from the government or inputs from a global economy.

But what about those people who live at the edge of our economy? Is the system fair for them, and can we provide better access to healthy food for all? As I got into this local food movement, I started to wonder if local governments, with the help of nonprofits, could do more to help promote local healthy food to food insecure households?

Many low-income households use SNAP benefits (food stamps) to buy cheap, processed food that only exacerbates chronic health problems and adds more costs to the already financially strapped health care system. Can government provide a different kind of subsidy, in addition to the snap program, but used exclusively for healthy local food purchased at a farmer's market? This would support the healthy eating habits of low-income residents while it supports local farmers at the same time. It would encourage better eating habits which might help reduce health care costs associated with poor diets, like diabetes and heart disease.

While food stamps are now accepted at many farmers markets, because the produce might be more expensive than conventional or processed food at the supermarket, and it requires a separate stop at the market, many low-income people do not normally shop at a farmer's market or use the stamps there. But a program that is separate and in addition to the food stamp program, where these 'market stamps' are only redeemable at a farmer's market or local food co-op, might encourage more people to use those additional dollars and start eating healthier diets that include more fruits and vegetables. Local governments would also have to make certain that farmers markets are accessible to inner city and low-income people by public transportation. But for every dollar spent on a local food assistance program, two very important things are accomplished with the same dollar; healthier eating habits for low-income households and healthier local farms and infrastructure.

It would take some work to figure it all out, but if a city like Asheville started its own version of the federal SNAP program for local food, call it 'market stamps', and funded it with, say $250,000, and distributed those market stamps to needy households in the city to be used solely at farmers markets and local food coops, that money circles back to local farmers and food processors and stays in the community. A program like this would help create healthier eating habits for low-income residents while it helps build the local food infrastructure. The program might become self-sustaining because it could reduce some health-care costs currently paid by the government (because of better eating habits) while it creates local jobs for farmers and the food industry.

As I started looking into this idea, I discovered that there is already a similar program for young mothers and senior citizens operating in many states. A program under the USDA called the Farmers Market Nutrition Program (FMNP) is associated with the Special Supplemental Nutrition Program for Women, Infants and Children (popularly known as WIC). The FMNP program was established to provide fresh, unprepared, locally grown fruits and vegetables to WIC participants, and to expand the awareness, use of, and sales at farmers' markets. A similar program for low-income senior citizens is called the Senior Farmers Market Nutrition Program (SFMNP). Can we expand programs like this to encourage more food insecure people at all ages to eat healthier foods?

Trying to get the federal government behind a program that expands the FMNP program beyond new mothers and seniors would take a monumental effort and a lot of time, if it could be done at all. But developing a more local or regional program might be possible. We're researching possible program options and funding now at the Creekside Farm Education Center, with the key issues related to how the monthly farmers market 'coupons' are distributed and easily redeemed by farmers for cash. An electronic debit card system would be most efficient, where funds could be deposited directly into the farmers account like other credit and debit card transactions at the farmers market (most farmers use Square with their cell phone now at the market). MANNA FoodBank could help us identify at-risk homes and distribute the electronic 'market stamps.' How the funds are distributed to the food insecure, used, and redeemed must be efficient and limit manual processing and paperwork. It's a big project to be working on, but there's some smart people in our little community at Walnut Cove, including retired bankers, financiers, IT guys, lawyers and doctors who can dedicate some time to the problem. We formed a little think tank, a "junto" as Ben Franklin would call it, and started having regular meetings at the education center to study the best options for funding and implementing a program like this. If we could do anything to improve access to healthy food for low income households, and improve food justice, it was worth our time.

CHAPTER SEVEN

ON SELF-RELIANCE

If a man empties his purse into his head, no man can take it away from him. An investment in knowledge always pays the best interest.

-Ben Franklin, on purchasing books

VICTORY GARDENS

Independence and self-reliance are core values and traits of the American people. Our country was founded on these values. But can communities become more independent and self-reliant in food production, and how much food can they really produce? In my father's generation, during World War II, as much as half the fruits and vegetables consumed in the United States came from small, local gardens that popped up in parks, vacant lots and backyards. Known as Victory Gardens, they helped reduce the pressure on the food supply brought on by the war.[54]

With many young men leaving the farm to go off to fight in the war effort during World War I and World War II, many nations feared that there wouldn't be enough farmers and food producers left to feed the hungry troops going off to war, or to feed the people back home.

Victory gardens, also called 'war gardens' or 'food gardens for defense', were vegetable, fruit, and herb gardens planted in back yards and public spaces like parks in the United States and other countries to increase the food supply. Commercial crops were diverted to feeding soldiers overseas, and food rationing that began in the Spring of 1942 became another incentive to get Americans to grow some of their own food in backyard gardens and plots of land wherever they could find it. Along with aiding the war effort by allowing more food to be allocated to the troops, these gardens were also considered a civil "morale booster". The average citizen gardeners could feel empowered by their contribution of labor to the war effort and rewarded by the produce that they could grow and sell.

Victory gardens quickly became a part of daily life in towns and cities across America, and neighbors often got together to work in gardens that popped up on sports fields and city parks, along railroad tracks and vacant lots, and in Great Britain, even on golf courses that were requisitioned for farming and agriculture. New York City had as many as 800 people working in one large Victory Garden. The U.S. government also encouraged raising chickens in your backyard to increase the egg and protein supply. The US Department of Agriculture and other organizations printed instructional gardening pamphlets and even issued shovels and other gardening tools. Gardening radio shows encouraged gardeners with helpful tips on growing vegetables. Posters popped up everywhere with slogans like "Our food is fighting", "Grow your own, Can your own" and "Sow the seeds of Victory!"

Victory gardens made no small contribution to the war effort and keeping Americans fed at home. It has been estimated that approximately one-third of the total vegetables produced in the United States during WWII came from victory gardens.[55]

It helped to lower the price of vegetables needed by the US War Department to feed the troops, thus saving money that could be spent elsewhere on the military. By May 1943, there were an estimated 18 million victory gardens in the United States with over 12 million in cities and 6 million on farms and in rural areas.

The trend continued to grow, so that almost half our vegetables came from these victory gardens in the year 1944. Fruit and vegetables harvested in these home and community plots was estimated to be between 9 and 10 million tons in 1944, an amount equal to all commercial production of fresh vegetables.[56] Other estimates suggest a slightly lower percentage, but that at least 40% of the fruits and vegetables consumed in the United States came from these Victory Gardens.[57] Having more food grown locally in neighborhoods also reduced the need for trucks and transportation, including fuel, that could be redirected to the war effort and transporting valuable military equipment and supplies.

In Great Britain, County Herb Committees were established to grow and collect medicinal herbs when German blockades created shortages, for instance in Digitalis Purpurea (Foxglove) which was used as heart medicine to regulate heartbeat at the time.

The Victory Garden movement also united and energized the home-front and gave people feelings of empowerment at a very fearful and uncertain time. Local communities would have festivals and competitions to showcase and celebrate the produce people grew in their own gardens. As we'll see later, growing your own food creates feelings of self-reliance, confidence and community strength. More people got off the couch and did some exercise working in these gardens, so there were other benefits to our national health from the Victory Garden program. But what the program really tells us is that we can grow a lot of food locally if we had to, or chose to, even in densely populated areas.

While this book is largely about the agricultural neighborhood, the same principles discussed here apply to backyard gardens. The eat your view, grow local movement, and all reasoning behind it, can apply to your own 5 x 10 garden bed in your own backyard, or tomatoes in a pot on your apartment balcony. We can become a nation of gardeners again and take back some food sovereignty and independence right at home.

Contrast the Victory Garden movement during WWII with current trends in food supply. More than half of the fresh fruit and nearly one-third of the fresh vegetables that Americans eat now come from other countries. The big change in where our food comes from happened gradually over the past 40 years, and it wasn't all bad. It did help to satisfy a year-round demand for fruit and it did supplement our domestic supply during winter and between harvesting seasons. Having more variety of fruits and vegetables throughout the year is a good thing if it gets people to eat more of them. But it also allowed importers to capitalize on lower production costs elsewhere in the world, and the problem arises when foreign food supplants or replaces our own food supply that is readily available, particularly in the summer time.

The proportion of the imported fresh fruit eaten in the United States rose to 53.1 percent in 2016, up from 23 percent in 1975, according to the Agriculture Department's Economic

Research Service. Fresh vegetable imports rose to 31.1 percent from just 5.8 percent in 1975. And the trend continues to grow. It should be noted here again that the United States remains a net agricultural exporter, with grains, soybeans, meat and nuts accounting for most of the trade surplus. But do we want to turn production of the rest of our food over to a foreign nation, like we've done with another basic necessity, our clothing?

Here's more on how the trend played out over the years. The import share of fresh fruit grew from 1.4 percent in 1970 to 30.4 percent in 1990, reaching 45.3 percent in 2008, and 53.1% most recently in 2016. The import share for vegetables grew from 3.9 percent in 1970 to 8.0 percent in 1990, reaching 17.2 percent in 2008, and then nearly doubling to 31.1 percent in 2016 (less than a decade).

We grow tomatoes year-round in the US, and in the winter months primarily in California and Florida. But Mexican imports supplement the supply (most heavily in the winter when domestic production is lowest) and Canadian imports arrive throughout the summer months, so that over 57% of our tomatoes are now imported from outside the United States. That's a huge percentage for tomatoes! It almost seems un-American, like importing apple pie.

Asparagus and oranges provide for some contrast here. Asparagus is imported throughout the year (mostly from Peru and Mexico), with just a brief domestic season here in the United States, so that we now import about 95% of our asparagus. Oranges are mostly produced domestically throughout the year (in California and Florida), with relatively little outside supply (only about 9%). But the supply that we do get comes from very faraway places – Australia and South Africa. We're also importing a lot more apples from New Zealand, and I'll tell you something, mate, you can't get much further away than New Zealand.

Commodities like asparagus that are of high value and highly perishable are generally flown in on commercial airplanes as the standard means of importation. Air transport, by the way, consumes three and a half times more fuel energy than truck transport (per pound and mile). Below are the current percentages of common produce imported and consumed in the US in 2016. Big export countries for this produce are Mexico, Canada, Chile, Peru, Honduras, Costa Rica, and Guatemala.

Produce Imported from Other Countries as a Percentage of the Produce Consumed in the US

Asparagus 95.6% Mostly from Peru and Mexico
Avocados 85.9%
Garlic 75.2%
Cucumbers 74.2%
Squash 64.7%
Bell Peppers 60.2%
Blueberries 57.2 %
Tomatoes 57.2 %
Eggplant 56.9%
Grapes 50.0% Mostly from Chile, some from Mexico
(Source: U.S.D.A. Economic Research Service)

Cucumbers, Bell peppers and blueberries on this list were another big surprise to me. I don't care much for eggplant, so I don't really care about that one. But really, 74% of our cucumbers and 60% of our bell peppers coming from another country? Don't tell me that it's because we needed to make room in California to grow more almonds that we can ship to the Netherlands – then I'd get really mad. But the scary thing is that imports of foreign produce are likely to continue growing. According to a recent U.S. Agriculture Department report, fresh produce imports will rise 45 percent from 2016 to 2027, implying that a decade from now, three-quarters of our fruits and almost half of our vegetables will be imported.[58] In other words, we could end up getting our produce as we do our fish — more than 90 percent of which is imported from somewhere else.

The rapid rise in imported fruits and vegetables over the last 40 years was probably the result of better roads (through Mexico and the US interstate system); the development of climate controlled, refrigerated containers for cargo ships; and better, more frequent air transportation routes. Cheaper labor in foreign nations also contributed greatly to the expansion of foreign produce in the US markets. The growing wealth of Americans also had something to do with it- Americans could afford to eat asparagus in the winter, something unheard of in my grandfather's day.

There is no question that the global produce business has allowed US citizens to eat more fruits and vegetables throughout the year, and not just when they're in season here. It is undeniable that this is a good thing. But relying too heavily on foreign food, and increasing our imports now to levels where most of our produce comes from far-away places, is just risky business.

With all this food traveling far distances around the globe, what happens to our food costs if fuel prices rise rapidly? It has been estimated that a 100 percent increase in diesel prices (where the cost of fuel doubles) could lead to an average wholesale produce price increase of 28 percent, but it could be more.[59] Transportation makes up a significant part of the cost of produce. Some studies have shown that over 70% of the cost of produce comes after the food has left the farm in transportation, storage and handling costs (including the grocer). You might say that 100% of the cost comes from handling, since

God and mother nature do most of the actual manufacturing work to create the product. But overall, as fuel prices rise, so do food prices, that's clear. Relying too heavily on fossil fuel-based transportation and storage creates its own risks, particularly as energy prices continue to be far more volatile than food prices. And what happens if a hurricane, or a drought, wipes out crops or infrastructure in the country we depend on. What about political unrest in Central or South America, and how could that affect our food supply? I don't know what can happen, but I just don't like the idea of giving up control. It's like handing my car keys over to a shady looking valet with a big tattoo around his neck. Something doesn't feel right.

BIG AG VERSUS SUSTAINABLE AGRICULTURE

There are some big, obvious differences between conventional, industrial farming and sustainable agriculture, including many psychological differences. The stark differences can be clearly seen between cows raised in knee deep mud and manure on massive Confined Animal Feeding Operations (CAFOs) and grass-fed beef raised on rolling green pastures. Industrial farming sees a domination of nature versus harmony with nature. Conventional agriculture is based on commodities and specialization, where huge farms grow a limited number of products, and usually just one, like corn or soybeans.

Conventional agriculture is driven by multinational corporations focused on profit, which comes from speed, higher volumes and lower labor costs. Sustainable agriculture is more labor intensive and more concerned with the quality of the soil and produce, and the long-term health of the environment and the local community. Sustainable agriculture focuses on diversity and crop rotation, and farms grow a much wider variety of produce for local consumption.

Sustainable agriculture attempts to provide all the fresh, safe and locally produced food a community needs at the same time it creates local jobs and stronger community ties. It brings production, processing and consumption closer together in a tighter feedback loop that encourages local business. Conventional, industrial scale agriculture focuses on the centralization of management and capital, huge farms concentrated in certain regions of the country, and large national processing centers to achieve scale and reduce costs.

Commodity based big ag also receives huge subsidies from the government, while small scale sustainable agriculture is a grass roots movement supported by the local community and receives very little help from the government, if any. Research by Brian Riedl at the Heritage Foundation found that the largest commodity growers of corn, wheat, soybeans and rice receive more than 90% of all farm subsidies, while growers of the 400 other domestic crops are pretty much shut out of the farm subsidy program. His research showed that the largest growers and agribusiness, including Fortune 500 companies, received the overwhelming distributions of farm subsidies from the US government. The top 10% of recipients, says Riedl, received 73% of all farm subsidies in 2001. It's a system that helps the big get bigger, and it moves us in the wrong direction and away from local food sustainability and resilience.

A study of the food processing industry revealed that just 138 men and women sit on the boards of directors of the top ten corporations that produce over half the food sold in America. Just 138 people have the decision-making power over most of our food supply. And given the more recent consolidation in the food industry since 2000, that number is likely less than

138 people now. I'm not sure if the researchers actually counted the number of board members at each of the ten largest food corporations that produce over half the food that we eat, but to check the math is pretty simple. The average number of board members on a corporate board of directors is about ten people. Times that by ten companies, and you get one hundred board members. The number could be smaller, but in any case, a lot of decision-making power has been concentrated in a very few individuals.

In our global food system, these large, multinational companies have taken control of where, when and how our food is produced and grown, processed and delivered. A small handful of companies are making these decisions. Many of the same companies are taking control of the food genes by legal patents. Companies like Cargill / Monsanto, ConAgra, and Novartis / ADM control most of the plant genes in Genetically Modified Organisms (GMOs) that are rapidly becoming staples in the food industry.

By some estimates, the ten largest multinational food processors control over 60 percent of the food and beverages sold in the U.S. They're led by companies like Nestlé, PepsiCo, Coca-Cola, Unilever, Danone, General Mills, Kellogg's, Mars, Associated British Foods, and Mondelez. And because these companies require massive quantities of uniform, standardized inputs, they can dictate how, when, where and by whom products are grown and produced.

According to an August 2014 story in USA Today, the agriculture and food production industry employed more than one billion people, or a third of the global workforce. And while the industry is substantial, says USA Today, only a relatively small number of companies wield an enormous amount of influence.

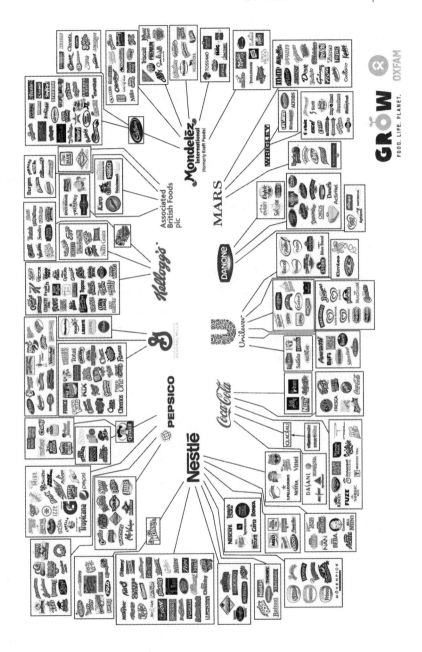

Map of the largest multi-national food corporations and the brands they own.
Source: OXFAM. For a full view of the map, visit www.eatyourview.com/whylocal

The article cites a 2013 report, "Behind the Brands," from Oxfam International that focused on 10 of the world's biggest and most influential food and beverage companies. The article and the report suggest that these corporations are so powerful that their policies can have a major impact on the diets and working conditions of people worldwide, as well as an enormous impact on the environment. The above Oxfam graph shows the 10 companies that control the world's food.

In an interview with 24/7 Wall St., Chris Jochnick, the director of the private sector department at Oxfam America, described the impact that these 10 companies have on the world. "If you look at the massive global food system," said Jochnick, "it's hard to get your head around. Just a handful of companies can dictate food choices, supplier terms and consumer variety." Another 2016 article related to the Oxfam report in Business Insider is titled, "These 10 Companies Control Everything You Buy." Just the title of the article says a lot about our current food system.

It's hard for the average person to really know and understand the corporate ownership of the popular brands that they purchase, but here's a very brief example to show the diversity of unrelated food brands that companies own. Kellogg's owns Pringles; General Mills owns Haagen-Dazs ice cream; Dannon owns bottled water companies; Mondelez owns Oreos; Mars owns Uncle Ben's rice; Unilever owns Hellmann's mayonnaise; Pepsico owns Quaker Oatmeal; Nestle owns Gerber baby food. These ten companies also own hundreds of other companies and unrelated food brands and employ hundreds of thousands of people around the world. Their supplier companies employ millions more. The scope and reach of these companies are enormous in a worldwide web of people and food.

Like any large, multinational corporation, those in industrial food and agribusiness continually search for lower cost production areas and methods. Labor and capital move around the country and the world to places where maximum profits can be generated or extracted. Money and capital migrate from one place to another in search of cheaper labor and cheaper food production, just as it does for making clothing, like a t-shirt. There is no real sense of place, or real value placed on the land, like a farmer would feel toward his own land. Because the capital, and the migrant labor force, can be quickly picked up and moved, the land becomes irrelevant, and can be used, abused, and left at any time. There are plenty more places to send your capital and find labor. It's a different mentality, a different psychology, then traditional farming and food production.

The industrialization of farming in my state of North Carolina can be seen from the numbers over the last half of the 20th century. Since 1950, North Carolina lost half of its farm land and 80% of its farmers while the number of farm workers, including migrant workers, more than doubled from 54,000 to 127,000. The traditional family farm was already showing signs of industrialization back in the late 1950's.

In the year 1900, there were nearly 6.5 million farms in the US; today there are fewer than 2 million. Most farming has been concentrated on a relatively small number of very large farms while some regions of the country that once grew a lot of food have seen agriculture all but disappear. And the important local food processing centers, like companies that can grind and process wheat, are long gone in most regions of the country. Most of that processing has moved to very large, industrial scale, national processing plants, like the large spinach factory that processes and packages most of the spinach grown in California for national distribution.

Communities can gain some resilience and self-reliance only if they develop the necessary infrastructure that includes processing food, protecting usable farm land, and encouraging the spread of knowledge and the technical capability of growing food.

If a farmer is growing food on a large scale for far-away corporate processors, he loses connection with the local community. Growers for local consumption contribute to the health and vitality of their community on several fronts, including economic, social and political ways. They create connections between producer and consumer and increase the knowledge and understanding of healthy food and where it comes from. Money and profit stays in the community and circles through the region several more times, which adds jobs and wages that bring further economic benefit to the area. The profit and economic benefit do not go straight off to some large, far-away multinational corporate office at harvest time. In the old days, the wheat grown would go to a local processor to be ground and processed, then to a local bread maker or bakery for further processing into finished products for consumption within the local community or region. That model is long gone in most regions of the country, and product and money doesn't continue to circulate throughout the community to create jobs and incomes.

Massive farms owned by just a few individuals or corporations doesn't do much for the local community. Thirty or forty years ago, the wealth and income from a farm was spread out among many farmers around the community, and they all shopped and supported other businesses in that community. When these small farmers were put out of business, if affected everyone else in the community.

Wendell Berry described the collapse of small farms and small farming communities in America in the 1970s because of the growth of large multi-national food processors and the move to massive farming operations. US farm policy under the direction of Earl Butz, Secretary of Agriculture, was "Get big or get out." Small farms couldn't compete and were swallowed up by larger and larger farms, many of them corporately owned and using modern industrial farming methods, chemicals and equipment. It devastated small farming communities, and small towns began losing grocery stores and other local shops, which eventually became boarded up ghost towns. There just wasn't any money floating around the local economy anymore once Big Ag took over and thousands of small farmers lost their farms and jobs. So did local shop owners.

Farms that produce for the local economy are integrated into the local economic structure and economic development far more than those that produce for far away markets. Growing and selling food locally contributes to the social and economic health of the larger community in more ways than we can fully understand. Americans need to gain a better understanding of the benefits from a local food economy, and the dangers that come from relying completely on big ag and faraway places. The leaders of the sustainable and local food movements have learned some of these lessons and are trying to teach them to the rest of us. Small, local farms are good for the community and local economy while they improve our food security and resilience.

Building the local food movement, with more direct sales and profit going to farmers, makes the small farm operation more profitable, but according to the USDA census of agriculture, the majority of the nation's 2.1 million farms are very small in terms of sales volume and income from the farm. About 75 percent of farms sold less than $50,000 in agricultural products in 2012, and 57 percent had sales less than $10,000. Take out the costs of production and the property taxes, and there's not much left for most of these farmers in terms of profit.

The fact is, the farm does not provide most of the household income for most farmers. The USDA says that for 1.5 million farm households, or roughly 75% of the farms out there, less than 25% of total household income came from their farm. Most of these farmers must work other jobs. In 2012, 61% of all farmers worked off the farm at least some days, and 40 percent worked off the farm for 200 or more days. And they made a lot more money off the farm than on the farm.

In 2012, of the 2.1 million principal operators in the United States, roughly 13.7% – 88,264 – were women. This was a 6 percent decrease since 2007 and was a larger decrease in numbers than male principal operators, which means we're losing female farmers like my neighbor Lynn Bonham faster than male farmers. The total number of U.S. farmers declined between 2007 and 2012 by 4.3 percent.

We're losing new, younger farmers at a faster rate, and now only 5 percent of American farmers are under the age of 35. In 2012, the number of new farmers who have been on their current operation less than ten years was down 20 percent from 2007. Those newer farmers that were on their current farm operation less than five years was down 23 percent from 2007. We have fewer new farmers coming into the business, and many young people are not following in their father's footsteps because they're finding better paying jobs with more 'prestige' off the farm.

With the overall aging population of farmers, and a decreasing number of young, new farmers taking up and staying with the trade, we're losing the knowledge and technical skills for farming. More corporately owned, massive farm operations will continue to take over farm production in the US. The difficulties of getting into the business, the prices of land and equipment, and the capital required, are the biggest barriers to entry for young people who might be interested in getting into the business.

CORN NATION

Products derived from corn make for a pretty easy sugar in our bodies, and we're getting way too much of it. We've become a corn nation without even knowing it. In his 2006 book *The Omnivore's Dilemma*, Michael Pollan takes us on a fascinating walk through a typical grocery store to help us understand a big part of our farming and health problems, which are related, and how we became a corn nation. Derivatives from corn are in just about everything we eat, and corn even feeds the animals that feed us: cows, chickens, turkeys, pigs and sheep. It also now feeds some of the fish that we eat, like farm raised salmon. [60]

Because the animals are eating it, it's in the eggs, milk, cheese, and yogurt. It's certainly found a nice home in the middle aisles of the grocery store, where all the processed foods live, because just about all of it includes corn bi-products or derivatives, including modified corn starch, corn flour, corn oil, mono-, di-, and triglycerides (from corn).

Most soft drinks have corn sweeteners as the number two item on the label, after water, in the form of high fructose corn syrup, and it's in the beer too, in the form of alcohol fermented from glucose that was refined from, you guessed it, corn.

You'll find corn in most of the small print ingredients from xantham gum to maltodextrin to lecithin and lactic acid. It's also in everything from diapers to toothpaste to glue. It's in yogurt in the form of high fructose corn syrup (on top of the corn the cow ate), and fortified milk gets the double whammy also, with vitamin D from corn. Bubble gum and make-up have corn additives, and as Pollan tells us, if this list is starting to give you a headache, the coating on aspirin is often derived from corn. The list goes on to include roughly 25% of the items in the grocery store, says Pollan, or about 12,000 products.

This isn't the first time in our nation's history that we found something to do with our excess corn, or the government had something to do with it. We've been finding uses for corn from the very beginning of America.

Farmers living west of the Appalachian Mountains distilled their excess corn and other grains into whiskey, which was much easier to transport to markets on the other side of the mountains than bulky grain like corn. A few bottles are a lot lighter and easier to carry than bushels of corn, and probably made the traveling a bit more enjoyable. It was also more profitable.

Colonial farmers could make whiskey from surplus barley, rye, wheat or corn by fermenting the grain's sugars into alcohol. And people in the early days of this nation drank a lot of whiskey, as much as a pint a day or more on average. Whiskey was often used as a currency or medium of exchange because there wasn't a lot of hard (minted or printed) U.S. currency floating around some of the more remote areas of the colonies.

Alexander Hamilton convinced congress and George Washington to put an excise tax on distilled products and producers to help pay off some debt that was incurred during the Revolutionary War. It became known as the Whiskey Tax. Other than duties from imports, there weren't many other sources of income to this new nation, and taxes on any product or industry was going to be met with resistance anyway. The western farmers of course thought this tax on whiskey was unfair to them, and it led to what is now called the Whiskey Rebellion.

These western farmer distillers fought the tax with sometimes violent resistance, and often attacked, tarred and feathered the tax collectors who had the difficult and dangerous task of collecting the whiskey tax. In 1794, a large contingent of western farmers rallied in western Pennsylvania and threatened to take their cause right to the new capital city, Washington, DC. President George Washington stepped in and ordered troops to quash this rebellious group, and he even put on his old uniform to travel west and review the progress of the military expedition. Historian Joseph Ellis says that this was the first and only time a sitting American president led troops in the field, all over derivatives from corn. General Washington was a striking figure on a horse, tall and majestic in the saddle and decked out in a military uniform, and not the kind of guy you wanted to mess with. The Whiskey Rebellion was quickly put down.

How did all of this happen? How did corn get into everything? And what are the risks from that? One big reason is that the United States government has been subsidizing corn for a long time now. It often costs a farmer more to produce a bushel of corn then he gets for it at market price. The cost-to-price disparity is due in large part because we're growing way too much of it now, but the government subsidies pay the farmer a set rate for every bushel and so make up the difference and give him some profit. As much as half the net income to a farmer growing industrial corn comes from this government subsidy check.

With so much readily available and cheap corn out there, food scientists have found many novel ways to use the abundance. That's why it's in everything. And feed lot operators and Confined Animal Feed Operations have also benefited greatly from the cheap excess of corn. Cheap corn led to the CAFO's in the first place and make it profitable.

The problem is that cows were designed by nature to eat grass, not corn. Corn can cause ulcers in their stomachs that require antibiotics to keep under control. The massive use of antibiotics allows bacteria and viruses to build up immunities to the antibiotics, making them resistant, which reduces their effectiveness in humans. We're running out of useful antibiotics for human use fast. Resistant strains are developing faster than we can create new antibiotics.

Chickens do better on corn than cows but spending their entire life in a cramped and confined space in a massive warehouse with tens of thousands of other chickens creates other problems and risks for humans. For egg layers, living in a tiny cage where she can't even flap her wings, let alone turn around, with a conveyor belt of corn running in front of her, is just another moral issue that many people aren't aware of, and producers would like to keep it that way. Out of sight, out of mind. Salmonella outbreaks at large chicken egg facilities are not uncommon events. When it happens, and eggs are distributed nationally, the result is a large, national scare over a wide geographic region.

The onslaught of cheap corn in the '50s and '60s made it

economically feasible and more profitable to set up massive feed lots for cattle and large factory warehouses to grow chicken. Small farms couldn't compete, and farm animals started disappearing from the typical small farm at about the same time. It wasn't always like that. Small farms across the country had varied operations that included different crops and animals. The farm looked like an entirely different place back then, and it wasn't just corn fence-row to fence-row. It was varied and interesting, and pretty because it was varied in color and texture. The modern farm-scape looks monotone and monotonous; a single shade of green, "corn green", in endless miles of sameness. I like to see a red chicken break that color up once in a while.

At the beginning of the 20th century, one quarter of Americans lived on a farm. A typical farmer was able to feed his family and about 12 other Americans. Today the average American farmer, all 2 million of them, feeds an average of 129 people. Unfortunately, he can barely support his own family on it. Typically, he can't even eat what he grows because it's not sweet corn but commodities like feed corn for animals, or corn that needs to be processed. We've already noted how big agricultural states like Iowa now import over 80% of their own food and are otherwise a "food desert" because it's all corn and soybeans.

We became a corn nation just after World War II when a huge munitions factory at Muscle Shoals, Alabama, converted from making ammunition explosives to chemical fertilizers using the same raw product, ammonium nitrate. The process requires a tremendous amount of fossil fuels to create the intense heat to convert ammonium nitrate into the nitrogen rich fertilizers, the end product. The government happened to have a tremendous surplus on the raw material and encouraged it, and the industrialization of our food had begun. Corn sucks up nitrogen from the soil in a big way, and the industrial production of nitrogen fertilizers allowed for the industrial production of corn.

Even with massive amounts of fertilizers and the artificial replenishment of nitrogen, the soil loses all its other minerals and nutrients, becoming organically lifeless. The pesticides, herbicides and fungicides kill everything else.

DOING JUSTICE TO CORN

While corn derivatives are in everything now in the form of cheap sugars, it's only fair that I give corn its just deserves and rightful place in the vegetable kingdom. There's eight acres of it growing on my farm for a good reason − it's a high calorie food. Corn gets a bad rap all the time because of the high fructose corn syrup used in many processed foods and soft drinks, and that's true, it can be made into cheap sugar. But corn is a great source of good calories, and some scientists use the metric "calories per acre," in which corn ranks highest in crop yields.

Corn has been a very important plant in North America for a very long time. It helped the pilgrims and first settlers survive the early years on this continent. If the native Americans didn't show and help these early settlers how to grow and store corn, they would likely have starved. The native corn was much better adapted to the local climate and environment than the European wheat that the settlers brought with them.

Calories matter because every one of us needs about one million of them each year. They certainly aren't the only thing we need; we also need vitamins and minerals, fats and protein.

But if we don't have those 1 million calories, other needs start to fade into the background.

In the calorie department, corn is king. In 2014, the average yield in the United States was 171 bushels per acre for corn. The world record is 503 bushels, set by a farmer in Valdosta, Ga. Each bushel weighs 56 pounds and each pound of corn yields about 1,566 calories. That means corn averages roughly 15 million calories per acre, so theoretically, each acre would provide the annual caloric intake for about 15 people. This estimate is related to field corn, or dent corn, which is dried before processing. Sweet corn and popcorn are different varieties, grown for much more limited uses, and have slightly lower yields. If you had taken the United States 2014 corn harvest of 14.2 billion bushels and used it to feed people, it would have met 17 percent of the entire world's caloric needs. With some easy math I could quickly determine that instead of feeding corn to dairy cows, my eight acres of corn could feed roughly 120 people their caloric requirements for a full year (eight acres times fifteen people per acre). We'll come back to that eight acres later.

By contrast, wheat comes in at about 4 million calories per acre, and soybeans at 6 million. Rice is also very high-yielding, at 11 million, and potatoes are one of the few crops that can rival corn because they also yield about 15 million calories per acre. Other vegetables, while much more nutritious than corn, wheat or potatoes, are far less calorie and energy-dense. Broccoli yields about 2.5 million calories per acre, and spinach is under 2 million. We all need those vegetables, but we get our full days' worth of vitamins and nutrition from them in a fraction of the 2,000 daily calories that we need for energy. That leaves plenty of room for inexpensive, easily grown calories that aren't as nutrient-dense, like corn. The problem occurs when we get too much of those easy calories in the form of processed foods, snacks, soft drinks and beer, all from corn.

Many people throughout North America are interested in the social, economic, and environmental benefits of community-based farming, and because of that I believed that the agrihood concept is sellable. But the financial side of the agrihood model is the biggest obstacle to developing these communities for real estate developers and land planners. Keeping most of the land in farming creates a financial burden, particularly in markets where land prices are rising quickly. We need to create a financially viable business model.

The farming activity in the agrihood model is generally a break-even proposition at best, with the farm making just enough to support the farmers who do the work. As described previously, the developer must offset the cost of the land dedicated to farming by a limited number of lots that he will sell. Most developers would just opt to develop the whole thing; that's what they're used to doing. At today's land prices in popular, growing regions of the country, close to modern towns and amenities, it's difficult for a developer to pay rising prices for land, decide not to develop a large portion of it for resale, and still make a profit.

The key is how the developer markets the project. The agricultural aspect of the community must be viewed as a true and valuable amenity, and a premium must be paid by the lot buyers to live in such a community. I've tried to explore the financial nuts and bolts of a small agricultural development to show that the agricultural community can be profitable and reproducible in different areas of the country. It's hard to do in a rapidly growing area like Asheville, North Carolina where land prices continue to escalate at an increasing pace, but if it can be done here, I think it can be recreated in other areas of the country experiencing similar growth trends.

Asheville and Buncombe County have been experiencing urban sprawl for so many years now that it threatens to overwhelm what is left of its rural, farming heritage. There are few working farms remaining in Buncombe County; most are small scale, less than half are profitable. The ongoing boom in housing has chipped away at what little farmland remains, with commercial and residential development driving land values so high that purchasing land for the purpose of farming is a losing endeavor. In many cases, the tax value of the land is so high, the families who have lived on and farmed the land for generations cannot shoulder the tax burden each year. The rural landscape and pastoral beauty of rolling farms were integral in attracting new residents to this beautiful region of the country, but it's vanishing at a cost much higher than just its value per acre.

This is why agricultural land and other open spaces tend to disappear quickly. South Buncombe County has already lost most of its farmland, and what remains is financially out of reach to young farmers starting out. It's a terrible loss in more ways than one.

Unfortunately, the sellers' market for farmland is not the only economic force driving the conversion of agricultural land to residential and commercial developments. Preserving farmland is hard to justify if farmers still can't make a living on it. Because of the topography and the surrounding hills and mountains, Buncombe County farms tend to be smaller and steeper than those outside the mountains, and they compete poorly against bigger, flatter farms in the Midwest for the production of bulk commodities.

Even relatively flat portions of Buncombe County never had many large farms or large fields of row crops, and except for Burley tobacco and milk, no significant production of major commodities ever existed. Most farms are now, as they have always been, small, specialized producers. Sam Bingham compiled an agricultural development protection plan for Buncombe County that included some interesting historical information about farming in the county.[61]

Bingham says that originally all farms in Buncombe County were small subsistence farms created by the original settlers of the region. With the earliest dirt roads, such as the Buncombe Turnpike and "The Drovers Road" in the early 1800's, cattle and other livestock including pigs from Kentucky and Tennessee were driven through Asheville and down along the French Broad river to markets in Spartanburg and Columbia, South Carolina, and as far away as Charleston. Local inhabitants along this dirt interstate started planting Indian corn to feed and support those large herds of cattle and the men who came through on the trail in the fall.

Farmers started setting up stock yards and pens along the way to feed and support the herds being driven down the Drovers Road. Eventually the Civil War and the railroads put an end to the Drovers Road and the local corn farms that fed the cowboys and animals along the way.

Many Buncombe County farmers in the 1960s and '70s tried to join the national trend toward highly-capitalized, large scale farming production models but, says Bingham, they couldn't compete with larger farms in flatter regions of the country. Chicken and milk production couldn't compete with other regions because too much feed had to be imported from outside the region at too high a cost. Grass fed beef on pasture couldn't compete with the massive CAFO's out west. Tobacco had been a fairly reliable source of income for many farmers in the county, but it got squeezed in the national trend away from smoking.

Real Estate development is now the primary reason for the loss of agriculture in Buncombe County. Almost 100 percent of the population growth in the county comes from people moving here from out of state for the climate and to get out of larger metropolitan areas and into a more rural and natural setting. The natural beauty of the land and surrounding area is what is driving the in-migration and causing its own disappearance. As land prices skyrocket, the beauty of the landscape goes from farming and rural to urban/suburban sprawl. Once beautiful and rural areas of the county, like Fairview, have lost much of the pastoral views that drew people there.

There are a few examples left in the county that prove a farmer can still make a living off the land in Buncombe County, but it requires a lot of direct marketing and support from the local community by people who understand the importance of local producers with direct purchases from the farm. Hickory Nut Gap Farm is one farm just east of Asheville that illustrates how mountain land and farming can generate enough income to support a family. The farm has become somewhat of a tourist destination, and offers pasture raised beef and other farm products for sale at its roadside store, along with a large barn that they rent out for events. They also sell beef and other farm products wholesale to grocery stores in the area and have a cooperative arrangement with other farms to raise cattle to their specifications. The Hickory Nut Gap Farm beef brand is now sold in many grocery stores and restaurants and is well-known in the region. The farm was passed down through the family to its current owners, and as strong a business as they have now, I still wonder if the income generated from the farm would pay off a mortgage on that land if it had to be purchased at current market prices. And no new farms are likely to pop up in that area because so much farm land is now gone to development, and that means gone forever. It's not feasible to knock down houses to create farm land again.

The other pressure on farming in the region comes from an aging population of farmers. As he looks toward retirement, the farmer knows that he could cash out quickly and sell to a developer or chop it up into smaller homesteads himself. His children may want the farm to stay in the family but can't afford to buy it from Dad at its current market value. Even if Dad had a son or daughter that wanted to keep farming the land, it puts him in a difficult situation. He must decide if he wants to allow his children to try to scratch out a living on a small farm, as he did, in which they all struggle, including him in his golden years, or does he just sell it all and become a millionaire and live out his remaining years comfortably. That's a tough question to answer honestly.

If a farmer dies, the significant money involved and the difficulties of splitting up assets among multiple heirs makes liquidation the easiest and most efficient way to settle a farm estate. The housing is needed anyway, you could argue, and Asheville is currently struggling with a serious shortage. Farmland, once taken for granted in this region, is now seriously threatened and vulnerable. The same scenario is playing out all over the country. And without farm land nearby, it's impossible for a community to be self-reliant and resilient.

The most effective way to preserve farmland may be to just try to help keep these small farms in business by supporting them through farmers markets and CSA programs. But keeping it going for the long-term means finding ways for young farmers to gain access to the farm land. Younger farmers with new ideas and energy can't afford to get into the business right now.

There are supporting organizations out there that can help young farmers learn and do the work. The Buncombe County Extension Service helps young farmers with technical advice like soil fertility and pest control, and several nonprofit organizations are also nearby to help with the marketing and promotion of produce, including the Appalachian Sustainable Agriculture Project. Creekside Farm is a proud member of ASAP because it is organizations like this that form the critical infrastructure to resilient and sustainable communities that can grow their own food and fend for themselves.

I described ASAP in a previous chapter, but I think it's worthwhile to revisit this organization for a moment. I believe it is this type of organization that adds exponentially to the local food infrastructure, and if an organization like this exists in your area, join it. If one doesn't exist in your region, start one. ASAP helps by promoting direct sales from the farm so that more of the retail value of production comes back to the farm and the farmer. They continually promote local Farmer's Markets and CSA programs, and help to organize sales to local bulk consumers like restaurants and institutional buyers such as schools and hospitals.

The ASAP website is a clearing house for people searching for locally grown food. The site lists numerous CSA programs and Farmers Markets throughout the region. ASAP has regularly scheduled events every spring where people can meet the farmers offering CSA programs, and where they can ask questions about the farm and farming methods. The farmers set up tables for the event, just like at a farmer's market, and for several hours people can stop by and get to know the farmer who will be growing the food, and if they like what they see, they can sign up for the season right then and there.

There are 122 farm members from Buncombe County alone on the ASAP web site, and they include everything from small scale farms to small grain mills, aviaries (bee farms), flower growers, wool fiber producers and hops growers. Businesses include Hickory Nut Gap Farm, Carolina Bison, and The Biltmore Estate. Sixty-five of the producers are large enough to sell wholesale.

ASAP understands that community-based farming benefits both the farmer and the residents of the community, and they have become the bridge that brings everyone together. By helping to build lasting relationships between local food producers and local residents, they show how farms are the invested interest of the entire community. ASAP probably does more than any other organization in our region to facilitate the entry of new farmers into agricultural jobs because they help to support the sale of their produce. I don't think I can say enough about how important this is to local food resilience.

Local farms and food are dependent upon the entire community. Knowing the person who grows your carrots, beets and greens, and being able to buy them fresh-picked that day at the Farmers Market, creates a personal connection and bond between farmers, local food and consumers, which keeps the whole system viable and alive. At the same time, it keeps farm land productive and in its natural, rural and pastoral state.

Keeping Creekside Farm as a working, productive farm was a major goal, and a CSA program is what helps make it all happen. The entire community, including all our neighbors, can continue to enjoy and benefit from the natural beauty and fertility of the land for, hopefully, the next several generations.

Our primary goal in the whole project was to keep an agrarian landscape that remains fertile, biologically diverse, uncluttered to the eye, and productive. But it takes a community of people buying the food to support it and keep it going.

The agrihood community that we were trying to create, with a CSA model for food production and distribution, will become economically self-sufficient after only a few years of operation and hopefully serve as an innovative model for community-based farming and development in Western North Carolina and beyond. Hopefully it will be a model for vibrant, thriving, and beautiful communities where farming and a return to a deep appreciation of the land will be at the forefront. That's the plan, anyway.

Alberto Cirri was the perfect traveling companion for my frequent tours through the Italian countryside. He was bookish, highly intelligent, and naturally optimistic. Generally quiet, soft spoken and reserved, except when it came to wine and after drinking it, he was always pleasant and cordial to his friends as well as strangers. He would often sing to himself, and almost always when he was riding his ATV around his small farm outside of Prato, near Florence.

He loved to eat, but was slender and, although he sometimes wore his clothes a little disheveled, rather stylish in demeanor. He loved reading travel books, and when he toured Europe or America, he would write down and describe in detail the cities and countries he visited, their environment, customs, climate and culture. He took notice of the structure of a region's economy, its primary industries and the types of employment, and nothing escaped his curiosity.

He had a particular interest in farming techniques, soil types and seed varieties. He told me that whenever he traveled he "loved rambling through the fields and farms, examining the soil and crops very closely." He told me, "I might stay out in a field for hours, so that some people think I'm crazy, and others might think I'm really smart, which I'm neither." He was always looking for a new plant or vegetable that he might be able to try growing on his little farm, or some organic technique to help him avoid pests.

Alberto described farming in an email as "well planned and well executed experimentation by trial and error, with expectancy for lots of error." Sometimes success was attended by joy, rapture and bliss, and often it happened by just dumb luck, he said.

"Farming usually requires study and hard work to understand what is really going on in the soil and in the plant," Alberto once said to me. "Creative passion and dedicated purpose are the mother of all knowledge, and without it nothing great was ever achieved. To have a great garden, you need these two things."

Alberto had passion and purpose. He also worked very hard when he set his mind to something, and hard work is truly the mother of invention. Michelangelo, the Italian renaissance painter, sculptor and inventor who lived not far from Alberto's home and was a sort of hometown hero for Alberto and his people, wrote, "If people knew how hard I worked to achieve my mastery, it wouldn't seem so wonderful at all."

Alberto came to visit our farm and to do some hiking in the Blue Ridge Mountains in the fall of 2017. After a day hiking, I sat drinking wine with him at the farm and asked him what he thought about the agrihood that we were developing. I trusted his opinion and wanted to know what he made of it all. We were still in the early stages and I was feeling a little worried about the idea and if it made economic sense. Alberto didn't really make me feel any better, at least not at the beginning.

First, I gave him a little background on my thought process and why I thought this might be a good idea. I had just finished reading Duany and a lot of his ideas were still fresh in my head. There are plenty of emotional reasons to build an agrihood and for people to want to live there, I told Alberto. Anyone who is aware of the way food currently comes to our dinner tables probably has the emotional motivation, particularly with meat products. But the reasons for building an agricultural community must also be logical, I said. Logic reigns supreme when it comes to money and investment, for the developer and the home buyer.

Alberto said, "I agree, the way animals are treated is very disturbing, and all the chemicals used is not good also, but you're right, it must be logical."

I said that the most logical reasons can be related to health, environment, economic and social needs for the prospective buyer. Then I went into a long discourse about the logical justification for putting every nickel I had into a new urban agricultural village.

For health needs, I gave him a list of benefits. The benefits of an agrihood, I told him, are fresh, healthier food without all the chemicals and humanely raised meat; it preserves open land and green space which has psychological benefits; it promises some food security by protecting the capacity to grow food locally; and it provides opportunities for healthy exercise and recreational activity in the garden.

"Take out half the population, right there," Alberto said. "If you want to be logical, and try to see if this idea will work, let's be logical. Half the people won't care about the health benefits."

He cut out half my potential customer base just like that, and I thought it was a bit high, but I continued to my list of economic benefits for the agrihood. The economic benefits include the cost savings on fertilizers, pesticides and herbicides; maintenance expenses for normal landscaping of common areas could be used for agriculture; recreational gardening activities by residents becomes productive food producing activity. With a composting program, it closes the food-to-waste-to-food loop and saves food disposal costs while enriching the soil. There is also the reduction in long term economic costs to the environment that future generations will inevitably have to pay. And it pays young farmers a living wage that allows them to learn a valuable trade, providing meaningful jobs, while keeping more money in the local food system.

"Who's going to save all this money?" Alberto asked. "Yes, it may make long term economic sense for the region, but it will be hard to explain the economics of it to your buyer. Take away another half the customers, and I'm being generous to you on this one. That leaves you with 25% of the potential buyers." I think the wine was kicking in because he was having too much fun with this.

I went on to explain my thoughts on the social benefits. The social benefits from the agricultural neighborhood come from the gathering spaces provided by the garden and the food support buildings- the food processing, storage and preparation facilities. It enables social benefits through regular gatherings and events like pick-up day at the CSA program, farmers markets, farm to table meals, regular cooking and canning classes, and annual events like the Fall Harvest Festival. The whole idea of the agricultural community is geared to people coming together to share and celebrate food, I told Alberto. It also provides training to young farmers which has its own social benefits. The agrihood fosters a sense of community while at the same time it creates a new kind of economic system. Surely he couldn't counter this argument and slash my potential customers in half again.

"You assume that people like each other, but I'll give you that anyway." Now he was just being facetious. "The farm is very beautiful, and if people wander down to admire it, and if they happen to run into someone they like, then what you're saying is true. But I'm sorry, I must cut the number in half again. Not everyone will attend your little harvest festival. You're at twelve and a half percent. And to be clear, we're talking about the percentage of people who are looking to buy a new home in the first place, which by itself is a small number."

Friendship means you can play the devil's advocate until it hurts. I mean really turning the screws. You can't do that with strangers. "Environmentally the agrihood has numerous benefits," I continued. These include less pollution to soil and water; closed cycles of food-to-waste-to-food; the restoration and rejuvenation of marginal farm land into healthy, living, organic soils; better, more intensive crop yields from organic, close-up hand work of the soil; significant reduction in transportation costs to the environment, including less petroleum and CO_2 emissions. The logic was perfectly clear.

"More than half the Americans voted for Trump, correct?" said Alberto, "so they don't believe there is anything wrong with the environment or don't care, so cut it in half again. That leaves you with six and a quarter percent of the potential home buyers." Then he surprised me.

"That's actually a pretty big number when you think about it," he said. "If there are 1000 potential home or lot buyers out there in Asheville, which I'm sure there are, then that means 60 of them might actually consider living here. You only need 12, right?"

I'm not sure our math could be verified in any real statistical way, particularly when I counted two bottles of wine on the table, but there is a logical argument to the agricultural community. It makes long-term health and economic sense, and Alberto agreed. But it's also a values-based decision to live there, which tends to over-ride logic sometimes. Environmental justice, human, animal and social justice, and a desire for some independence and self-reliance, all these things play a role in motivating someone to move to an agricultural community.

CHAPTER EIGHT

―――

IT'S A TRANSCENDANT THING

"Who is truly free? The wise man who can govern himself."
- Horace (65-8 BC)

My discussion with Alberto about the reasons for people to move to an agrihood were mostly based on logic, but there are other more transcendent things that I thought about and did not bring up with him in that conversation. There is a group of people, I believe, that have deeper, spiritual connections to nature, and this spirituality underlies many of their deepest values and decisions. These transcendent and spiritual beliefs and values could be a strong motivation to someone looking to live a simpler, more connected life in an agrihood, but it's tough to describe, and probably would not appear on anyone's marketing plan for an agrihood. Even so, I think it's real, and I can try to describe this spiritual connection by describing a person who I view as very spiritual, our farm manager Melissa.

Melissa was looking for a new helper for the 2018 growing season. She handed me a resume for one applicant that she seemed to like, and as I scanned the resume one of the listed job experiences caught my eye. It read, "Assistant Goat

Milker". The description of the experience read, "Tasked with weekly goat milking shifts and feeding chores. Execute small-scale safe raw milk production." The professional wording to describe such a seemingly menial task as milking a goat was humorous and impressed me greatly. "That's our girl", I said.

Anna was her name, and she was a recent graduate from Warren Wilson College just outside of Asheville. Warren Wilson College is a small, private liberal arts college, and tuition and fees are about $35,000 per year, so it's not inexpensive to attend. The college operates a small farm, and requires all students to work somewhere on campus (which helps students pay down some of the tuition costs), so many of them work on the farm. Probably beats working in the dining hall. Anna also worked in the vegetable gardens on campus and helped take care of some draft horses that could be used for plowing, along with milking some goats, and this must have spurred her interest in farming.

Newly graduated with a degree in History and Political Science, Anna chose to look for a job in farming and agriculture. She could have found a job at much higher pay, but she seemed to be looking to find a higher purpose or to fill some intrinsic need, and perhaps she was looking for a spiritual connection to the land and nature that comes from growing food. She may have been trying to find some meaning or purpose right out of college, truly free for the first time in her life with no commitments to schools or her parents. She didn't just want to make a living, she wanted to learn how to live. John Adams once wisely said, "There should be two educations. One should teach how to make a living, and the other how to live."

I knew that Melissa was going to become Anna's spiritual mentor, of sorts, and I knew Melissa would teach her form of spirituality by action and not so much with words. Melissa is a kind and good person, but I have never asked Melissa about her spirituality or for her thoughts on virtue and goodness. She probably does not think of virtue as a struggle. She probably does not think or know about her virtues at all, and I admire her more for that. It is a relief to one who has spent so much time thinking and struggling to understand what virtue is and how it expresses itself in human beings. To her, it all comes naturally, simply and quietly in her garden.

If I did ask her about her spirituality, I imagine that she would say something like this; "Either God is there, or he is not there. But I see signs in small green things coming up in my garden."

Melissa sees things in ways that are pure, honest, unassuming, and humble. She has no grand plans or schemes of men. There is no want, no ego, vanity or arrogance. She desires only to plant a seed and help it grow. She works to create an environment in this little garden that is uncontaminated, unpolluted, pure. Her faith comes in moments, when a seed germinates or green things first sprout from the ground. There is a depth in these brief moments that is more real to her than other experiences of life. In the silence of her garden, at these small moments, an extraordinary sense of hope overwhelms her. The hope brings happiness. This is sacred ground and the source of her spirituality.

In the summer of 2007, we packed up the kids and headed to Williamsburg, Virginia. Williamsburg is a town that reenacts life during colonial times and it's a great place to bring kids to learn the history of early America. It was capital of the Virginia Colony from 1699 to 1780 and played a fairly significant role in the American Revolution. It's part of what is called the "Historic Triangle" together with the other historic Virginia sites at Jamestown and Yorktown.

The historic homes and buildings were preserved for posterity only because the capital of Virginia moved to Richmond in 1780 and Williamsburg became a backwater town, so buildings weren't knocked down and replaced with more modern structures over time. Colonial Williamsburg is a living-history museum where actors in period costume depict daily Colonial life in the streets and in the stores and workshops that make up the historic district. Bands in colonial costume march down the street, and street actors stage protests against British rule and taxation. It's good, clean fun for the family.

At the edge of the historic district is the College of William and Mary. Thomas Jefferson attended the College of William and Mary which was to become an important influence in the development of his lifetime love of learning. We walked around the historic campus, where students in summer school were still marching off to class. We ended up at the college bookstore, which lies at the end of the colonial main street, and it happens to be in an excellent location to sell tourists t-shirts and souvenirs, a great source of revenue for the bookstore, far above the profit from textbook sales to students. I purchased a book on Jefferson's gardens at Monticello, and the kids got a Colonial Militia hat and a plastic sword (which turned out to be a big mistake.)

While visiting Colonial Williamsburg gives us a good feel for what a colonial town looked and felt like, it's important to remember that in colonial days, just outside of this small historic village boundary was a vast stretch of wilderness, dangerous and largely unexplored. It wasn't four lane roads lined with miniature golf courses, clothing shops, and fast food restaurants like it is now. The thirteen original colonies were really city-states with huge stretches of untamed wilderness between them for hundreds of miles. And outside of this village of Williamsburg, which was originally cut from the woods and wilds like all colonial towns, lived an indigenous group of people that saw the natural world quite a bit differently from these colonial city dwellers.

Indigenous groups like the Indians of North America believed that everything in nature was alive and had its own spirit. The animals, the trees, streams and rivers, and even the mountains and the rocks had a living spirit. It must be a beautiful and wonderful connection to believe such things.

This same connection to Mother Earth has appeared in almost all early civilizations across the planet. This spiritual connection to the living world appears across every continent and every prehistoric culture so that it seems to be an almost innate human perception of the world.

Kirkpatrick Sale is a prolific writer about political and environmental issues, and he says, "In virtually every hunter-gatherer society that archeologists have discovered from the Paleolithic past, in almost every rudimentary society that anthropologists have studied in recent centuries, one of the central deities- in many cases the primary god, worshiped before all others- was the earth". It's not that surprising. Peoples very existence depended on it.

A deep connection and respect for the natural world was inevitable. The belief that the world and all living things were enveloped in an invisible force helped early humans to understand and navigate their environment. All things were endowed with a spirit, and if you showed the proper care and respect, you could tap into that great spirit, and it would help you as you hunt and forage for food. If you didn't show the proper respect, then you're on your own.

After killing a seal, Inuit Indians of Alaska and Northern Canada would immediately cut open the seal's scalp in an effort to release his spirit, and the hunter would give thanks to the seal for willingly allowing the hunter to catch him. The seal's spirit would go out into the world and tell other seals that he was treated with respect, so they should allow themselves also to be caught by this hunter in the future. Almost all early cultures had elaborate ceremonies connected with the hunting, gathering or harvesting of food. A sacred respect for the land and its animals helped people connect to the natural environment and live in harmony with it, which helped to ensure their own survival.

How do we find spirituality in the modern, natural world? Our scientific and extractive worldview today has become the all-encompassing and irrefutable domain from which we see all things. Science is king. In fact, as Kirkpatrick Sale says, "we almost do not have the methods of thinking, the very language, with which to challenge it" or to see it any other way. The spirit world must have died when we invented the microscope.

We learned how to control the world, and how to maximize the extraction of its resources through industrialized food production as well as more efficient and more effective mining and drilling technologies. The world became our apple, and we took a big bite out of it in the 20th century. We forgot or disregarded any concept of the connection of all things, and in the name of self-interest, human-interest, we plundered.

APPRECIATION OF BEAUTY

Humans seem to need a regular dose of beautiful imagery in order to be satisfied and happy. As noted previously, research has proven that immersing yourself in nature for just 20 to 45 minutes will dramatically reduce stress levels and anxiety. There's scientific research now that shows how living in a more pastoral, natural setting can affect health and happiness and so would support the choice of an agrarian lifestyle. But there's even benefit from sitting on your patio and tending a small herb garden or sitting in a city park on Saturday mornings.

Something new and aesthetically pleasing seems to fill an innate aesthetic need and helps us touch some higher plain of existence. It is as if humans need to refresh themselves in the presence of art, beauty and nature. While in the presence of great beauty we seem to carefully observe and absorb our surroundings in order to extract the beauty that the world has to offer.

Jesus Christ said that "Heaven is spread out upon the earth, but you do not see it." The appreciation of beauty in nature is a means of connecting to the universe and to the transcendent. A true appreciation of beauty brings with it a sense of awe, wonder and elevation. You feel a oneness with the universe and a sense of truth, vividness and clarity in the sensation. There can be a spiritual sense of awe, wonder and elevation in not just the experience of nature, but also at the experience of art, music, physical or athletic performance, and even just witnessing good moral deeds.[62]

As esoteric as this may sound, it's quite simple: spirituality and connecting to the transcendent is the ability to spot beauty in our daily lives and to truly appreciate it on a regular basis. Some people have the ability to do that, and the sense of awe that it brings usually generates a feeling of overwhelming vastness. Ben Franklin made a telescope that was superior to others at the time, and with it he could gaze into the awe-inspiring beauty of the universe and feel over-whelmed at its vastness and the sheer number of stars that he could see with this instrument. Those same stars are still there for you to admire.

It might be surprising to learn that you can develop this ability to notice the beauty around you if you just focus your mind on it and practice. Look for the beauty and you'll start to see it more often. Happiness comes from an aesthetic sensitivity to nature, from just taking the time to stop and smell the roses. It's like strengthening a muscle in your arm, and sensitivity to beauty in nature can be developed with practice and exercise. There's scientific research and evidence from the field of positive psychology to back this up.[63]

Since the beginning of time, people have experienced a hunger, a deep instinctual need to make sense out of life, to transcend the ordinary and often painful experience of life and find meaning in their experience in the world. This desire to connect, to make contact, is a sensation that brings with it the question of whether there is something to which we can make contact. This connection is always available in nature. You can find it in the beauty of the mountains or a sunset over the ocean. You can find it in a garden, or in the love and care for animals. It's everywhere you choose to look for it.

In Melissa's CSA garden, I claimed a small patch of earth at the outer edge for my "Jefferson Garden" experiment where I planted some heirloom seeds that I purchased at Monticello. Not having a green thumb like Jefferson or Melissa, the garden failed miserably and turned into a brown patch of dirt with a few stems and some weeds. I'm quite certain Melissa and a few CSA members must have looked down upon it with some regret and pity.

But I did grow some squash that came up beautifully for some reason beyond my capacity to understand. To anyone else looking at the squash, they might have seen a side dish. To me, it was a feast. This was my spot of earth, and I was happy and proud of it. I may not have the ability to find the deep spiritual connections that Melissa does in her garden, but I think I may have touched upon it once or twice. In a tiny little spot of earth, I worked with nature and created something from nothing.

It is as if, while getting the physical exercise planting this garden, I was strengthening some muscle in my head. New connections of synapses in my brain were forming, new transmitters and receptors. The squash suddenly wasn't the same squash I'd seen in a grocery store. It took on a new, deeper meaning that I could now begin to understand. And the synapses in my brain extended down into the tangled roots in the earth. I was learning.

THE COW PASTURE

There is something almost spiritual about riding a tractor through rolling hills and cutting hay. Doing work on a farm like this, which isn't really work to me, creates a transcendent connection to the beautiful scenery around me, with the blue-green mountains in the distance, and the bright green grass in front, and a job that promises a couple hours of peaceful contemplation. With the dull hum of the tractor engine, and a light breeze on my face, my mind is free to wander off in forms of deep meditation on nature.

I am a grass farmer. It's probably all I'm really qualified to do as a farmer. But I know 20 cows and a couple miniature donkeys are going to eat this hay next winter. And I have a regular dinner guest now that waits patiently for his next meal while I cut the grass.

A black hawk lives in the trees adjacent to the farm. I never really trusted that guy, because I know he's always eyeing my chickens. But that was before we really connected and became a team, a pack, hunting partners. One day while I was cutting tall grass with a bush hog, I noticed out of the corner of my eye this hawk dive down into the row I had just cut and grab a field mouse. About a half hour later, I spotted him on top of a dead tree very close by and watching intently the row of cut grass just behind the tractor. Mice and other small creatures would get scared by the tractor and scurry out of the tall grass and run across the field of freshly cut, shorter grass behind the tractor. Bad idea.

I turned the tractor around at the end of a row and there he was again. That hawk was on the ground just 30 feet from me, incredibly close, with another mouse in his talons, and for just a second or two, he stayed there and looked right at me, right into my eyes, so close and so strong and confident. I could see the muscles in his chest and his legs, and the power of this hunter that I'd never seen at a distance, and the fierce but beautiful features of his face, his beak, his brow and his eyes. I stopped the tractor and we just looked at each other for a moment.

That day we learned to hunt together. I scare them out, and he swoops down and grabs them. And every time I get on the tractor now to cut tall grass with the bush hog, that hawk is sitting in a tree nearby, watching and waiting.

We're fortunate to have a farmer in the area who helps us with managing the livestock at Creekside Farm, Josh Martin, and he keeps a few of his own cattle on our land in return for the help. The cows get to roam around on about 30 acres of land with a creek, about 3 acres of woods for shade, and a high meadow for when they want to walk up and check out the view. They've got a pretty good life here and are very healthy cows. They walk through their salad bar all day, the way God intended. This picture contrasts sharply with the way most beef cattle are raised and my cows probably don't know how lucky they are, but I feel lucky to have them.

The two miniature donkeys, about three feet tall, also live in the pasture and are a big hit for all the visitors that stop by the farm. Their names are Darla and Pedro, and everyone in the neighborhood knows their name and stops by from time to time to bring them apples and scratch behind their long ears. They earn their keep in the pasture by keeping the coyotes away from the young calves. Donkeys, even miniature ones, are very territorial and can injure or kill a coyote with a swift kick from their back legs if one comes into the pasture and threatens a calf.

We bought a large chicken coup on wheels, the egg mobile, and Melissa pulls it and the 75 chickens that call it home around the pasture where they scratch up bugs and fertilize the pasture. She moves it around about every week or two following the cows from one pasture to the next, and for that effort the chickens reward her with about 75 eggs every day in the summer, less in the winter.

We put up a short electric fence for pigs around an old tree line, and six pigs spend their days digging up roots and keeping the brush down. Pigs can sunburn easy, so they like where they're at in the shade. Melissa will move their electric fence down the tree-line every couple of weeks. Like the chickens, they also eat organic food, which is twice as expensive as regular food, but it's all part of what she's trying to do here with this farm. The wealthy, gated golf community, The Cliffs at Walnut Cove, borders the farm on two sides, and it's kind of funny to have cows and pigs and chickens so close to homes that sell for a couple million dollars, but the animals don't seem to mind.

We divided up the 30-acre pasture into three roughly 10-acre parcels so that we could rotate the cattle often enough and let the different parcels all rest for a few weeks at a time. Depending on the rain and the heat and the season, we adjust how long they might stay on any parcel. It means more work managing and moving the cattle around the different sections of pasture all the time but letting pasture rest is a proven technique to improve the overall quality of the soil and the grass. We try to use Joel Saladin's "cow days" math to determine how many days a certain number of cows can stay on a given area of pasture, depending on the rain and the season. Usually they get moved about once every two weeks. That means they'll be off a section for about a month while the grass recovers.

The most important part of keeping cattle is making sure the fence is always intact, and that requires running the fence line, which I do a couple times a week, and for that I use the Gator, a two seat ATV. Deer will often damage the fence when they jump over or try to get through it. Bears don't bother jumping and just go through it. Inevitably the hot wire on the fence will get tangled or cross one of the barbed wires and short it out.

Riding the fence line gives me a chance to ride around the farm with a purpose, and it becomes another spiritual connection point for me to the land, the animals and to nature. I usually do it later in the day, and sometimes I'll bring a couple beers with me, because as Ben Franklin says, "Beer is proof that God loves us and wants us to be happy."

Standing in awe at beautiful scenery, like a sunset over the mountains, and truly appreciating it, savoring it, helps to build or increase the innate character trait of spirituality and connections to the transcendent world. But I think working with and within nature, immersing in nature with a job that promises a few hours of peaceful contemplation, helps to build deeper spiritual connections to the earth and then the universe. It's part of the peace and joy that comes to many people from working in a garden or on a farm.

EVERYTHING IN MODERATION

Temperance, like spirituality, is another trait or strength that makes up the human character. Temperance is the strength that protects us, often from ourselves. "Everything in moderation" perfectly describes the virtue of temperance. Many of our problems in America – like obesity, alcoholism, drug abuse and overwhelming debt – are related to intemperate behavior. Temperance is the ability to look out for your "future self". You strengthen this muscle in your head in simple, small steps, like pushing away from the table, closing your tab, and holding your tongue. Controlling your emotions, and not over-reacting, builds the strength of temperance. It means trying to temper and control your emotions, needs, wants and desires in order to protect yourself and your future self. Moderation in our diets is critical to our future health. We cannot keep eating high sugar, high salt, high fat processed junk foods and sugary snacks. At some point our "future selves" will regret it and have to pay the piper for this intemperate behavior.

The age of mass consumerism and the need to keep buying more stuff can also be seen as intemperate behavior, particularly when we're using up limited resources and polluting the planet in the process. Having more "stuff" will not make you as happy as you think. Becoming healthier and more active, with a healthy diet and some exercise, will go much farther to improving overall happiness over the long term. John Seymour, the environmentalist and rebel against consumerism, once wrote, "It's time we cut out what we do not need so we can live more simply and happily. Good food, comfortable clothes, serviceable housing, and true culture- those are the things that matter."

Can we cut back on excessive consumerism? Can we buy less stuff? And can we afford to spend a little more for healthier foods? Let's take a look back 100 years to see how much we were spending then on food and other stuff. We spent a much bigger percentage of our annual income on food back then, which leads me to believe that most of us can spend a little more on healthier food today. A trip to Whole Foods or the farmers market, or the purchase of a CSA share, won't really break the household budget, particularly if we cut back on some of the other unnecessary "stuff".

According to an April 2012 article by Derek Thompson in the Atlantic, spending on food and clothing went from half the family budget in the year 1900 to less than 20% one hundred years later in 2000. Food alone went from about 43% of the family budget in the year 1900 to about 9% in 2000, and it continues to drop as a percentage of income as wages rise.

Although it was really not that long ago (my grandfather was born in 1898), the year 1900 seems like a completely different time and place. Thompson says that only one quarter of US households had running water in the house. Even fewer owned the home they lived in, they mostly rented. Fewer still had flush toilets. Just one out of twelve households had gas or electric lights, one-twentieth had telephones, one-in-ninety owned a car, and, of course, nobody had a television. It's hard to imagine how much things have changed since then. It's also important to recognize how far we've come in a little over 100 years, and how much better we have it now. Historian Brad DeLong said that in the year 1900 we lived closer to the 16th century than we did to the 21st century. And the average life expectancy was about the same: the ripe old age of 50.

In the year 1800, 90% of Americans were farmers. When my grandfather was born one hundred years later, that number dropped to about 40% of the labor force. When my father was born, it dropped again to 21% of the labor force. Today it's about 2% of the labor force in America.

In the year 1900, says Thompson, more than twice as many households reported income from children (22%) than wives (9%). The average annual income was just about $750, but over the next century it would go up about 68 times. Household income (unadjusted for inflation) doubled six times in the 20th century, or once every 15 years, on average. We're far better off than we were in 1900.

By the year 1950, the population doubled to 150 million, and the number of farmers had fallen from 40% to 10%, due largely to the tractor. At the same time, food has gotten much cheaper compared to wages, and its share of the family budget declined from 43% in 1900 to 30% in 1950. Today that number is about 9% of the family budget. That's a reduction in food cost from 43% to 9% of our household budget since 1900.

It's eye-opening to think families used to spend more than 50 percent of their income on just these two basic necessities, eating and clothing ourselves. Now, the average household spends well under 20 percent on those same basic needs, and we own a lot more clothes, closets full of clothes. The down

side is, today we spend more than half of our money on housing and transportation. In 1900, no one had a car and the gas
expense that comes with it, let alone insurance and repairs.
More people didn't own a home either but rented. And the
homes themselves were more modest, not the "castles" we
expect today.

The cost of food continued to drop over the last half of the
20th century. According to the U.S. Department of Agriculture, the average share of per capita income spent on food fell
from 17.5 percent in 1960 to 9.6 percent in 2007.

Americans spend less of our cash as a percentage of income
on food than any other country, and half as much as France,
Belgium and Spain. If you consider spending on food at home,
the most important measure of social welfare, it takes much
less from our budget than every other country in the world.
We don't have to eat like the French, but surely many of us can
spend a little more for healthier food.

Americans now spend more money eating out than at
home. We spend just over half of our food budget – 50.1% in
2014 - on food consumed away from home. This was the first
time American food spending crossed that threshold.

But the averages don't really tell the whole story. In 2016,
upper income households spent about $11,000 on food, which
was about 8% of their earnings. Middle income households
spent an average of $6,224 on food, representing 13.1 percent
of income, while the lowest income households spent a lot less,
$3,862 on food, representing a much higher 32.6 percent of
their income. One third of poor U.S household income goes to
food. That's comparable to India and Uzbekistan, where they
also spend about one third of their income on food.

WANT FRIES WITH THAT?

We're spending a lot more money eating out, and that usually means lower quality fast food for lower income bracket households. Over the last half century, Americans began to spend a lot more on food they didn't prepare at home. Americans in the lowest 20% income bracket spend a high percentage of their food budget eating out, nearly one-third of it, and it's usually less expensive fast food.

What most studies don't show us is what we're actually eating. Many researchers believe our food system in the U.S has become corrupted in the last several decades. We're rushing through drive-through fast-food restaurants and eating unhealthy processed foods and were eating and drinking massive quantities of sugar in the form of corn-based derivatives.

Unfortunately, other countries like China are starting to eat like us, and it's starting to show in weight gain and obesity rates. The obesity rates in Chinese cities is now reaching 20%, and if you go to a Chinese city these days you'll recognize the image Colonel Sanders on many city blocks. KFC, and McDonalds, are now popular restaurants across China. Heart disease, diabetes and other health problems related to obesity are on the rise in China, and government officials are very concerned about it. The development of rapid transportation in China has greatly reduced bicycle transportation, which is the other side of the story (less exercise).

Our Americanized fast food diet is encroaching on cultures all across the planet. Almost all nutritionists believe we need to get back to healthy whole foods cooked fresh at home. Bringing family, friends and neighbors together around the table is what creates community, but it also creates healthier lifestyles that protects our future health, our future selves. In the future, you can look back and thank yourself for eating that salad today.

PRUDENT BEHAVIOR FOR FOOD BIODIVERSITY

Farmers by the very nature of their occupation must be prudent. They make serious financial and personal sacrifices in the spring, hoping for a good crop in the fall. There is no immediate gratification from the challenging work that they do. They get up with the sunrise to begin working for, and watching out for, the future of their families. It's prudent behavior. But there are some imprudent, even careless things that are happening on the American farm these days related to our seed stock and genetic biodiversity.

Most people are aware of and concerned about the rapid loss of biodiversity in our oceans and rain forests, and rightly so. But most people are not aware of the devastating loss of biodiversity in our food supply over the last 100 years. As with other businesses over the past century, there has been a great deal of consolidation of seed suppliers and the growth of huge companies like Monsanto and Cargill. It is dangerous to grow and store a limited number of varieties of any single crop, and it is prudent behavior to save and keep crop genes we might need in the future.

A group of researchers went through the commercial seed catalogs from 1903 and found that farmers back then could order 307 different varieties of corn seeds to plant in their fields. By 1983 that number had dropped significantly, to less than a dozen varieties that were commercially readily available for planting. Just twelve varieties were found in the National Seed Storage Laboratory. The same kind of drop in the number of varieties was true for all other commercial vegetables. The same has happened for chickens and livestock- consolidation to a limited number of producing breeds. Here's a list of the number of varieties of vegetables that were available to growers in 1903, and those that appeared in the National Seed Storage Library just 80 years later, in 1983.

VEGETABLE	1903	1983
Beets	288	17
Cabbage	544	28
Sweet Corn	307	12
Lettuce	497	36
Peas	408	25
Squash	341	40
Tomatoes	408	79
Cucumbers	285	16

Every variety of plant has developed its own unique genetic defenses that help it survive different challenges in its environment, whether that is resistance to some pest, fungus or heat. If we lose that plant, we lose the genetic trait it has developed over thousands of years, and a genetic trait we may need at some point in the future, particularly with the risks of climate change and global warming.

Many food scientists believe it is prudent behavior for a people to protect the biodiversity of their important food seed stocks. There may be wheat varieties out there that have genes which make it more resilient to drought, and they may turn out to be invaluable given a warming climate. Protecting the gene pool of food plants is like an insurance policy.

The clearest example of the risk in growing a limited number of varieties of a plant, and the one most people are aware of, is the potato famine in Ireland in 1845. A potato fungus swept through the country and caused massive starvation and migration. Another potato variety might have been more genetically resistant to the fungus and mitigated some of the starvation. Keeping a larger gene pool going in our food supply is a sensible thing to do, but we've been going in the other direction to our great peril. With the rapid consolidation of seed suppliers and a concentration on growing a limited number of high yielding varieties over the past couple of decades, and the growth of a limited number of patented GMOs, we are reducing our available gene pool for the fight against future disease.

It's happening elsewhere on the farm. People eat more eggs and poultry than ever, but the world's reliance on a few high-yielding chicken breeds is edging out hundreds of others. Nearly a third of all chicken breeds are at risk of extinction. That's alarming because many varieties have traits, like heat or pathogen resistance, that could also be invaluable in the future.

We're trying to do our small part at Creekside Farm by growing several old heirloom varieties of vegetables through membership in the nonprofit organization Seed Savers, based in Iowa. Melissa is growing and saving seeds for older vegetable varieties that are no longer available commercially but have been kept alive and in circulation by other small growers and members of Seed Savers.

Nonprofits like Seed Savers and other groups are helping to protect varieties of vegetables through the sharing, sale and distribution of heirloom seeds, and Melissa is dedicated to growing as many heirloom varieties as possible. A large portion of the farm and gardens are an experiment in finding the best varieties for our native soils and climate, with a focus on bringing back seeds and vegetables grown here in Appalachia in the early days. She's growing for variety and for taste, but also to save and share seeds. Melissa has already collected many varieties of heirloom tomato, bean and squash seeds that were grown in this Appalachian region 100 years ago.

Some groups and organizations are trying to save rare seeds and their stored genetic information by freezing and storing them in remote locations, like the Svalbard Seed Vault buried in a mountain above the arctic circle. Other groups like Seed Savers use a network of members and growers to save and share heirloom seeds as part of one large community of concerned citizens. It's like having the genetic information out on the internet and stored away in hundreds or even thousands of computers, but in this case, it's growing in small gardens and stored away in mason jars across the country. It's a good idea to have this genetic information stored in multiple locations.

I started learning about seeds from the farm manager, John Cuykendall, at Blackberry Farms near Knoxville, Tennessee. John is an older guy that likes to talk and tell stories more than farm the land, but he still does a lot of that. There's plenty of help for the farm work, so John mostly just likes to tool around and test some of the old heirloom seed varieties and talk about seeds with visitors to the farm.

Blackberry Farm is a high-end resort centered around a working farm in the mountains of Tennessee. The farm and gardens supply much of the produce, cheese, jams and jellies used at the wonderful restaurant at the resort called The Barn, which is housed in a huge barn structure. Blackberry Farm can afford to pay John to just sit and chat with visitors, so that's what he does a lot of the time. He'll invite guests in to his warm and rustic garden shed to sit in front of the wood burning stove and just talk about the farm, what's coming up, and what they might be working on right now. But mostly he likes to talk about heirloom seeds.

John has a story about almost every bean seed or heirloom tomato that he grows. "Provenance" he calls it, and every seed has its own history and story: how he acquired it and where it originally came from. There's a story John likes to tell about a bean variety that he got from a farmer in Tennessee. That farmer said he found a few seeds in the stomach of a goose he shot for dinner one fall as it was flying south for the winter.

"No telling where that goose flew in from", John told me, "could'a been a few hundred, or maybe a thousand miles away. But the farmer had never seen these kinds of seeds before, so he threw them in the ground that next spring to see what came up."

"Turns out they grew the best beans he had ever tasted, so he kept saving seeds and growing more, till I got my hands on some of them," John said with a big grin on his face.

John Cuykendall is an avid member of the Seed Savers organization and was proud to show me his seeds that were listed in the annual catalog of seeds. They keep a huge printed and on-line catalog of seeds that growers across the country are offering for the sole purpose of distributing to other growers, many free of cost, so that other growers might plant, harvest and save more seeds which should increase the overall stock of that variety across the country. John is a modest and prudent man who believes that saving seeds like this is a wise thing to do. He also finds seeds fascinating and loves to do it.

It is the proneness of human nature to do things that are harmful to ourselves and not always in our own long-term best interest, and so moderation and self-regulation can be the virtue that saves us from ourselves. The message from the organic and grow local movement is all about moderation. Use less, eat less unhealthy foods, have less impact on the planet in any way you can. Reduce, reuse, recycle is another underlying mantra from the environmental movement. It all relates to moderation, self-control and prudent behavior.

Growing a limited number of varieties of plants and growing them using destructive industrial production methods with massive amounts of chemicals might represent short term gain and an overabundance of certain food stocks, like corn, but at a greater long-term cost. It would seem then that we're not doing a very good job of looking out for our future selves as a nation, which isn't very prudent behavior. Building stronger connections and appreciation for the wonder and beauty of nature may help us see the error of our ways.

CHAPTER NINE

———

CULTIVATING RESILIENCE

"A life of leisure and a life of laziness are two things. There will be sleeping enough in the grave."

-Ben Franklin

WESTWARD EXPANSION

In the early days of America, at the western edge of human expansion, a man chops away at the forest with his axe, taking down one tree at a time. The sound of American expansion into the wilderness is the rhythmic chopping, the sudden snap and a swoosh of branches rushing through the air toward the ground. The tree falls hard and loud, then silence rushes in. Sunlight fills the ground around the stump, and civilization has just expanded another 200 square feet into the vast western wilderness.

What was called "the West" during the early years of our nation was everything west of the Alleghany Mountains, which was in fact a vast continent of total wilderness stretching for thousands of miles. Prior to the American Revolution, the simple act of westward expansion was hotly debated between the colonists and the British Parliament. England did not want the colonists moving beyond the Blue Ridge Mountains, they claimed, to protect Indian lands. The colonists believed that this was just an excuse to save choice land for another handout to the British aristocracy, and by the time of Washington's presidency, people were already flooding across the Alleghenies and into "the Ohio country".

In England, most of the land was already owned by members of the aristocracy. To the colonists of North America, the continent was so huge and unexplored, that it made no sense not to allow the growing population to spread out. The issue rose to become another symbol of the unjust tyranny of England over America, and this conflict contributed to a sense of independence and self-rule across the colonies. The natural lay of the land in America came to breed the virtues of self-reliance and independence in its people. Before there was an outward liberty and independence, there was an inward liberty and independence – an independence of spirit and a sense of self-reliance and self-determination.

George Washington encouraged the inevitable western expansion, writing, "If I was a young man just preparing to begin in the world, I know of no country where I would rather find my habitation than in some part of [the west]".[64] To Americans, the west was filled with the hope and dreams of a bigger and better future. Hope is an American virtue, and it first came to us from the very land itself.

Thomas Jefferson believed that the vast open spaces of this continent would help to keep the American people virtuous. He believed that a rural, agricultural society was a more virtuous society than an industrial one like in England and the rest of Europe. In a letter to Washington, Jefferson said, "Agriculture is our wisest pursuit, because it will in the end contribute most to real wealth, good morals and happiness."

He believed that a country of farmers and an economy based on rural agriculture would keep us virtuous as a nation, and this may be why the Louisiana Purchase was so important to him. More land would help to keep our country rural and agricultural for a long time to come. Another reason that he sent Lewis and Clark out to explore this new, vast interior was to find a means to export all the agricultural goods out of the future heartland of the nation.

"I think our governments will remain virtuous for many centuries," wrote Jefferson to James Madison, "as long as they are chiefly agricultural; and this will be as long as there shall be vacant lands in any part of America."[65] Jefferson was already looking westward and counting on the "vacant lands" west of the Alleghenies.

Jefferson clearly stated his idea that an agriculturally based economy was more virtuous than an industrially based one in another letter he wrote to Abbe Salimankis. He writes, "That there is much vice and misery in the world, I know; but more virtue and happiness I believe, at least in our part of it; the latter being the lot of those employed in agriculture in a greater degree than of other callings."[66]

Jefferson believed that the dirty, industrially based cities of Europe were the breeding ground of vice, exploitation of the poor and uneducated and the suppression of human rights and dignity. A free man that harvests the fruits of his own labor in the wide-open spaces, a healthy lifestyle in a pastoral setting, a man or woman connected with the earth and with nature, this is Jefferson's idealistic vision of life and liberty. Jefferson believed that connecting with the natural world leads naturally to a more virtuous life.

To roam freely in open spaces, to be your own boss, to survive by your own wits and labor, these are things that spawn the ideas of freedom, independence and liberty, and will protect us from the threat of tyranny in the future. Jefferson believed that freedom and independence are the cherished values that come naturally to those living in a rural, agricultural setting. At the time of the Revolution, most Americans were strong nonconformists and self-made men living in a rural, pastoral setting.

Our remoteness from Europe, our colonies on the edge of a vast expanse of land and natural beauty, inspired Thomas Jefferson to believe that God had a hand in creating this new nation. Man was born free to roam this vast continent and make his way in it, and this inspired his writing, "The God who gave us life also gave us liberty at the same time."

He also wrote famously, "Rebellion to tyrants is obedience to God".[67] Liberty and freedom are God given rights, and when other men will try to suppress these rights we are obligated to stand up against them. Freedom and independence came naturally to these new Americans, and rebellion against any perceived tyranny was a natural response.

Jefferson of course valued the high ideals of independence and freedom more than anything, and he hated any form of tyranny. Independence of mind, body and spirit were, he believed, the key character traits of Americans that would promise our success. And he believed independence was a natural progression brought on in large measure by the natural surroundings of our environment. This wild and free continent full of wondrous beauty and natural abundance bred a free and independent spirit in the human beings that lived here. This is our common heritage in America. This is where we come from.

THE RESILIENT COMMUNITY

Kara and Melissa believe that local food is mostly about healthy, better tasting food without all the chemicals, and I think that's probably true for most of our CSA members also. But to me, it's about a lot more than just fresh vegetables, something much deeper and more primitive. To me, local food is more about keeping the food producing capacity close to home. It's what drives me more than anything else in this whole farm project. It's my underlying motivation for everything. And it relates to the concept of resilience, which is what this chapter is all about.

Resilience is about being able to take a hit and not break in half. It's about taking a punch and getting back up. If something bad and unexpected happens, you're not sitting dead in the water. Over the course of my whole life, and certainly my business career, I've always been on the lookout for where the axe is going to fall. This psychological tendency may come down to me through evolution since our ancestors were probably always wondering if there was a tiger lurking behind the next bush. After thousands of years asking, "Where's the tiger?" it started to get embedded in our genes. Resilience is being able to take care of yourself (and your community) and preparing for the worst. Resilience may be a new term or concept, but the idea of watching out for future problems and taking steps to prepare, avoid or mitigate them runs deep in human evolution. We're conditioned to respond to crisis.

How does a community become more independent, resilient, and self-reliant? If you imagined placing a big dome over your community, how big would that dome need to be to provide all the resources that you need to live? Would it be a small local dome, or a much larger dome encompassing a larger region, or perhaps your entire state? To be truly self-reliant, the dome would probably have to be larger than the local area if we want to maintain our standard of living and the modern conveniences that we've grown accustomed to.

But it could be much smaller to provide the truly basic needs of food and water.

Self-reliance also means being resilient enough to be able to bounce back after some disturbance or unanticipated event. In order to build a more resilient community, we need to ask ourselves what resources do we use and expect? Water, food, shelter, heat, and electricity are the first that come to mind for most people. But to be truly resilient, we also need to ask, what happens if we flip the switch and the lights don't come on? What if we turn the faucet and no water comes out. Are we prepared for disruption? Do we have a backup plan, or are we working toward creating one? This is how we begin to create a more resilient community.

When it comes to food, we need to ask the question, how did it get to me? Most likely the food chain went from the farm, to the processor, distributor, and retailer, but often other actors are involved. And where and how far away are each of these players in the distribution channel? If there were a disruption along the food chain due to an oil shortage, which might be caused by a hurricane knocking out a couple refineries in the Gulf of Mexico, or a solar flare that disrupts the power grid, how would the food come to us? Is there a backup plan?

Researchers involved in resilience science suggest that we're about to overturn industrialization as we know it. Just as the grow local and farm to table movement is changing our food system, communities and regions will become more resilient and self-sustaining at the regional level and won't count on national or global sources of supply. If that's true, that's a good thing. But there is a right size to resilience, and it's not local, and it's not national. Once again, it's about scale. Resilience is about being able to take care of yourself and your community in the event of some serious disruption.

I attended a lecture by soil scientist and researcher Laura Lengnick held at the Organic Grower's School Spring Conference, and she suggests that the roots of community resilience are found at the regional scale and is dependent on three things: diversity, self-reliance, and community wealth. Diversity in this way of thinking includes both the social and ecological aspects of community.[68]

Resilient communities have high functional diversity, says Lengnick, which means the practical and efficient ability to provide critical resources like water, food, power and transportation. Resilient communities provide for all their basic needs, and they have a strong plan in place for any kind of disruption or adversity that might come their way.

According to Lengnick, a resilient community has a "high response diversity," meaning that it can react to changes quickly in order to sustain critical community resources. Lengnick also says that networks of people and processes increase a community's ability to react and respond to different threats and situations. Lengnick believes that having some exposure to mild disturbances actually helps a community learn how to respond to change and to develop proactive resolves for the future, so it's good when some bad things happen—as long as they are not too bad, and the community has a plan in place to learn from them.

The key to a sustainable and resilient community is to be locally interdependent and globally autonomous; in other words, not dependent on global supply chains. You can still source products from places outside of your region, or even globally, as long as you're not dependent on them. As I said before, I like coffee, but I could live without it for a while. I wouldn't be very pleasant in the mornings, but I could continue to exist. Basic food calories are a different story entirely.

Resilience is bigger than just bouncing back, it includes the ability to respond to change so that you can limit negative impacts or avoid them entirely, or even capture new opportunities. And some things can sneak up on you slowly. Here's an example. Given the aging population of farmers in the US, a full 50% of our farms will turn over or change ownership in the next 10-12 years. Resilient communities will plan for this to make sure they have the training and resources in place for a younger generation of farmers. This is one of the objectives of the Creekside Farm Education Center; building that knowledge base and the people who are willing to learn. Resilience means spotting potential problems or threats before they happen.

Resilience also includes a transformation capacity; the ability for a community to change or "bounce forward," says Lengnick. It is the ability of a community to transform completely, to find a new dialog and new way of looking at things and to innovate completely new and novel solutions. The grow local movement is a bounce forward. It's a new way of looking at food and how it gets to us; it is a vision of an entirely new kind of food system.

A resilient community will take an inventory of its assets, and not just financial wealth. Human capital, the shared learning and social bonds that cultivate social capital, the built environment, the natural environment; all are important to the accumulation of a balanced portfolio of assets that are the foundation of a more resilient community. A resilient community has a plan to create jobs and fuel the local economy all along the local food processing, distribution and sales channels. It encourages cooperation between local governments, nonprofit organizations and businesses, communities and farmers, in order to build a new food culture so that we can grow, process and distribute food in a way that promotes the local accumulation of wealth.

Because of nationally centralized processing and distribution plants, salmonella, E. coli, mad cow and avian flu epidemics have caused illness and death over vast distances. In just one year, 2018, there were two national recalls on romaine lettuce. Every head and every leaf of romaine, from every store and every restaurant, and every home across the country, was to be pulled from shelves and destroyed, just to be safe. While the problem likely started at one farm, people over a broad region were getting sick, including 18 states and Canada, because of how the lettuce was centrally processed and distributed. Those incidents created a lot of wasted food across two nations, but they also killed people and made many more people sick.

And given the centralization of our food production and processing, the Pentagon and other national security agencies have been studying the threat from agri-terrorism and the intentional disruption or contamination to our national food supply. Just having more local and regional processing and distribution points reduces that risk while it builds stronger, more resilient local food production and processing capacity. Building these local food processing and distribution assets will make us safer now and stronger for the future. I know it seems silly, but I bought an old hand crank grain grinder and an old butter churn at an antique store once, and I felt a little better about myself when I brought them home; a little more self-reliant, a little more resilient. But we need food processing assets at a much larger scale and at the community and regional level to become truly resilient.

The deeper truth is we're just not that resilient when it comes to our food systems. When food is grown and processed in far-away places and must travel long distances to get to us, we risk food shortages if a disruption occurs in our oil, gas or electricity supply. Global climate change can result in more catastrophic weather events like hurricanes that can not only cripple a region but can take out oil refineries which drastically affects the gas and oil supply in a much broader region of the country, just as Hurricane Katrina did. Grocery store shelves in far-away Asheville, North Carolina, were already thinning out just two or three days after that event. Most gas stations ran out of gas within four days, and long lines began to form at those stations that reported having some gas deliveries. If another hurricane followed Katrina in the gulf, and a third went up the east coast taking out more refineries and storage facilities there, the problem would have become devastating for us and a lot more Americans along the east coast. Without the fuel to deliver food or to drive to the grocery store, hunger starts setting in very quickly. We're getting multiple hurricane threats, and larger storms, every year, and it just takes the right combination in the wrong places to create havoc in our fuel supply.

Russia and other groups are attempting to hack our power grid which the CIA and NSA acknowledge as a very serious threat. Devices that can be exploded above our atmosphere, including smaller nuclear warheads, can generate an electromagnetic pulse (EMP) that would cause our power grid to fail over vast distances, and take out satellites, telecommunications, banking and financial infrastructure at the same time. The sun itself presents a very real threat to the power grid from solar flares and coronal mass ejections (CME) that can damage the power grid to such an extent that it might take months, or even years, to repair and get back on line. One such CME took out the US telegraph system in 1859 and shut down all communication for months while the wires were replaced or repaired. That same event would have devasted the current power grid, and without refrigeration, fresh food spoils very quickly. An event known among scientists as the Solar Storm of 2012 was of a similar magnitude and passed the earth's orbit but fortunately missed the earth. The timing was lucky. In this digital age, it would have been devastating to our power, information, banking, health care, transportation and communication infrastructure.

Up until now, most of the recent, serious catastrophic events in the United States have been weather related regional events, and the people affected were able to get help fairly quickly from national resources outside of the region. But what if an event affected a much larger region or the entire nation, or was a global event, and no help was coming? Do we have the infrastructure, capacity, technical capability and human capital at the local or regional level to fend for ourselves for any length of time?

Extreme weather events, likely caused by climate change, are already impacting agricultural and food distribution systems worldwide, and officials need to consider how we can make our towns and cities more resilient. When Superstorm Sandy hit New York City back in 2012, it woke a lot of people up to how vulnerable we can be in our food supply. If Sandy had hit that area a few hours earlier, at high tide, the Hunts Point Food Distribution Center in the Bronx could have experienced major flooding and power loss. Nearly 50 percent of the food supplied to the New York City region comes from the Hunts Point massive distribution complex, and almost a third of it sits in a flood plain.[69] Hunts Point feeds over 22 million people, and severe damage to the facility or to infrastructure like road or rail lines would have had serious ramifications and adverse impacts on people throughout the northeast. [70]

Threats don't have to be sudden catastrophic events; they can creep up on us. Farms in the Southwest United States are predicted to feel the effects of climate change as temperatures rise and droughts become more frequent, and they'll become less productive.[71] The other side of that story is that the farm land values will drop, because they are less productive, and since farm values are the collateral for farm loans, it will become harder for farmers there to get the loans they need to stay in operation. It becomes a vicious circle.[72]

LOCAL VS. ORGANIC

Having the ability to grow and process some food at the local level increases our resilience and ability to withstand and recover from some unforeseen natural or manmade disaster. It's also much healthier for humans over the long term.

In a nine-year study, the United States Food and Drug Administration (FDA) reported that between 33 and 39 percent of our food contains detectable amounts of pesticides, including 54 percent of our fruits and 36 percent of our vegetables. Scientists really don't know much about the long-term effect of these chemicals on our health.

Organic food is grown on farms committed to environmentally friendly agricultural methods that use none of these harmful or synthetic chemicals. In order to label produce as organic, farms and farmers must meet rigorous government standards and the process of becoming certified organic can become an intensive multi-year process for an organic farm. Most local growers at the Farmers Market are not certified organic because of the time and expense of going thru the process, but they usually grow using organic methods just the same. But what if you were faced with the choice, buying organic food from California or local food grown by conventional methods using chemical fertilizers and pesticides? What would you buy? What's more important to you?

I had a conversation with Melissa about this organic versus local food subject over the summer. I caught her packing vegetables into CSA boxes at the cold storage shed and I started the conversation by saying something like this, "Food from California can be organic, but heavily dependent on fossil fuels for transportation. What's more important to most people. Organic or local?"

I continued, "I mean if I were in a store and had a choice between organic tomatoes from California and non-organic tomatoes grown locally, I'd choose the local ones. Mainly because I know that decision supports the local food infrastructure and jobs for local farmers and the money will circulate through the local economy a couple more times. It also makes us more resilient in case something bad happens that might disrupt our national food distribution."

In truth, we're rarely faced with this dilemma or have this choice because local food is almost always grown using organic methods. And I know organic from California carries the burden of carbon monoxide and other chemicals put into the atmosphere from the truck that brought these tomatoes all the way across the country, and I breath those chemicals and they make their way into my body, so these tomatoes are not chemically innocent. I also know that there is a great deal of consolidation in the organic farms in California with organic growers getting bought up by larger and larger companies. If it keeps happening, we'll end up with just a few very large organic companies controlling most of the organic food, as happened with conventional food. Organic is becoming the huge, mono-cropping fields in Mexico that produce lettuce in plastic trays to be shipped thousands of miles in refrigerated trucks. Organic red seedless grapes shipped 7000 miles from Chile does nothing to help a small farmer here live a simpler life raising a family on a farm right down the road. And with all the food miles associated with this kind of "organic", what good are we really doing for the environment? I didn't say all that, but I knew how I would answer the question. I'd buy local.

"Both are important to most people, and you can have both," Melissa answered. "Organic food from California goes into supermarkets and Whole Foods all around the country, and that's good because it reduces chemicals in the food and in the soil and streams in California. It's good. It's healthier food for people to eat."

She continued, "Local organic food is better, better because it reduces food miles and fossil fuels and CO_2 in the atmosphere. It's taken a while for people to learn about eating healthier organic food, and it will take a little while longer for people to really understand how important eating local is, but they're learning." She smiled.

Then Melissa added, "Growing local food was actually started as a reaction to industrial agriculture and all the chemicals being used a few decades ago. People didn't trust Big Ag and started to grow their own food, and then started sharing and selling it to others in their community. They were inter-related concepts, local and organic were the same thing, until large companies jumped on the organic band-wagon and set up massive organic farms in California. Now they've become separate ideas, organic and local, when at first, they weren't separate. Understand?"

I said I understood, but I still thought to myself, it would be great to see survey to find out what is more important to most people from an ideological standpoint, local or organic. If you had to choose I mean. Anyway, I changed the subject back to something we've discussed on many other occasions, and we never really came to terms.

"OK, let me ask you another hypothetical question. If you had a good crop of tomatoes that was getting close to harvest, and all the sudden you found a blight attacking the crop, would you ever consider spraying that crop with a chemical if you knew it would save the crop. Otherwise you're wiped out, no tomatoes. My inclination is to save the crop. Isn't that yours?"

I could see the frustration on her face immediately. She looked at me like 'you just don't get it do you', although she said nothing at first.

Finally, Melissa said, "If you farm organically and build up the soil health you won't need any pesticides or herbicides or chemicals. And once you start spraying, you kill everything else that is good in the soil, the helpful organisms, and you're locked in, and you have to keep spraying because your soil becomes depleted and unhealthy. Once you start down that path, there's no turning back."

She continued, "I've read studies and been on organic farms that prove that an organic farm can be just as productive as a conventional farm that sprays, if the soil is built up and healthy."

"Besides, if something bad happens, as you say, then you're not going to be able to get your chemicals anymore, are you, so you're really in trouble with unhealthy soil and no chemicals and that isn't very resilient, is it?"

Brilliant! She just used logic that was undeniable, irrefutable, and geared right to me. She's so smart, she hit me right where I live. Chemical production is not resilient because you won't be able to get the chemicals if there is some serious, catastrophic disruption in our society, so you better know how to grow organically. It wasn't just about preserving the health of our soils for the future or reducing chemicals to become more sustainable. Knowing how to grow food without the chemicals is resilient and prudent behavior. It doesn't even take a calamitous event to see the logic. The long, slow depletion of oil reserves means chemical fertilizers (derived from fossil fuels) are also on a slow march toward extinction, and it's prudent to learn how to grow food without them. The chemical question, to use or not to use, would never come up again between us.

SOIL HEALTH, MICROBES AND HUMAN HEALTH

I knew also that it went much deeper with Melissa. She had a better understanding of soil health and all the organisms that call it home, particularly the microbes (or microscopic organisms). A garden has its own microbiome, a collection of bacteria, fungi, one-celled archaea, and viruses, and new research suggests how important this is to soil health, and in turn, human health. Our health depends on the flourishing and diverse microbiome in our own gut, the stomach and intestinal tract—and that depends on natures microbiome. Human health is inextricably linked to the health and diversity of microbes in the soil. A five-year study by the National Institute of Health's Human Microbiome Project suggests that we should think of ourselves as a "superorganism," a residence for microbes with whom we have coevolved over human history, and these microbes perform critical functions and provide valuable services to our bodies and our health. The microbes in our bodies outnumber our own human cells ten to one and collectively they weigh about three pounds – or about the same as our brain.

Just as we have unwittingly destroyed vital microbes in the human gut through overuse of antibiotics and highly processed foods, we've devastated soil microbiota essential to plant health through the overuse of chemical fertilizers, fungicides, herbicides, and pesticides. And we failed to add organic matter back into the soil (upon which the microbes feed). These soil microorganisms, particularly bacteria and fungi, cycle nutrients and water into plants, into our crops, and ultimately into our bodies. Soil bacteria and fungi serve as the "stomachs" of plants. They form symbiotic relationships with plant roots and break down or "digest" nutrients for the plant, providing nitrogen, phosphorus, and many other nutrients in a form that plant cells can assimilate.

These soil microorganisms do much more than nourish plants, and were just starting to understand some of these relationships. Just as the microbes in the human body both aid digestion and maintain our immune system, soil microorganisms both digest nutrients and protect plants against pathogens and other threats. For over four hundred million years, plants have been forming a symbiotic association with fungi that colonize their roots, creating mycorrhizae, literally "fungus roots," which extend the reach of plant roots a hundred-fold. These fungal filaments not only channel nutrients and water back to the plant roots and cells, they connect plants and actually enable them to communicate with one another so that, together, they can set up defense systems. A recent experiment in the U.K. showed that mycorrhizal filaments act as a conduit for signaling between plants, setting off an alarm that allows the nearby plants to start building and strengthening their natural defenses against an intruding pest. When attacked by aphids, for instance, a broad bean plant transmitted a signal through the mycorrhizal filaments to other bean plants nearby, acting as an early warning system, enabling those plants to begin to produce a defensive chemical that repels aphids and attracts wasps, a natural aphid predator. Another study showed that diseased tomato plants also use the underground network of mycorrhizal filaments to warn healthy tomato plants, which then activate their defenses before being attacked themselves. The fungus becomes a telegraph system that helps plants communicate with each other and warn each other about a potential threat in the garden. That is truly amazing, and there is so much more that we have to learn.

There are more living organisms in a teaspoon of healthy soil than there are people on the earth. Over 6 billion plus of them. What's just as incredible is the variety and variation of organisms and species. Over one million different organisms (most of which remain unidentified) can be found in an acre of earth. Many of those organisms are important to human gut health. The incredible complexity of the gut and its importance to our overall health is a topic of increasing research in the medical community. Numerous studies in the past two decades have demonstrated links between gut health and the immune system, mood, mental health, autoimmune diseases, endocrine disorders, skin conditions, and cancer. The term "gut microbiome" refers specifically to the microorganisms living in your intestines, and a person has about 300 to 500 different species of bacteria in their digestive tract. While some microorganisms are harmful to our health, many are incredibly beneficial and even necessary to a healthy body. Since the immune system development is influenced by these microbes, studies show that growing up in microbe-rich environments, such as a traditional farm, can have protective health effects on children as it encourages immune development. They even affect brain processes, psychological health and wellbeing, and behavior.[73] These microbes can be "hitchhikers" in the food that we eat and water that we drink, but they originate from the environment, from the very soil beneath our feet. Our diet is an important source for these helpful microbes, and interaction with the soil, just digging in it with our hands in the garden, can be bring us into contact with them, which may improve the health of our gut.[74]

Urban living in a sanitized world, antibiotic overuse, and simple separation from the outdoors limits our exposure to these microbes and it's been shown that individuals who grow up in city environments have a less diverse gut microbiome. But on the farm today, poor land management practices and the use of chemicals have reduced soil microbial biodiversity there. Some studies have shown that urbanites are more prone to inflammatory disorders like diabetes and multiple sclerosis as well as allergic diseases such as asthma, but the full impact of the loss of diversity in the microbiome is not fully understood yet. Enough solid evidence suggests that soil biodiversity provides benefits to human health indirectly through suppression of soil-borne pathogens and exposure to soil microorganisms that improves our immune system. Working in a garden has more positive health benefits than we fully understand. Eating vegetables grown in microbe rich, healthy soils also shows benefits to our gut health and in turn, over all health.

Spraying chemical pesticides, herbicides and fungicides kills many helpful microbes and other larger living organisms in the soil, like earthworms. Adding organic matter back into the soil by composting and other means feeds these microbes and keeps the soil alive and healthy, and in turn, you too.

FIGHTING HER BATTLES

In the early spring of 2017, it happened. Plants started wilting before Melissa's eyes. The young onions and tomatoes that were just transplanted from plastic trays into the garden two weeks before were dying. So were several other vegetable rows that were direct seeded early in the spring. Melissa pulled plants up to look closely at the roots and there it was: a little white maggot chewing away at the seed and the soft delicate root base that sprouted from it. Her heart sank, and I could see the fear and sadness in her eyes when she told me about it. Hundreds of dollars in transplants, and hours of arduous work, about to be ruined and wasted. All the sudden, rows of crops and entire sections of the garden were now threatened by this little invader who seemed to come out of nowhere.

Like a scientist that all growers must become, Melissa quickly began her research to identify this little bug so that she might find an organic solution to the problem, if there was a solution. Melissa called out the representative from the farm extension office, talked to Jason Davis, and went by several gardening shops with samples in a plastic bag, until there was a consensus about what exactly this little bug was. It was the dreaded seed-corn maggot, a voracious and all-consuming pest. The result of years of growing corn and not rotating in other crops gave this little pest an opportunity to find a home and infiltrate the soil. Although it may have had 'corn' in its name, and corn seeds are a delicacy for this little creature, it wasn't really all that particular about what seed or root stem it ate, and it would and did attack most of the vegetable varieties that Melissa had planted.

Some conventional farmers might immediately spray the field with a toxic chemical that requires a special license to purchase and use (most conventional farmers have that license). The application of heavy chemicals like that requires protective gear, including coverings over your clothes and head, waterproof gloves and a mask. Using intense chemicals, part or most of the crop might be saved, assuming the problem was caught in an early stage. It basically kills on contact, and within a couple days the corn seed maggots are dead, along with just about every other living organism in the soil. The seedcorn maggot has natural predators that would be killed, including many species of spiders, wasps, beetles, dung flies, mites and ants that feed on the maggot eggs and larvae, which may create more problems in the future if they come back (so you have to keep spraying chemicals since you killed off the natural predators).

This is obviously not an option for the organic gardener. After her research, Melissa determined to use bugs to kill bugs, and ordered some little creatures called nematodes that arrived a few days later through the mail. They're so tiny that you can't see them, these nematodes, and Melissa mixed them with water and walked through the garden with a backpack sprayer to disperse them. These little bugs then search out and eat the corn seed maggots. I always find it curious how organic gardeners have figured out so many ways to get nature to fight your battles for you in the war against pests. And they have a lot of allies that can do the job. Melissa's little army of nematodes did a fair job saving some of the crop that year, but there was still a big reduction in yield. It's nothing new to an organic farmer. If it's not a bug or a fungus, it's deer, rabbits, ground hogs or other hungry animals out to ruin you.

DISRUPTION CAN BRING CHANGE

Community food security comes from a sustainable food system that enhances or maximizes self-reliance and social justice (so that all people can have access to it and can afford it). It's a place-based food system, or a sustainable community food system that improves the health of the community and the environment over the long term. It involves building the economic framework and strength of the local food system and building a localized farming and food network economy. It means having fair livable wages for local producers and processors so that they can continue to produce food for the community.

Having a self-reliant food system means that food is produced, processed, and controlled locally as much as possible. Food sources are multiple and must be varied, and community members need to be involved in the decision-making. And because unpredictable environmental, political and economic factors can greatly impact food systems, another important component to food security is the ability of a system to withstand and adapt to change or disturbance, such as climate change. Sometimes a disturbance or disruption can bring on necessary change for the good. The rapid rise of the grow local movement in Western North Carolina was brought on in some measure by a major disruption in farming in the region; the demise of big tobacco.

The Appalachian Sustainable Agriculture Project (ASAP) published a report in March of 2018 titled "The End of Tobacco and the Rise of Local Food in Western North Carolina."[75] Researchers analyzed Census of Agriculture data to understand and trace shifts in agriculture over a 15-year period, from 1997 to 2012, to determine what changes have taken place since the fall of big tobacco as a cash crop in the region. Tobacco had been the major cash crop for 20 Appalachian counties in the region because growers found it more profitable to grow it under a system of federal subsidies and price supports.

It seems crazy to us now that the federal government would subsidize a crop that would do so much damage to our national health and cause so many deaths, but it's not the first or last time. As noted already, the government is currently subsidizing corn that is sold cheaply now as high fructose corn syrup and causing serious health problems related to obesity, such as diabetes and heart disease. The financial supports for tobacco had effectively discouraged farm diversification in North Carolina and other places, but that all began to change in 1998 when the Master Settlement Agreement started holding tobacco companies accountable for tobacco-related medical expenses.

The ASAP report says that the tobacco industry took another hit in 2004 when the Fair and Equitable Tobacco Reform Act finally ended all federal support for tobacco growers and producers. As a result, the number of tobacco farms in nine Western North Carolina counties that were studied plummeted from 2707 to just 74 over those fifteen years between 1997 and 2012. Revenues from tobacco farming dropped from over $20 million to less than a million dollars over the same period.

ASAP was formed in large part to help these farmers find other crops and markets to sell to. Their mission from the beginning was to find ways to connect local people to farms and encourage the cultivation of more diverse crops like vegetables that could be sold into local and regional markets. A disruption in the farming status quo forced change in the region toward a more sustainable and resilient local food economy, and ASAP led the way. Is it possible to remove subsidies for corn processed into high fructose corn syrup? And what disruption might that cause?

CULTIVATING RESILIENCE

Local government officials need to understand how essential it is to support local food production for the health and security of their residents as the threat of climate change continues to grow. They need a long-term plan, 10 to 20 years out, and they need to start working on it now. Anything that can support local farms and food production must be considered, including the processing and local distribution systems. Figuring out ways to make local food production more cost effective and making sure that there are enough stores carrying this local food will build the necessary infrastructure and entrepreneur base to support a stronger local food base. Finding ways to encourage and promote local stores, restaurants and markets to feature local food will go a long way to help get it started. Looking for ways to conserve farm land, such as the agrihood concept, is also important, as well as encouraging food growing within any neighborhood or development. This also creates jobs and training in the farming sector.

Asheville's efforts to brand itself as a "beer city" and "Food-topia" focus on promoting local foods, local beer, local (non-chain) restaurants, and the food bounty of the region. City officials continue promote Asheville as a Foodtopia which is a very good initiative that helps build the necessary food infrastructure.

A resilient community needs to couple its natural resources and capital with an environmentally friendly approach to those resources to make certain they are sustainable for the long term. It needs to assume something will happen, and the lights won't always come on, so prepare for it. It needs to develop a focus from national dependency to local capacity, with a "learn as you go" mindset. You can't do everything at once, but a plan should be in place to ensure the community and the region is becoming more self-reliant in the basic needs of its citizens. It is a transition from imported to place-based resources, and it's a long, steady process to get there. It means adding redundancy and working towards a local economy where more resources and wealth stay within the community. It's a change in mindset from producing products to producing community assets and building more capacity at home for our basic needs. Laura Lengnick would add that it's a change in mindset that looks for opportunity in change and takes advantage of it. For instance, given the aging population of our farmers, we can take advantage of the fact that there has been a disconnection in transfer of farming between generations to teach the new generation of farmers sustainable practices. If they have been taught by the current generation of farmers, they would have learned conventional practices. We are not burdened with the task of retraining a generation of farmers – we can simply teach them how to farm using sustainable practices. That more resilient thought process puts a more positive and proactive spin on the problem of an aging farmer population.

At the other end of this logic, we should be asking ourselves, do we really need to import food just to save a few pennies? What are the risks and potential costs of doing this, and the threats of becoming dependent on it? The risks and threats of dependency far outweigh the cost savings for most of our basic food needs. But is local necessarily resilient? How big does the dome over your community have to be in order to eliminate the importing of resources or exporting of waste?

Bioregionalism is an ecosystem-based way to look at this question that was developed in the 1970's and 80's. Some researchers used the theory of bioregionalism as a way to divide the country up into smaller, self-sustaining regions. They suggested that each region of the country (or ecotype) will have its own ecosystems and water resources and will find its own way to manage them to support its residents, and many suggested that we could divide the nation by watersheds. State lines become irrelevant on their maps. They would put a theoretical dome over a water shed, one that might include the

Southeastern states of the US for example, and suggest that region work to building its own self-supporting infrastructure that is not dependent on national resources. Researchers would suggest then that food and other resources would be located closer to those who consume them, with less dependence on national or global inputs. Resilience thinking is newer but leans on some of the early ideas that came from bioregionalism.

By 2050, there will be an estimated 400 million people living in the US, and 70% of Americans will live in mega-metropolitan regions, say modern regional planners. Many of these metropolitan areas fall within differing watersheds already that could support that region.

However you break up or define different regions into self-sustaining units of the country, resilience is about developing the potential of available resources and the human capital to become stronger and more self-reliant at a more local level. It's a plan to approach sustainability and self-sufficiency. It means gaining a better understanding of ecological systems in the region, and taking an inventory of available resources, and finding a way to provide for all people in the region their basic human needs using those resources.

At a smaller scale, just below the regional level, we can build food security and resilience at the city and community level. To build more resilient communities, sustainable food supplies and local food systems should be on the agenda of every town council and city board in the country. Not just because food and food spaces relate to quality of life, but because it is life. Food systems need to be an integral part of long-term planning at the county and even township level. Local governments need to be key players in creating sustainable and resilient agriculture systems and the means to deliver that food to citizens. Cities should be supporting these new local food systems and food webs because they have a significant impact on health and security, which should be the primary concern of any local official.

Local governments can create impact by encouraging local food production and increasing access to markets. They can establish farmers markets in central and outlying areas of the city. They can try to encourage restaurants to buy and promote local food, along with the larger institutional buyers like schools and hospitals. All of this helps build an infrastructure that may be vitally important in the future.

There are a lot of ways to help the local food infrastructure, such as municipalities assisting with local food affordability (through SNAP-like programs) or supporting programs that distribute local food through financial or material donations, and several ways that haven't been thought of yet. Local food production and sustainable farming practices also help municipalities by reducing transportation and the amount of CO_2 emissions, thus improving air quality in the city. This, in turn, impacts the respiratory health of citizens and reduces the funds now spent on that health care. Additionally, it reduces a municipality's use of fossil fuels, a limited resource, providing a financial savings and reducing the overall burden on the energy infrastructure.

Protecting agricultural land while still allowing for growth will be the most difficult issue that cities and regions will have to deal with in coming years. Looking for ways to condense and manage growth within existing boundaries and the built environment will be the challenge, so that cities don't keep spreading out into valuable near-by farm land. New urban planning tools will be helpful, like defining areas for 'infill' and creating dense mixed-use projects with housing above retail shops and office space, which helps to contain sprawl and keep open land open for potential farming.

CHICKEN FROM CHINA

United States agriculture policies often move us away from food safety, security, and resilience. The U.S. Department of Agriculture, in July 2017, proposed a rule allowing China not only to send cooked chicken into the United States, as they have been, but also allow them to raise and slaughter the birds that it ships here. I need to ask again, "Do we really need to import chicken from China?" Are we losing food security and food safety, while at the same time we move away from resilience and self-reliance at the local and regional level?

In March of 2018, the Trump administration started negotiating a deal with China that would allow the US beef industry to export more beef to China with a reciprocal agreement to allow more cooked chicken to be imported into the US from China. Under current regulations, China may only export cooked chicken products to the United States and it will likely enter the US as chicken nuggets. And while those products can be processed and packaged in China, under current regulations the birds must be raised and slaughtered in Canada, Chile or the United States (why Chile?), then frozen and shipped over to China for processing. Those rules are based on long-standing concerns about China's poultry farming and slaughter operations, particularly regarding avian influenza.

Many question China's ability to enforce food safety standards given its poor track record. According to a May 2017 report by National Public Radio, that record includes rat meat being sold as lamb, oil recovered from drainage ditches in gutters being sold as cooking oil, and baby formula contaminated with melamine that sickened hundreds of thousands of babies and killed six. One Shanghai food-processing factory that supplied international restaurant brands was caught selling outdated meat, repackaged with new expiration dates.

Here's one truism from economics- you get what you pay for. Are we willing to take on more food risk to save a few pennies? Forget about local food resilience and keeping the capacity to produce food at home, are you willing to feed your children potentially unsafe food to save a few pennies or so that the US beef industry can sell more meat to China? No FDA inspectors, no US government oversight of the food factories for food safety and cleanliness, like here in the US. These are the kinds of decisions that are often being made for us by the government and the food industry.

When we become dependent on far-away places for our food, it leads to a cycle of dependence that's hard to break. It's hard to rebuild the infrastructure. One extreme example of this dependence is Haiti after the devastating 2010 earthquake. So much food aid flowed into Haiti, and for a long time after the quake, that it completely disrupted local farming on the island nation. Farmers couldn't compete with all the free grain and other food products coming into the country, and it put many of them out of business. Many gave up working the land and moved on to other businesses or means of income. While the immediate food aid was a good and necessary thing to save lives, prolonging the aid without helping farmers to grow their business again affected Haiti's recovery. The country found it more difficult to get back on its own feet and became dependent on the food aid.

If the United States becomes dependent on other countries for certain food types (like vegetables), we lose the infrastructure and capacity to produce that food type. The basic laws of economics tell us that price has a direct impact on sales. If the price on imported food is lower than domestic production than it will reduce demand for that domestic product. The reduced demand will result in lower production volumes on these goods as producers switch over to other products that promise higher prices and margins (or guaranteed subsidies, like corn). The reduction in overall capacity includes losing the necessary equipment and labor to plant, irrigate, harvest, process and distribute the product. Every country, and every region within those countries, needs to do whatever it can to build its own food producing capacity and infrastructure for the long-term food security of its people. Dependency is not security.

THE FOOD RESILIENCE AND SELF-RELIANCE OF ASHEVILLE

As an experiment, I wanted to see how big the dome would need to be over Asheville for it to become a truly resilient and self-reliant community, without any dependence on national or global inputs for our basic needs and survival. How big is that dome?

To recap from a previous chapter, researchers have analyzed the average American diet to determine how much land it would require to feed the average American. They came up with an average 20,000 square feet of land per person, or .45 acres, with the bulk of the land necessary for cattle and meat production. A vegan diet would require significantly less land at about 7000 square feet, or roughly one-sixth of an acre. More agriculturally intensive farming would require even less land.

Based on these numbers, Asheville, with a population of nearly 90,000 people would require 40,500 acres of farm land to support all its citizens if no food were imported into the city. Because most of the city of Asheville has been developed, and there's not much farm land left, and certainly not enough to support that population, we need to move our dome outside of the city limits.

Buncombe County has 253,000 residents and so would need 116,321 acres of farm land to support its food needs. It falls short with just 71,400 acres of farm land. According to the 2012 USDA census of agriculture, Buncombe County has 1060 farms that make up that 71,400 acres of land. However, 38% of what is considered farm land is actually woodland, leaving just 32% as pastureland and 24% as cropland. Taking out woodland, Buncombe County has just shy of 40,000 acres in pasture and cropland. That's a far cry from the 116,321 acres the county needs to produce all the food required to sustain its citizens. We must go a little farther out with our dome, beyond county lines.

While Buncombe County is roughly 35 miles wide and 25 miles in length north to south, by expanding our dome out to a 50-mile radius, with more rural and agricultural land available as we move away from the city, we would likely achieve a local, self-reliant status as far as food is concerned. Water resources easily fall within our 50-mile radius dome. But what about other necessities?

A coal fired power plant also falls within our dome, located on the south side of Asheville, so we'd have electricity, as long as we could import coal from West Virginia or other regions. Natural gas and petroleum products would still need to be imported. Unless we move our dome out to a larger regional area, it would be difficult for any community to become fully self-contained (fully resilient). The key would be to work towards local sustainable and renewable energy sources, like solar and wind, to become more self-reliant for the longer term. It would also be important to have some backup power source for emergency needs, like a stockpile of coal or natural gas, and plenty of fuel to run generators at the hospital, for instance.

At 65 miles out from the city center of Asheville are both a hydroelectric dam and a nuclear power plant, located across the border in South Carolina. So power is available at the larger regional level that isn't dependent upon importing coal from outside the region. Food, water and power are all within reach of a regional, resilient community with a diameter of 65 miles from the city center of Asheville. But unless we're all driving electric cars, we'll still be dependent on importing gasoline to get around. It's very difficult for a community to be fully resilient and self-reliant. But on the other hand, we don't really need to import chicken from China. We can at least work on feeding ourselves.

Looking at resilience from a national level, how can we build hundreds and even thousands of more self-reliant and resilient communities, at least where food, the basic necessity of life, is concerned? While there are profound social and environmental benefits to eating locally, can we as a nation actually do that, all of us eat locally? The popularity of the farm to table movement has skyrocketed but local food potential (the number of farms) has declined over the past 50 years. We covered up a lot of farm land under sprawling cities and suburbia. Given limited land resources, growing populations and mass suburbanization, can we still feed everyone locally?

While definitions of "local" vary widely, most in the grow local movement would consider a 100-mile radius as "local" food. Recent research shows how much potential remains for grow local on a national basis. One study found 90% of people could eat local and within 100 miles.[76] New farmland mapping research shows that most Americans could actually eat within a 50-mile radius.

Professor Elliot Campbell with the University of California Merced Department of Engineering used data from a farmland-mapping project funded by the National Science Foundation and information about land productivity from the U.S. Department of Agriculture. His research showed that most areas of the country could feed between 80 percent and 100 percent of their populations with food grown or raised within 50 miles.

Campbell's research looked at the farmland near every American city, and then estimated how many calories those farms could produce. By comparing the potential calorie production to the population of each city, the researchers found the percentage of the population that could be supported entirely by food grown in the region.

Large coastal cities would have to reach out to a larger region to feed its inhabitants. For example, the research shows that New York City could feed only 5 percent of its population within 50 miles but as much as 30 percent within 100 miles. New York would have to reach out to a couple hundred miles, into more rural areas, to feed most of its residents. The greater Los Angeles area could feed as much as 50 percent within 100 miles, so 200 miles would likely cover their needs.

Other conflicts, of course, would have to be resolved. For instance, water would have to be redirected from almond production in the central valley to water other crops in the LA region. New York would have to work out something with Philadelphia for available farm land as their radius encroaches on that city. But in theory, these cities could feed themselves within a larger dome of food production.

Campbell's research showed how diet can also make a difference. For example, local food around San Diego can support 35 percent of the people based on the average U.S. diet, but as much as 51 percent of the population if people switched to more plant-based diets.

Campbell's research would suggest that careful planning and policies are needed to protect farmland from suburbanization and to encourage local farming for the future, if we're to become more food resilient in our metropolitan areas. If there were ever a serious oil shortage, more serious than the OPEC oil embargo of the 1970's, then we need food closer to cities that doesn't require long distance transportation.

One important aspect of food sustainability and self-reliance is the ability of a region to recycle nutrients, water and energy. For example, if we used compost from cities to fertilize our farms, we would be less reliant on fossil-fuel-based fertilizers. Campbell says, "But cities must be close to farms so we can ship compost economically and environmentally. Our maps provide the foundation for discovering how recycling could work." His research might help to close the food-to-waste-to-food cycle, building another layer of resilience.

Why is resilience important? A changing climate, rogue states like North Korea, global terrorism, cyber-attack, take your pick, any of these could devastate the food network in the United States and in most first-world nations. Just as an exercise in resilience, imagine a large comet or meteorite hits the earth. It's about the size of the one that hit Siberia in 1908, causing the famous Tunguska Event. That air-burst explosion was equivalent to 10 to 15 megatons of TNT and is estimated to have been around 1,000 times greater than the energy released by the atomic bomb dropped on Hiroshima, Japan. The Tunguska Event flattened 2,000 square kilometers (770 square miles) of forest. Depending where it hit the United States today, it could disrupt oil, gas and electric supplies over vast regions of the country and seriously affect the distribution of food. Who do you think would be better off handling and surviving the event, the Americans living in 1908 when it hit, or the America of today? Almost all food was local back then. It was all organic also, by the way.

Independence and self-reliance are the key strengths and virtues of the American people, and this has been true from our very beginning as a nation, and it continues to show itself. Homesteading is the ultimate socially-acceptable expression of independence and self-reliance.

CHAPTER TEN

COURAGE

Homesteading is a lifestyle choice of self-sufficiency and trying to live "off the grid." It takes some courage to do that, to live by your own wits and labor. It usually means subsistence agriculture which would necessitate the knowledge and work of gardening, canning and food preservation. Many homesteaders build their own homes or natural buildings, and many pursue crafts or the small-scale production of textiles, clothing or other useful items that they can sell for cash when they need it. They usually try to find renewable energy sources including solar and wind power. Many try to grow heirloom vegetables and heritage livestock as another act of sustainability.

Some homesteaders come to this lifestyle after a successful career that afforded them the financial capability to buy land, build a home, and purchase necessary equipment, like solar panels, generators and farm equipment. A lot of young people come to Asheville these days with the hope and dream of homesteading themselves. They feel this intense desire for freedom and independence, and many of them want to become homesteaders because of what it represents, a self-reliant and sustainable lifestyle choice. What holds a lot of them back from pursuing this dream is the cost of land and the lack of the necessary knowledge and skills. Homesteading classes and workshops are offered on a regular basis by different groups in Asheville that teach some of these self-reliance and homesteading skills.

Modern homesteading doesn't just relate to rural living, but refers more to a lifestyle choice, and there is a big movement in urban homesteading right now. All you need is a backyard to grow some vegetables, cancel the cable, sell the car and take a bus when you need to go somewhere. A wood burning stove and a place to collect wood is helpful for these urban homesteaders. It's all about self-sustaining, self-reliance, and ultimately independence. And it can be done within city limits.

In line with this sense of independence and self-reliance, I wanted to see if my small farm could independently feed the same number of people that the average large-scale, conventional farmer feeds, or 129 people. If we all ate seasonally and relied on canned food for out-of-season goods like we did 100 years ago (and we wouldn't be flying in asparagus from Argentina in January or any beans from Chile) could we provide the necessary calories, vitamins and minerals required to sustain 129 people?

Our CSA program supports much of the vegetable needs for 80 households for about six months of the year, which comes to around 200 people. We offered cooking and canning classes so residents could learn and participate in canning beans and other produce for winter months, which could extend the food year. The bulk of the protein could come from legumes and the eggs from our 75 chickens, the number of which could easily be increased. We had enough cattle on 30 acres of pasture that would supplement some of the protein needs, assuming people cut back to what is probably a healthier intake of red meat, like the old days, or how meat is consumed in Europe, where it isn't expected with just about every meal. Meat-eaters require a lot more land than vegetarians, so I ran the numbers there.

A cow usually goes off to the meat processor at about 1200 pounds, and from that you get about 500 pounds of meat, off the bone and fat trimmed. If 129 people ate one pound of meat per person, per week (or about four "quarter-pounders" per week), one cow would last about a month. At that rate of consumption, we'd need to slaughter 12 cows in a year, and given the carrying capacity and birth rate of our pastures and existing herd of 20 cattle, that might be a strain. We'd probably have to cut down red meat intake to a half pound of meat per week, maybe a little more. The six pigs hanging out in the tree line would add about 1200 pounds of pork in a year. We would supplement protein with chicken eggs and legumes, and could add a flock of broiler chickens that would run on the pasture with the cows for another protein supply, which we've been thinking about anyway.

But to support our fictitious community of 129 people, we needed to increase carbohydrate production from corn and wheat, and rice in our climate was not a possibility.

The land had already been producing feed corn on 8 acres, and by switching that over to sweet corn we could have easily filled our caloric needs for 129 people. But it wasn't going to be that simple. We were letting our neighbor, Lynn Bonham, the dairy farmer down the road, continue to grow feed corn on that 8-acre parcel. She was a hard-working farmer and needed it and counted on it to support her dairy operation. I knew that she followed the best conservation practices, didn't overspray it with chemicals, used no-till methods and planted cover crops in the winter time to help replenish the soil. She cared about the soil, and never tilled or planted too close to stream and creek beds but left a swath of grass to limit any soil erosion.

Most of the milk Lynn's dairy produced went to a local processor and distributor in downtown Asheville to be eventually processed into milk, butter and cheese. I was surprised when I discovered where the milk processor was located, right downtown, and I felt pretty good about that. Lynn told me that she brings about 1000 pounds of milk to the processor every day, along with several other dairies in the county, but even with that our region was still considered "milk deficit", meaning we drink more milk here than we can produce. Lynn raised her dairy cows in a smaller operation with about 250 working dairy cows, and they did have access to pasture on a beautiful 120-acre farm she owned. It was close enough that I could walk there from my farm in about ten minutes, and I occasionally did to visit Lynn and check out her operation and her young calves. She usually kept another 200 young cows and calves that she was raising to take their place at the milking stations in the future.

I didn't want to take that 8 acres away Lynn who needed the feed corn to supplement the grass her cows were eating. Dairy cows need a lot of calories for their milk production, and I figured people like milk, cheese, yogurt and butter enough that it would be a valuable product from the farm, and certainly have caloric benefit. Theoretically I could trade the feed corn for dairy products in a three-way trade between me, Lynn and the local processor, just like the old days. So, I left it at that. We'd have butter, milk and cheese in our little self-reliant farming community.

After a little research I discovered that we might be able to squeeze in a winter wheat crop on that same 8-acre field that would provide a great deal of our grain needs for this fictitious community of 129. The crop could be made into bread or pasta and give us the carbs that we needed. We would plant in October and harvest in June, which would still allow Lynn to farm corn in the later summer months. She said she could still plant a 90-day corn in late June that she'd still be able to harvest in late September. A winter crop wasn't ever done in this area, summers aren't generally long enough and the climate in these mountains can get pretty cold. Usually feed corn farmers here like Lynn Bonham just plant a winter cover crop like wheat or barley to replace some nitrogen in the soil and prevent soil erosion during the winter months, but never harvest it. My little experiment in self-reliance would take more research.

BREAKING BREAD

The French ate bread as a staple in their diet for hundreds of years. Until the 19th century, it was the core staple in their diet that gave them the bulk of their necessary calories and filled the bellies of the working poor, and it took as much as 50 percent of their income. Bakers and bread making were so important in France that it was overseen by the local police. In fact, some historians suggest that one of the big underlying reasons for the French Revolution was a couple years of poor wheat harvests that led to a dramatic rise in bread prices. Some historians have suggested that the real start of the revolution was a Women's March in protest of the astronomical cost of bread for their families, and others who had other grievances against the government and the aristocracy joined in, later storming The Bastille.

During the bread famine, where bread prices rose to as much as 80 percent of the household income, and upon hearing about the uprising, Marie Antoinette supposedly said, "Let them eat cake." The phrase has been passed down to us but was probably not uttered by her. And the cake in question was really brioche, the rich man's bread made with eggs and butter, and the statement was used by others to show how disconnected and oblivious the aristocracy was to the suffering of the masses.

I didn't want to screw this up and have our CSA members coming at me with pitchforks and torches wanting to form a new CSA. With some research I discovered that there were a couple new wheat varieties that had been developed by scientists, hybrids, not a GMO, that could grow in the mountains of North Carolina. Being a hybrid, it was developed by crossing different varieties of wheat to gain the benefits of the genes from the different varieties. Crossing like this has been done for thousands of years, and it's not anything like the gene splicing done in modern labs to create an entirely new plant, a genetically modified organism.

I knew that we would need a way to process and grind the wheat to turn it into flour, and then someone to turn that flour into usable products like bread or pasta. So I actually went about the whole process backwards and started my research at a bakery. The whole idea in fact started at City Bakery in Fletcher, North Carolina, just outside of Asheville. I stopped by City Bakery one day in the spring of 2016 to meet with the owner, Brian Dennehy.

City Bakery produces bread for several wholesale accounts including Ingles grocery stores, the largest grocery store chain in western North Carolina, for other wholesale clients, and to supply bread to their own sandwich shops and restaurants in Asheville.

I went to ask Brian what he thought about baking bread from local wheat, something no one really did, yet, at least not at any scale from wheat grown right in the area. I wanted to see if he was willing to partner on a little experiment to see if together we could do it. I'd try to grow the wheat, and he'd see if he could make some decent bread with it.

He said right away that he'd be interested in trying it.

"It's going to take a lot of trial and error," he said, "there's a lot to figure out when it comes to getting the right taste and texture with different wheat flours and it may take us a while to get something good."

He didn't want to get my hopes up too much, so he said, "It might take days, maybe weeks, to figure out if we'll get something good from it." The moisture content, how the wheat reacts to different types of yeast, temperature, and a lot more went into it than I understood. It turns out that baking bread from a new variety of wheat was more difficult than I thought, but he was willing to give it a try.

Brian Dennehy is not the kind of guy that would make idle promises. He took over managing the wholesale baking operation for City Bakery, a business he and his father started several years ago as a sandwich shop that baked their own bread in the back. He's often covered in white flour when I see him, and he makes some of the best bread I've ever tasted. City Bakery is an institution in Asheville because Brian is obsessed with his art form and very critical of his products. To him, baking bread is part science and part art, and he takes it very seriously. He's a master of his craft, and I knew that if anyone could turn the wheat from my field into good, wholesome bread, he could do it.

Growing the right variety of wheat, Brian told me, was very important for bread making. He didn't know of anyone growing wheat in this area for anything other than a winter cover crop, but he suggested that I go see a gal named Jennifer Lapidus at a local company called Carolina Ground.

Carolina Ground, I soon discovered, was way ahead of me and my little project. Jennifer made a business of grinding wheat for local bakeries in a small space on the west side of Asheville. Jennifer describes her business as a milling facility devoted to grains grown in the South. It's all about locally ground bread flour, pastry flour, and rye flour, and her goal is closing the gap between the farmer and baker. Most of the flour she grinds comes from around the state of North Carolina, and some comes from nearby regions of South Carolina and Georgia, but nothing came to her from the immediate region here in Asheville or the higher elevations of Western North Carolina.

Jennifer owns a 48" stone-burr gristmill, built by Osttiroler, (a small family-owned business in Austria) that uses an ancient technology of stone grinding where the germ is crushed into the endosperm, spreading its oils and imparting both flavor and nutrients into the end product. Whereas most modern mills employ roller mill technology that tends to strip away and separate out the bran from the germ and endosperm, this mill rotates slowly in a process known as cold stone milling which helps to preserve the nutrients and integrity of the end product, the flour. Although roller mills mass produce flour with greater efficiency and a very long shelf life, cold stone milling produces flour with more flavor and nutrients and a shorter shelf life.

I must say that I loved the idea that she was there- Jennifer and this small business. Here was a major asset to community resilience, someone who could grind wheat, and I would not have known that she even existed had I not started this crazy experiment. Jennifer and Carolina Ground are the kind of capital (human and mechanical) that all communities need.

When I asked Jennifer if she could grind some wheat for me, she said that she was willing to give it a try, and there it was, I had my local mill to grind the wheat. Continuing to work backwards, I called Dr. Jeanine Davis, an extension specialist and researcher in the Department of Horticultural Science at North Carolina State University. I'd met her a couple of times because she worked at the Mountain Horticultural Crops Research and Extension Center near Asheville. I wanted to see if she knew of any wheat varieties that would grow well in this mountain region. She didn't, but she directed me to speak with another scientist who she had heard had developed a couple new wheat varieties that looked promising for our area. His name was Dr. David Martin, and in a collaboration between the U.S. Department of Agriculture and North Carolina State University, he had developed two wheat varieties that I might try.

I reached out to Dr. Martin and discovered that indeed he had helped to develop two new varieties that were both fairly resistant to a fungus that has devastated wheat fields for years and showed some promise in the eastern parts of North Carolina. He believed they might be hardy enough to grow up in the mountains where I wanted to plant it. These new varieties he called Nu East and Carolina White.

"They're hardy and I think can stand the climate in the western mountains of North Carolina and should be good in length of days and the amount of rainfall," Dr. Martin told me. Asheville is in a region considered a sub-tropical rain forest climate. He confirmed these varieties were hybrids, not GMOs, and born by breeders using age-old cross-breeding techniques.

When I asked David where I might find these two varieties of seed, he said, "Try Foundation Seed in Raleigh, they might have it. But it's still a new seed, and there's not a lot of it around." David told me breeders create new varieties of seed through a lot of trial and error.

"Trying to get the right traits to cross over between different varieties that are desirable is not an easy process. And whether that is heat or drought resistance, or resistance to a fungus, it takes time." David continued, "Then after a new hybrid is developed, it usually goes to testing in the field, where different farmers will plant acreage of it under contract with the USDA or a different research institution to find out how it does on a larger scale and in order to grow more seed."

David went on to tell me that if it passes this field test and shows the desired traits and a good yield, it becomes 'foundation seed', where it is grown again for production seed and larger distribution. Eventually it becomes certified seed and is distributed more broadly through seed supply houses.

Before we got off the phone, David had one warning for me.

"The moisture content had to be just right when you harvest." He continued, "It has to be right at 17%, no more. If you're ready for harvest, and it rains on you, the seeds might germinate, and your crop is ruined."

That was not an encouraging thing to say at the end. I had no clue what I was doing. Now I had to worry about crop failure on this magnitude; hours of work and thousands of dollars washed away with one ill-timed rain? Man, farmers are brave, I thought.

I contacted Foundation Seed outside of Raleigh and found that they did have some of both kinds of seeds that I wanted to try, Nu East and Carolina White. They were in fact the only seed house that had it in the state, and perhaps anywhere. I ordered nine fifty-pound bags of each, based on their suggestion for proper coverage on 8 acres. Melissa was excited to try this little experiment and jumped in the truck and drove the 10 hours round trip to pick it up. It was early October, and Lynn Bonham had already brought in her corn. Within a week she sent one of her helpers over with her tractor and a drill seeder, and we had the wheat in the ground in about four hours. Now it was all up to nature and the weather.

I ran the numbers. If everything went well, and the weather cooperated, and the fungus stayed away, we might get as many as 50 bushels of wheat per acre, which is the national average. Some regions average 80 bushels per acre. That meant our eight acres might produce 400 bushels of wheat. One bushel of wheat produces 90 pounds of wheat flour, which makes 90 one-pound loaves of wheat bread. Ninety loaves of bread times 400 bushels of wheat come to a whopping 36,000 loaves of bread from that little 8-acre parcel of land.

Divide that 36,000 loaves of bread by 365 days in a year, and you get about 98 loaves of bread per day. Brian could easily bake that much bread every day, and a lot more, and it might be enough to feed the 129 people in my little experiment. That is if people ate bread as a staple like the French did in the 1800's.

So it was possible, in theory, for one or two farmers to grow enough food on a small scale to give 129 people their daily intake of grain and carbohydrates, vegetables, and protein, and if I traded some feed corn right, they might get some milk, butter and cheese. All produced from within a 10-mile radius of the farm.

In April of 2018 the wheat was looking just OK, but a little short and thin in some spots. Because the field had been in corn for so long, it needed fertilizer. It didn't all come in, and there were bald patches and spots where some weeds were taking over. Then in May, the rains came. Asheville had the wettest May on record. The rains had flooded large areas of the field and there were more dead patches. Lynn had lost about 50 acres of corn in a field that she planted down by the French Broad River. Many farmers in the area took a bigger hit than that. When mid-June came around, the wheat field looked worse. We started to wonder if it was even worth it to bring in the combine to harvest the wheat. The time, cost and expense of the combine was becoming harder to justify. And I was holding up Lynn and her 90-day corn in that field because of my little failing experiment. Her loss of 50 acres of needed corn because of the floods made it even worse, and I felt bad for her, and so I decided to give up this year. I called her and told her to go ahead and plant her corn. But I did ask her to save a couple rows of wheat that were doing better along the edge of the field, near the tree line. It probably came to about a half-acre of wheat.

In mid-July when the weather was dry, I went after that wheat with a weed wacker. I didn't have an old-fashioned sickle, so I may be the first person in human history to harvest wheat with a weed wacker (technically a gas powered 'string trimmer'). Who needs a million dollar combine when you can say "I farm with a weed wacker." It just sounds cool and tough, like you do things the hard way BECAUSE it's hard, like chopping down a tree with an axe instead of a chain saw. I didn't even harvest all the wheat, but I wasn't quite ready to give up completely, so I laid out what I cut to dry for a few days. After it dried some, I thought I might have an old-time threshing party, but I was afraid no one would show up, so I threw out a large plastic tarp and started beating the wheat against the ground and the tarp to loosen the seeds.

I guess by now you're probably wondering how far this stubborn idiot is going to go with this whole thing. Well, that's about as far as I could go. I didn't want to give up, but this was getting ridiculous. What was I going to do, bring a couple buckets of wheat seed to Jennifer so she could grind it, and then ask Brian to bake me a half loaf? I determined that it was about a $2000 loss and left it at that. I learned an important lesson about crop failure, and as farming goes, I got out of it pretty easy. So much for my grand scheme of 36,000 loaves of bread.

Oh well, let them eat cake.

THE FOOD PRODUCING CAPACITY OF CREEKSIDE FARM

If I had harvested the wheat, I may have had one-third the expected yield from that eight acres, which still would have been a fair amount of wheat to produce a decent share of calories. Because the field had been in corn for so long, it really needed fertilizer which would have greatly improved the yield. I tried going without the chemicals, and it hurt my yield. It would take years to build up the soil nutrients properly using organic methods to really get a good yield of wheat, but at least I knew we could grow these two varieties, they were certainly hardy enough for our climate and would have done better without the record rain in May.

I went back to the drawing board to see how we could increase caloric production on the farm in order to really break the chains of the industrial food complex. Adjacent to the corn field is the 10-acre upper pasture that we rotated cattle on. It occurred to me that if we concentrated cattle production on the lower 20 acres and limited the herd to 20 cows, it would free up that pasture for more food production. We'd have to supplement the cattle in the winter time with hay from another farm, but we could grow a lot more calories on that 10 acres. We could easily plant sweet corn on five acres and potatoes on the other five, both of which grow well in our climate. With a winter wheat crop properly managed, the addition of sweet corn and potatoes would give us plenty of calories to feed our fictitious community of 129, since both are very high in the calorie department. Recall from an earlier chapter that both corn and potatoes yield about 15 million calories per acre, and since every human needs about 1 million calories per year, one acre would feed 15 people. Times that by ten acres, and you feed 150 people the bulk of their basic calorie requirements. The good news is that these calories could be grown with very little extra labor, since corn and potatoes could all be grown with machine equipment including a tractor and a drill seeder, and for harvesting a combine and a potato ripper (borrowed from a neighbor).

So theoretically, growing vegetables on six acres, corn and potatoes on ten acres, winter wheat on eight acres (rotated with Lynn's feed corn), and running cattle on twenty acres, we could feed a community of 150 people, which is slightly higher than the number of people the average farmer feeds (using conventional farming methods). And while the average farmer is monocropping one plant variety, our residents would have wheat, corn and potatoes as a staple, a wide range of vegetables for vitamins and minerals, with some meat, butter, cheese, milk and eggs to boot. Obviously, we'd have to relearn the old ways of milling, drying and storing grain, and canning produce for winter. But the production capacity was there at the farm to feed at least 150 people.

Understanding the calorie requirements for humans and the caloric yield of a few key crops seemed like a good way to determine how many people we could feed a balanced diet from the farm. And if 150 people is the number, then I can relate that back to my earlier discussion in Chapter Two about how much land a developer should set aside to feed everyone in an agrihood. My numbers would say 45 acres could feed 150 people a balanced diet, including some meat, so slightly less than one-third of an acre per person. With the average U.S. household at 2.54 people, the developer would need to set aside roughly three-quarters of an acre per household for farming operations, which conveniently falls between our previously determined minimum of one-quarter acre and the goal of one acre set aside for farming in an agrihood.

But back to wheat, where we started. It's become clear to me in this little experiment that we're not completely dependent on the massive farms monocropping one variety of wheat on thousand-acre tracts. We can grow different varieties of wheat locally on small plots of land in a lot more places. We can change the rules of the game and become a little more self-reliant when it comes to our daily bread. And let's not forget about pasta! I love pasta, and so I'm not giving up on wheat. I'm planting it again, and maybe we'll have better luck next year. But I think this hyper-local wheat thing is a growing trend, and as it turns out, many small farmers are trying different varieties on small plots of land all across the United States and Europe especially. Small farmers and breeders are bringing back heirloom varieties of wheat with traits that offer promise in various climates and regions, and they're creating a whole new paradigm for wheat. Artisan millers and bakers will be able to take these specialty wheat varieties and make craft breads and pastas that are unique and flavorful, truly enhancing the grow local movement with local grains from local farms. I think that's where it's going, and this local food thing isn't just about produce, meat, eggs, and dairy, it'll include local wheat for bread and pasta. It may take a little while longer, but we'll figure it out.

Jason Davis probably farms more land than anyone in Western North Carolina, and it's a small amount of land compared to the thousands of acres that a farmer in Illinois or Iowa farms. He owns 100 acres himself but leases another 1500 hundred acres from small farms scattered throughout two counties, and many of the parcels he farms are tiny five- and 10-acre plots of land. It might take him longer to drive his combine down a country road to get to a small parcel of land than it does to harvest the crop off it. Last summer he planted a four-acre patch of soybeans on my farm, but he harvested about 175 bushels of soybeans off the land and he was satisfied with that.

Jason employs a lot of young men and women to help him with his expansive operation. He grew celery on 300 acres under contract for a grocery store chain for the last couple of years and was the first farmer in the county to grow that cash crop in our region on that kind of scale. He also grows a lot of tomatoes and strawberries under contract. Jason says he doesn't plant anything unless he's already got a contract for it with a buyer. He grew soybeans and corn on a few other leased properties and raised over 200 hundred head of cattle on various pastures throughout southern Buncombe and northern Henderson counties. This is what it takes to make a decent living off farming in this area; varied and scattered crops over a broad area.

Over half the farms in Buncombe County are between 10-49 acres in size, with the overall average size of a farm at just 67 acres. Small farms constitute about 88 percent of all farms out there across the US and grow about 20 percent of the food sales.[77] That's one-fifth of food sales right now coming off small farms in the US.

The market value of products sold from small farms in Buncombe County rose significantly from 2007 to 2012, from $37 million to over $54 million, or an increase of 46%. This is due in large part to the increase in local direct food sales in the region where the farmer takes home a larger portion of the sale. The average per farm revenue rose from $34,578 to $51,333 over this five-year period (this is revenue, not net income after expenses). The grow local movement is definitely having an impact on small farm sales in our region. Still, when you add up the input costs of seed, fertilizers, petroleum, and labor, there's not much profit left for the average farmer in Buncombe County. Jason Davis grows commercially on a larger scale and sells mostly wholesale and probably does better than most Buncombe County farmers.

Jason is a stout man about 40 years old, and he's a good man. He was brought up right, and you could tell right off that his parents raised him to be considerate and polite to the people he meets. His demeanor is always courteous and professional, and he always says "Sir", as in "Yes Sir" or "No Sir". I've asked him to call me Bob a few times, but he still says "Mr. Turner".

His young son is being raised the same way, and he calls me "sir" and says "yes sir" and "no sir" to everyone he meets. Jason's son Harrison looks exactly like you'd expect a young farm boy to look: stout for a 10-year-old, round face, blond hair and a crew cut. He wears jeans and a short sleeve, button down shirt with the requisite checkered pattern.

When I first met young Harrison, he was driving a large tractor and pulling a huge hay rake onto my farm. He was following his dad who was driving another large tractor pulling a hay bailer. When I first laid eyes on him, I couldn't believe that this little kid was driving this huge tractor.

They set right to work, and Harrison circled a ten-acre parcel in our upper pasture and raked the cut and scattered grass into straight rows with the big rake. His father followed with the bailer scooping up the rows in the front and stopping every few minutes to dump a roll of hay five-feet round out the back.

After about an hour and a half they had bailed the entire field and stopped to chat for a minute before they went on to another field a mile or so down the road. I spoke to Harrison.

"You sure do handle that big rig pretty well. How long you been driving that thing?"

"I've been driving this one since I was little. It's pretty easy." His round face lit up with a proud smile.

"We've been bailing hay since seven o'clock this morning. My dad got me up at 6:30 and we started right after breakfast." He wanted me to know that. It was now getting to be about three o'clock in the afternoon, and they were heading on to another place, and maybe two more if they could get to it.

"You are a hard-working young man," I said, "Just like your father." His face lit up again with another big smile.

I ran into Harrison again about a month later during the ASAP farm tour. The Appalachian Sustainable Agriculture Project runs an annual farm tour every year, and participating local farmers open up their farms for a weekend so that visitors can stop by and learn about the farm and what they grow. ASAP publishes a map of participating farms around the county and promotes the event to get people involved in the grow local movement, famers markets and CSA programs.

My wife and I visited several farms that weekend and made a point to stop by North River Farms to say hello to Jason and his crew. When we pulled up, Harrison was sitting at a table where people would sign in as visitors. We recognized each other right away and I spoke to him again.

"Hey Harrison, I'm thinking about getting a bigger John Deere like the one you got." I was thinking about it. Harrison lit up again with a big smile.

"What you want is the M series," he replied. "C'mon, I'll show you."

He jumped up and ran toward some tractors that I could see lined up next to a large metal building. His mom who was sitting at the table raised her eyebrows and probably wondered how Harrison happened to have my acquaintance. I quickly introduced myself and followed Harrison over to where the tractors were lined up in a row.

It turns out Harrison is the best tractor salesman I've ever met. He jumped on and off the tractor, showing me levers and switches and gears, and went about showing me the differences between the M series and the E series, and the specific reasons why the one was better than the other.

"A lot more power for one. And it comes standard with hydraulic hose connections up front," he said. Half the time I didn't know exactly what he was talking about, and this kid was 10 years old.

After sufficiently convincing me that the M Series 5058 was the tractor I wanted, I asked Harrison if he wanted to be a farmer like his dad.

"Yes sir, you bet" he replied.

I could see Harrison's father making his way back to the barn towing a large hay wagon full of farm visitors. He'd been taking people on a tour of the farm and showing them how they were growing celery and some of the other vegetables. As he pulled up to the barn, the farm tour visitors all jumped off the trailer and shook his hand and thanked him for the tour. Jason saw me and my wife over talking with Harrison and came over to greet us.

After some small talk and praising Harrison for being such a terrific salesman, I asked Jason how he kept track of his far-flung operation. I had already seen many of the fields and crops he had scattered around the county. With fields all over the place and different types of crops coming in all the time, different things that needed to get done at different times, "How did he stay organized?"

Standing with him for a few moments, I started to get an

idea. He wore two different radios and a cell phone on his belt. One radio – for the local volunteer fire department – was beeping while another one squawked. Garbled voices came through from a field way off somewhere else in the county. Jason would answer with "bring that over to the south field and pick up the spreader" or "head over to Mills River and give Josh a hand." Jason is one of the few, larger scale conventional farmers left in our region of the country, and I feel privileged to know him. He can grow food on a much larger scale and feed a lot more people than I can. It's different farming than our little CSA operation, or small local growers like us producing organic food on one to five acres of land. Jason uses big tractors, and big equipment like combine harvesters and large trucks to haul all that food. And he has several large barns and metal buildings to store it all.

Jason uses a migrant labor force when he has to for the more labor intensive and temporary projects like staking tomatoes in the spring, and it's the same group of people that come through at the same time every year as they make their rounds and follow the planting and harvesting seasons as far north as Michigan. He knows most of these workers by name and considers them friends and partners, and Jason says they can stake five acres of tomatoes in just a couple days because they're very experienced and good at what they do. Jason's farm is one of the many American farms still growing tomatoes that make up the 43% of tomatoes still grown in this country (reminder – 57% of the tomatoes consumed here are grown in another country). He's a big-time producer in our area, and my farm is the little guy supplementing on the edges of the food chain. I'm OK with that, and I'm just glad he's my neighbor—someone who can still grow food locally at a larger scale.

A year before, when I asked Jason if he'd like to put some cattle on my land, Jason said, "Yes sir. I never turn down land.

It's getting harder to find." Short, straight answers revealed the no-nonsense mindset of an efficient, effective manager. The deal was done that quickly.

The week after that conversation, Jason arrived at the farm with his livestock manager, Josh, to look at the land and fencing. We had barbed wire in place and Jason thought it would be a good idea to add a line of electric wire as an extra precaution. Josh came back a few days later with a crew of four guys and they ran an electric wire around the whole perimeter of the 30-acre pasture.

A week later, Jason and Josh returned with a trailer full of eight cows and two calves, and a second trailer with a bull named Big John. The cows that didn't have calves were pregnant, so I learned that our little farm was going to become a nursery for a while. Kara was thrilled.

We wanted a few cattle of our own, and Josh helped us to find a couple cow-calf pairs we could use to start our own heard. Josh also helped us to find a couple miniature donkeys to go with them. Within a year, our momma cows gave birth to another set of calves, so we had six cows of our own, and Jason's cows gave birth to another five calves, and the herd had quickly grown to 21 head in a years' time.

Jason stopped by our farm one afternoon to check on the cattle, and as we walked the pasture I asked him about how he manages all the risk of farming. He has a lot of money going out there every spring, and his payroll of ten full-time employees and more part-time must be a tremendous burden for a small farmer. He has to make payroll every week, plus all the costs of seed, fuel and supplies, and he won't see any revenue coming in until the summer and fall. Money going out all year, with money only coming in for a brief period. It takes a brave man to manage all that risk.

"Well Mr. Turner, I pray a lot," he said and smiled. "It can be a pretty nerve-racking experience, and we're just crazy busy in the summer trying to keep up with everything. I just try to stay organized." Then he said, "The timing on the rain can wreak havoc on us when we need to get crops in, so luck plays into it some."

NATURAL DISASTERS

Natural disasters are a constant threat to a farmer in Western North Carolina, particularly heavy rains and flooding off the mountains. In the fall of 2017 we had rains that wouldn't stop. It rained for three days until the ground was so saturated it couldn't take any more. Then the heavy rains started.

It came down hard and heavy for hours. Water ran swiftly down from the mountains and the hillsides around Walnut Cove and into already swollen creeks and streams. The water rushed into the Spain Branch and other tributaries and from there into Avery Creek.

Avery Creek is normally about twelve feet wide in most parts, and a foot or so deep. In some parts where it widens a bit, it might be just a few inches deep. But on this day the water rose so quickly, taking up all the water from mountains all around us, that it became a raging river more than ten feet high and broke over its banks and across my bottom pasture. It was 50-yards wide and running fast across the entire bottom field, bringing with it branches and tree stumps and old tires and anything else it could pick up on its way down the mountain.

The cows of course were smart enough to get to higher ground, but the logs and stumps that the river carried with it across the pasture tore up the barb wire fencing and completely took it out in places.

Within a couple hours the heavy rains let up some and Avery Creek started to subside so that I could get out into the field to check out the damage. Just then two pickup trucks pulled into the pasture, and Jason, Josh and a couple other guys got out. The cavalry had arrived. They knew my pasture would be susceptible to flooding and fence damage after such a heavy rain because Avery Creek ran along its entire northern edge. I didn't call them, they just showed up. Before they arrived, I was just standing there completely at a loss where to even begin, and I couldn't have handled it without them. I didn't have the skills or the knowledge to handle this by myself (I'm the guy who farms with a weed wacker).

Josh was the fencing expert. He had been out to the farm many times and he knew the land. As dusk fell, darkness was approaching fast, and clouds were hanging so low over the field that I could almost reach up and touch them. The fence was completely washed out in two places, where the creek came in and where it went out, and snarls of barbed wire littered the ground. Heavy metal t-posts were pulled out and twisted and would need to be replaced. Much of the river bank had washed out and debris was everywhere. We just needed to worry about getting a fence up to hold the cattle for tonight. Then the rain started again.

Josh had crossed the fast-moving creek several times back and forth by walking across a large tree that had fallen across the creek. It was a brave act. If he fell in, he'd get washed downstream quickly. After four hours in the dark and the rain, the fencing was replaced or repaired, and the pasture was secure again. Josh would come back in the morning to try to get the electric wire strand back on and working, but for tonight anyway, the cows weren't going anywhere. I shook hands with all the men and thanked them for the help, and they jumped in their trucks and drove away. Seeing them work with such efficiency, speed, and determination sent home a message for me: farming is hard work at all hours of the day, and if you want to make a career of it, be prepared to put in some grueling, muddy nights. But as bad as the experience was, I know also that I was extremely lucky.

This same story of the flood played out thousands of times on farms across North Carolina in September of 2018. Then hurricane Florence stalled out over the state and dumped record-breaking rains and terrible floods across a wide region. The loss of crops and livestock in the eastern portion of North Carolina was devastating to farmers, not to mention the terrible loss of human life. Just two years prior to Florence, in early October of 2016, hurricane Matthew inundated the eastern portion of North Carolina with massive flooding that took its toll on humans, farmers and livestock. This is our story in North Carolina, and the past few years have been very tough on farmers here. But there is clear evidence that violent storms and record heat are becoming more frequent and much more severe around the world. Scientists are convinced that its all related to global warming.

Global warming and the threats of flood, heat or drought are bringing some unwanted anxiety to farmers and a lot more people, and recent studies show that it's starting to have a negative effect on our overall psychological wellbeing as a nation. Numerous academic papers are now being published on the psychological toll that climate change exercises on our mental health; and the American Psychological Association recently described the term "eco-anxiety" as a clinically legitimate diagnosis.[78]

The research suggests that our psychological wellbeing is in some proportion related to climate change and extreme weather, such as heat, floods, hurricanes, fires and droughts, all of which are progressively becoming the norm. It's starting to create a lot of worry and anxiety for a lot of people, not just farmers. It takes a great deal of courage for a farmer to carry on in the face of these growing threats.

A CONVENTIONAL FARMER IN MISSOURI

While young Harrison had been driving tractors since before his feet could reach the pedals, when he sat in his Dad's lap to drive, the first time I did any work on a farm wasn't until I was 24 years old.

My first real job out of college was as a book salesman, and I called on bookstores for about two dozen small independent book publishers. I moved to St. Louis to take the job and had Missouri, Kansas and Southern Illinois as my territory, and I had more than one hundred bookstore accounts to call on and sell books to every season, twice a year. This was in the days before the internet put a lot of independent bookstores out of business. I'd carry in my big leather case full of the new book catalogs from the publishers, and I'd point out the new releases for the upcoming season and write down their orders for the new titles. What else is an English literature major going to do for a living?

When I was still new to my territory, I scheduled a sales call at a bookstore in Kirksville, Missouri, way up in the northern part of the state. Traveling salesmen always try to schedule their appointments in a big loop, so over the course of the week they can work their way out and back home and limit the driving between accounts. It turned out that Kirksville, Missouri isn't on the way to anywhere. It meant I had to dead head out to Kirksville and back for one appointment, about four hours driving each way, and there were no interstates to get there; it was going to be two-lane roads all the way, which meant a good chance of getting stuck behind a truck for miles.

I left early, before 6am, so that I could make it to the bookstore by 10am. Appointments usually took about 2 hours, sometimes more, but this one ended in less than an hour. The book buyer didn't buy anything. Nothing. Big goose egg. Not one book.

That was unusual for me. Usually I sold something. I represented publishers like Andrews and McMeel Publishing, who produced The Far Side books and Calvin and Hobbes comic strip books. I had Rand McNally, who created maps and atlases, and given there was no GPS or smartphone back then to tell you where to go, you found your way around the old-fashioned way: looking at a paper map or road atlas and trying to judge distances from the scale at the bottom. Maps were pretty good sellers.

But I got nothing on this sales call. Couldn't even pay my gas bill. I got back in the car and headed back to St. Louis and began to stew. As salesmen get older and a little wiser, they learn to take moments like this in stride and don't let it bother them too much. You take the good with the bad. Of course, I was still new and living closer to the edge and struggling to make the car payments. I regret it now, but I was stewing as I left Kirksville and kept asking myself why the heck I drove all the way up there in the first place. My butt was still sore from the drive up there and I wasn't looking forward to another four hours back in the car.

Just a few miles outside of Kirksville, still stewing, I caught an image out of the corner of my eye from the side window. It was just a blur of an image as I flew by at 60 miles an hour on this two-lane road in rural Missouri. It was a snapshot of an older lady sitting on a tractor with a big bonnet on her head. Behind her, she was pulling an old flatbed trailer with some bales of hay on it, and behind that, was an older guy in overalls bending over to pick up a square bale of hay.

I kept going for about a half a mile, and then suddenly something popped into my head and I don't know where it came from, and I said to myself, out loud, "I'm going to go help that son of a gun!" I felt trapped in the car and needed to get out. Without giving it another thought, I turned around at the next driveway, and headed back to the farm. I pulled into the gravel driveway that ran along the field where the old couple were working and parked the car half-way up the drive. I got out and started walking toward them in the middle of the field. I was wearing a nice dress shirt, khaki pants, and dress shoes as I stepped out into field.

The old couple had seen me pull in, and she stopped the tractor. The old farmer just stood there, and they both looked at me intently, and I know what they were thinking. "He must be from the bank."

As I got closer to them, I started thinking, "What the heck am I doing? These people are going to think I'm nuts." When I got about 20 yards from them, I picked up a bale of hay and walked over to the trailer, and said, "Hi, I just wanted to get out of the car for a while, so I thought I would come help you for a bit," and I tossed the bale up onto the trailer. The old guy stood there like I was speaking French. It didn't register.

I quickly went and grabbed another bale and tossed it on the trailer, and they both just sat and stood there dumb-founded. So I said, "I've been in the car for a few hours today, and I've never worked on a farm before, so here I am, free labor." I walked over to the old guy and put my hand out and said, "My names Bob".

The old guy realized that I wasn't from the bank after all, but still confused, he reached out his hand and said, "I'm George." He looked over at the gal on the tractor and said, "that's Helen." I said, "Hello Helen, nice to meet you." She smiled a curious smile, and I turned to grab another bale of hay.

George continued looking at her for a moment in a questioning manner, finally shrugged his shoulders, and turned to grab a bale himself. Helen fired up the tractor, and put it in gear, and began crawling through the field again. Within a few minutes, George and I started having to wait for Helen, so he told her she could speed up a little, which she did.

After a short while we were running out of places to throw the hay up on the trailer, so George asked Helen to stop while he climbed up on the trailer and started stacking up the bales toward the front of it. I walked to grab a few more bales while he did that, and when he was done stacking, I said, "George, why don't you just stay up there and I'll toss them to you?" I was a real farmer now. I had figured this out already, and now I was even giving instructions.

He stayed up on the trailer and I kept tossing him bales as Helen drove through the field and we were making progress! I was younger and in better shape than I am now, but the pace Helen was going at was not sustainable for one guy now, and I finally said, "Whoa, whoa, whoa, Helen! You trying to kill me?" She looked back at me, and smiled, and pulled back on the throttle a little.

George and I made some small talk as we made our way through the field, and I learned the difference between hay and straw. I must have called these bales of straw, because George corrected me and said this is hay, and he told me, "Hay is tall grass. It's what animals eat in the winter time." He'd store these bales of hay to feed to his cows next winter, but "straw is just the stems left over after you harvest things like wheat and barley.''. He said he used bales of straw as bedding for his cows and chickens. The animals didn't eat straw, and there was no real nutritional benefit from it.

George must have thought that I was a real city boy because I didn't even know the difference between hay and straw. It must have given him a chuckle. We talked a little about the farm while we worked, and I asked if it was very profitable running a farm. George said it was difficult for most farmers in this area to make any real profit at it, and many of his neighbors worked second jobs to sustain their families. George said that he drove a school bus to supplement his income on the farm.

After about two and a half hours, we had cleared most of that field, and the trailer was full, and George asked Helen to stop the tractor. It was getting close to 2 o'clock, and George said that he would have to leave soon to drive his school bus.

I brushed off the hay from my dress pants and looked out on the field with a sense of pride, and I knew that what we had just done, the three of us with our little system of driving and tossing and stacking, would have taken this older couple most of the day and probably most of tomorrow by themselves. And without saying anything, I knew they were still in shock about this stranger coming out of nowhere to help them, this city boy, and I knew also that they were grateful. Helen asked if I'd like to go up to the porch for a glass of lemonade.

We sat on the porch drinking some cool lemonade, which I remember tasted wonderful and washed down some of the hay dust that had been collecting in my throat. I told them about how my day started, and how I didn't sell any books, and Helen said, "that was a shame." They told me a little more about the farm and about their two kids who found jobs in Kansas City and Columbia, Missouri.

As we sat there chatting, I began to learn what modern, conventional farming was all about, and how financially difficult it had become for farmers to make a living at it. I was young and starting out in business for myself and asked George personal financial questions about how profitable this farm business was, which was probably impolite, but he was kind enough to answer them.

George told me about how it takes a lot of capital intensive inputs and some serious risk to run a farm business. George had a couple tractors that were much bigger than my little 5085 M Series, and I asked what one of his tractors cost. He said over $70,000 and back then that seemed to me like a lot of money, which it was. But that was just the start of it. Just to grow hay for his cattle he had to buy a side cutter and a hay bailer, which was another $30,000. Add to that the equipment to seed and fertilize the fields, a trailer and a barn or storage facility. This is just to grow grass, I thought. George told me that a large combine to harvest corn or wheat could run over $300,000 (today a large combine starts at $500,000). As most farmers do, George leased most of this expensive equipment and had that kind of debt and those payments hanging over his head most of his life on the farm. A couple bad years and those payments can ruin you.

Add to all this the cost of a home and the farm land itself, and unless the farm was passed down to George from his father, which I don't know if it was or not, now you're really piling on the debt. Hundreds of thousands of dollars, and in Asheville now, it's well into the millions. I began thinking that you would have to have a college degree in finance just to manage it all.

George also financed the seed, fertilizer and other supplies for his operational costs in the spring every year. The loans and debt kept growing faster than the corn. The debt pressure on

George and his wife must have been immense, and I wondered how they slept at night. A severe storm or a drought could wipe them out. Here I was just worried about a car payment. I realized that they had good reason to believe that I was coming from the bank or another creditor when I first stepped out onto their field. They were in debt up to their ears.

After a while George said that he had to get in his school bus and go, and I said it was time I headed back to St. Louis. Helen looked at me with a sad expression and said, "Aren't you staying for supper?" She said it in such a way that I thought I was talking to my mother for a second. I think they wanted to adopt me.

I said that I wish I could, but I've got a lot of miles ahead of me, and I better get going. I shook George's hand, and gave Helen a hug, and started walking down the gravel drive to my car, which was still parked halfway down the driveway. I looked back and waived, and they stood there on the porch waiving back and wondering what the heck just happened. So was I.

I got in the car and started heading back to St. Louis, but everything was different now. My mood had totally changed, and the miles ahead of me didn't seem all that bad now. I kept thinking about Helen in her big straw bonnet, and George in his well-worn overalls, and that warm feeling carried me all the way back home. But I was worried about them, and for months I thought about them and tried to keep an eye on the weather in northern Missouri from my local news.

Although it was not necessarily my intent to help someone out when I woke up that day, it just happened, but I got the benefit from it. I felt a little better about myself, and that is the real benefit of connecting with others and doing little favors for strangers. I also learned that day the difference between hay and straw.

CHAPTER ELEVEN

COMMUNITY

The Long-Haul Trucking Company travels the known routes along the interstates I-10, I-40 and I-80 to and from far-distant farms in California. Drivers sit in air-conditioned crew cabs, in front of air-conditioned trailers, bringing meat and produce to isolated communities 2500 miles away. Sometimes they go to more remote locations in Mexico or Canada as they crisscross the waving fields of grain. They have their known ports to call on, favorite truck stops where they fill up on steak and eggs and other supplies.

Sometimes the company will pick up apple juice that was grown and produced in China at a port in Long Beach, California and bring it to thirsty kids in North Carolina. The daring and intrepid sea captain aboard the massive container ship that brought the apple juice to Long Beach picked it up at a port near Shanghai and made the long two-and-a-half-week voyage across the Pacific Ocean using GPS and radar. The apples were grown in the remote Chong Dong Valley, 1000 miles west of Shanghai, and shipped by truck to the processing facility 500 miles away where they were turned into apple juice. From there, the juice went to a warehouse and distribution facility in Qing Dong Province, and finally on to the port outside of Shanghai.

The Long-Haul Trucking Company delivers the apple juice to a warehouse and distribution center outside of Hendersonville, North Carolina, now in a plastic bottle with a pretty picture of a red barn, rolling green pastures and apple trees on the front label. The distribution center is just across the street from a large apple orchard, as the region is well-known for apple production, and a little further down the road is a pretty, red barn and rolling green pastures.

COMMUNITY SERVICE AND MANNA FOODBANK

Food security and resilience thinking means everyone has access to healthy food, including low income households. It's also the right thing to do. Many Americans feel the moral and social duty to help those facing hunger in their community. The social dimension of being a good citizen, and the idea of service to others, is embedded in our society. Many serve through their church organizations by donating time and/or money, while others do it through nonprofit or other charitable organizations, and these charitable acts build community and connect you to it.

In the United States, more than one out of six children live in a household with food insecurity, which means they do not always know where their next meal will come from and don't always get three squares a day. In Western North Carolina, this number increases to one out of four children.

There is an organization in Asheville that feeds a lot of people facing hunger called MANNA FoodBank, and it works out of a huge warehouse down along the Swannanoa River on the southeast side of town. MANNA FoodBank is a nonprofit organization that has been serving Western North Carolina since 1983. MANNA is an acronym for Mountain Area Nutritional Needs Alliance. It's a member of Feeding America, the nation's largest domestic hunger-relief organization. MANNA in Asheville distributed 18.2 million pounds of food in fiscal year 2018 through 200 community-based food assistance agencies located in 16 Western North Carolina counties.

MANNA is the critical link between the food industry and the organizations distributing food in their immediate communities across the region; they collect, sort, store, and distribute food to accredited nonprofit agencies across the region. Their network of partner agencies, including pantries, soup kitchens, churches, and emergency food suppliers, then distributes the food directly to families in their local communities.

MANNA works with food industry partners, local grocers and national retailers, packing houses, farmers, and individual donors to acquire about 74% of the food they distribute. Other sources include the federal and state government (12%), food drives (2%) and food that they purchase in bulk (12%) with grants and private donations.

An incredible amount of food goes through their warehouse, with trucks coming and going all day long. The 18.2 million pounds of food distributed in 2018 was packed and sorted by more than 7000 volunteers who donated over 73,000 hours of their time, which is the equivalent of 37 full-time staff members. The community volunteers are critical to the entire operation.

Some estimates indicate that over 108,000 people in Western North Carolina don't have food security or continuous access to three square meals a day. To get food to those facing hunger, in the last fiscal year MANNA distributed enough to provide 41,000 meals every day of the year throughout the 16 counties it serves. MANNA also works closely with schools to identify students at risk for food insecurity and gives out more than 5200 'MANNA Packs' to kids every Friday to make certain the kids facing an empty kitchen have food over the weekend, when the school meals program isn't available.

MANNA says its mission is to involve, educate, and unite people in the work of ending hunger, and that means more than putting food on a plate – it means getting nutritious, health-supporting food to the people who need it most, and providing food with hope and dignity.

Nutritious, health-supporting food is important for everyone, but especially the individuals and families MANNA serves. Recent research showed 64% of clients seeking assistance from MANNA's network had to choose between paying for food and paying for medicine or medical care. It also showed that 31% of households seeking assistance from MANNA have diabetes and over half of client households have a member with high blood pressure. The correlation between food insecurity and chronic disease is becoming ever more evident in Western North Carolina. People experiencing food insecurity must often opt for cheaper, less healthy food just to have enough, and this increases their probability of chronic disease.

Because an agrihood can and should do more than just feed the community residents, I wondered if there was some way that Creekside Farm might be able to help organizations like MANNA by providing healthy, organically grown produce, and perhaps some free-range chicken eggs. With some help from residents at The Cliffs at Walnut Cove, I thought we might be able to do something, so I reached out to one resident I knew was already doing some volunteer work with MANNA, and she directed me to Jen Waite, MANNA's Director of Food Sourcing.

I met with Jen and her co-worker Justine Redden at the farm one sunny day in February of 2018 to see if we could come up with some ideas. We toured the farm and went over to the education center to talk. I started the conversation by suggesting that we might be able to provide some fresh, organic produce to MANNA. They both loved the idea right off.

Justine is a nutrition and health advocate, and she told me how getting people, especially kids, to eat healthier is her main goal at MANNA. "It's too common that children don't have access to fruits and vegetables at home" she said, and we both told stories about how kids don't even know the names of common vegetables or what many vegetables look like. Justine finally said, "Anything we could do would be helpful. It's so important to introduce healthier choices to children."

According to Jen, about one-third of the food they distribute is produce. The challenge with a lot of it is that the shelf life is short, or the produce is already starting to turn, when MANNA gets their hands on it. Larger grocery stores provide a lot of the produce that has been pulled from their store shelves, and the shelf life for MANNA is greatly reduced by the time they get it, sometimes to just a couple days.

"A lot of time we take the rejects from the large packing houses," Jenn said, "so it doesn't look perfect and it might have some slight blemishes. It may not look perfect or good enough to send to the grocery stores, but we're happy to take it. We don't care if a tomato isn't perfectly shaped. It all tastes the same."

"Most of our clients don't have access to really fresh food," Jen told me. "Of course, a lot of people haven't tasted farm fresh food. They don't know what they're missing. And if it gets our people to eat more vegetables, that's terrific."

"It'll at least last a lot longer, and that may give our clients a chance to keep it longer in case they don't eat it right away," Justine added.

I asked Jen where she got most of her produce and she explained that they work with the large grocery stores in the area, and a pair of packaging houses in Hendersonville and Mills River. I asked her if they get much produce directly from farmers in the area, and she said sometimes they do.

"Usually if they've got too much of something or don't have a buyer. We've received shipments from farmers that were rejected by the packing houses before, for whatever reason. But we get it from backyard gardeners too. No donation is too small." She went on to explain that changes in tax laws have helped incentivize farmers to donate excess produce rather than use it for livestock feed or till it back into the soil as compost.

The produce is sorted by staff and volunteers at MANNA for quality, then sent out in their fleet of delivery trucks. Any quality or freshness rejects go into a special large dumpster and is picked up regularly by another company to distribute as cattle feed. Very little is wasted. Most of those unused vegetables are going to end up on a plate as a steak someday.

The other 2/3 of the products that MANNA distributes include all the dry goods like canned goods, boxed mac and cheese, cookies, cereals and everything else you'd find in the middle aisles of the supermarket. It also includes some dairy products like milk and cheese. Like the vegetables, a lot of the dairy products have a short shelf life remaining so it's important for MANNA to sort, process and reship it quickly in refrigerated trucks, and they have large walk in coolers to store all the perishable products. MANNA also encourages families needing food support to sign up for the food stamp program; it's part of their overall mission of relieving hunger and is the most effective anti-hunger initiative in the country. But the truly wonderful thing that MANNA does is reclaim a lot of food that would be otherwise wasted. As noted previously, as much as 40% of the food in America is wasted and that would feed another large country. MANNA uses this perfectly good food to feed families who would otherwise go without right here in Appalachia.

I showed Jen and Justine around the Creekside Farm Education Center, including the commercial kitchen, and the wheels really started turning. I told them that we wanted to help any way we could, and that we were already having elementary schools out for a visit and for some classroom and field instruction, and Justine got excited.

"You could do food demos!" She explained, "You could do food demonstrations and show kids how to cook vegetables and let them taste them."

"After the demo, all participants do a thank you bite," she says. "Every kid takes a taste as a way to say thank you. But the rule is, no funny faces, just a thumb's up or thumb's down."

She's obviously done this before. She added something else.

"We have found that if kids learn about where their food is coming from, and are allowed agency over their own cooking, they are more likely to try, and enjoy, the food."

"I was at a school not long ago where we did a "Cook. Eat. Grow" program which featured an ingredient of the day to get kids to try different veggies," Justine went on. "We got more 'thumb's up' than we expected. Kids don't really know what they like and don't like because many of them haven't really been exposed to fresh vegetables that are properly prepared."

"If you could get the parents out too, like a family day, that would be awesome!" Justine added. "That way, the whole family can learn about fresh ingredients and cooking methods that they have not been introduced to before." What a great way to use this commercial kitchen, I thought. And the ideas kept coming.

"What about a 'Free Farmers Market' at schools?" Justine

asked. "We could set something up on tables after school and let the kids 'shop' for free with their parents. Setting it up like a farmer's market makes it fun for everyone." Another great idea, and I knew a couple ladies at The Cliffs who might jump on this one.

I asked Jen about meat products and whether they distributed anything like that. She said they did, but it was a little trickier. Meat had to be frozen and picked up and delivered in one of their freezer trucks. The agency that received and distributed the meat also had to have a freezer. Because the meat was getting close to an expiration date, freezing the meat and maintaining that condition was important.

"Warren Wilson College provided a whole pig once," Jen said. "The students operate vegetable gardens and a small farm, and they raised the pig and Manna purchased it. They made all the arrangements for the slaughter and packaging at an FDA approved packing house, and we got all the meat."

We got back to the subject of how the farm might help provide some fresh food to MANNA. I suggested that many weeks we have too much of certain vegetables because Melissa didn't always know how well a crop would do and so planted more than enough for our CSA shares. She planned to (and did) sell some of the extra produce at the farmers market, but we could easily divert some of that excess to MANNA.

I also said that many Cliffs residents have second homes and travel quite extensively, so there are extra boxes every week from people that didn't pick up, which we could add to our donation to MANNA. At the same time, I thought it might encourage some people to buy a share for themselves who may not have intended on doing so because they knew they would be traveling or out of town for a big part of the summer. Now they wouldn't have to feel guilty about buying a share and not using it, because what they don't pick up will go to a very worthy cause.

Then we came up with another idea. We'd just ask our CSA members if anyone would want to buy a share for MANNA. With one donation, a Cliff's residents can support a farmer and local food production and at the same time provide healthy food to households experiencing hunger. It was accomplishing two things with the same dollar. So in an email to our members the following week, we asked. Right away we received three replies from members eager to buy another share for MANNA. Melissa would plan and plant for those extra shares that same season.

MISS BRENDA

Jenn suggested that it might be smarter to just hook us up with one of their local food banks and save the food miles of bringing produce to their warehouse only to have it go right back out on a truck to a food pantry, and she said that there might be an agency close to us. As it turned out, there happened to be a food pantry and MANNA partner agency located at a church just down from the farm on Avery Creek Road, less than two miles away. I knew exactly where it was.

I went online and found a phone number for the food bank and called them on a Saturday morning when they had pick-up and I knew that someone would be there. Miss Brenda, who manages the food bank at the Avery Creek United Methodist Church in Arden happened to answer the phone that morning. I introduced myself and briefly described the farm and CSA program just down the road, and I offered to bring her fresh vegetables every week if she needed them. I said I could run down to her church that morning if she had time to talk.

Her answer was short and, surprisingly, not all that friendly. She said, "Well, you may have to wait, I have clients here." It wasn't what she said, but it was more the tone that surprised me, and I thought she might be a bit overwhelmed and stressed this morning with too many clients. I wasn't sure why I got that impression, but I went down anyway just before noon and just before they close the food pantry hoping to get some time to talk with Miss Brenda.

When I walked into the church and down some stairs into the lower level, I was greeted by an older gentleman who said to me, "Just go over to that table there and pick up a number, and someone will help you shortly."

"Oh, I'm not here to pick up food, I'm here to talk about dropping some food off," I said.

Just then a deep voice came from behind me.

"I'll give you my address and you can drop it off there," the voice said with a deep chuckle.

I turned around to see a very large, older black man with a big grin on his face sitting in a line of chairs next to the front door. He was a big man who could have been a defensive line-man at one time.

I replied with a smile, "I better talk to Miss Brenda first, but you got dibs on it if she doesn't want it."

Just then Miss Brenda, who was sitting in a nearby office, yelled out, "You'll have to wait. I'm with a client!" There it was again. Not the kind, friendly voice I had expected from the manager of a food pantry. Who was this church lady?

I stood there and waited my turn with Miss Brenda and noticed a kindly looking and very petite older lady was stand-ing in line and next to enter the storage room where the church kept the food pantry. She was so small, and wearing an over-sized white t-shirt that was several sizes too big for her, and she looked up at me and smiled, and I returned the smile and said, "How's the food in this joint?"

"It's good. It lasts me the whole week," she said with another smile.

I said, "Really, the whole week?"

"Yes, and it helps me out so much, so I can pay for rent and other things, you know."

I asked, "Do you ever pick up vegetables here?"

She scrunched up her face and said, "No, not really. Sometimes I'll pick up some cucumbers or something when I know it's in season and they're fresh. But not very often."

I glanced in the room and saw shelves full of canned goods and boxes of processed foods, like the easily recognizable boxes of mac and cheese. I wondered if these were her staples, and if she ever really ate any fresh food. Just then, Miss Brenda finished up with the old football player and called me in to her office.

Miss Brenda was wearing a pretty, floral pattern dress, had white hair and a kind, handsome face. It was a stark contrast to the tone of her voice and the short, direct language that she had been using with me, and I was confused for a moment, until she spoke.

"Why did you knock that old rock house down?" she said with a stern voice. I felt like a school boy and had no answer. The question came out of the blue as soon as I sat down. How did she know that I was the one that knocked down Gilbert's old rock home? How is it that these older ladies with white hair, ever since grade school, knew exactly when I did something wrong? What's with these people? How do they do that?

"I live just up the road from that farm, and have for my whole life, and I've driven by that old rock house every day since I was a little girl." It was becoming clear now. She knew where my farm was just from my telling her on the telephone that I had the farm on Avery Creek road, and she knew what I had done, and it was akin to a mortal sin.

Man, I'm in a tight spot. I thought quickly, and said, "Miss Brenda, if there was any way of saving that old rock house, we would have done that. But ya' know, Gilbert leased that to a couple boys who really trashed it. It was beyond repair, but if we could have, we would have."

She looked at me hard and cross, like my old third grade teacher Mrs. Jones (and I remember her name because it rhymed with "bones" which I thought was very funny back then). Turns out, Miss Brenda was also an old school teacher herself, so she had that look down and was good at it. I shrunk in my chair.

"How many houses you going to build there on that property?" she fired off. Now I'm really in trouble, this lady knows everything.

She knew Gilbert, she knew Lynn Bonham, she knew Tom Cochran, she knew all my neighbors, and I was on her 'bad' list, and I thought that I was going to have to sit there until I fully repented and atoned for my transgressions.

"Just twelve Mam," I said rather quietly. I didn't think it would be appropriate to go into a long diatribe about the agri-hood concept at this point. Just take my swat on the knuckles with her ruler and get out of there. That would be the smart thing to do at this juncture.

And just then, Miss Brenda's face and entire demeaner changed and suddenly lightened up, and she said in the kindest voice, "That girl, that girl working in the fields, I drive by her every day, God Bless her, she is such a hard worker."

I couldn't believe it. I was being saved by Melissa.

"She's out there every day working so hard in that field, rain or shine" said Miss Brenda, "and the garden looks so beautiful. It's so big, I can't believe she does all of that. God Bless her. What's her name?"

"Her name is Melissa," I said, and she was my savior, a saint, and she would atone for my sins, and maybe I wouldn't have to sit here forever, and maybe I wouldn't even get a rap on the knuckles with a ruler.

"She is about the hardest working person that I know, Miss Brenda," I added. "And you should stop by sometime to meet her. She's a wonderful person".

I continued by trying to steer the conversation away from me and on to the reason for my being there. "She has some extra vegetables that she'd like to donate to your food bank if you need them." I went on to describe the CSA program, our relationship with MANNA, and the CSA shares that a few people have purchased for a food-relief organization like hers. I may get out of this alive, I thought.

Miss Brenda, as it turns out, is truly a very kind and delightful person, and after she reprimanded me for tearing down that rock home she had known since childhood, she became the most pleasant and personable person that you could meet or talk to. Like all good teachers, after you've been reprimanded and taken your punishment, they welcome you back into their loving arms and forgive you and make everything seem OK again. She must have been a great teacher for young, adventurous boys that tend to misbehave occasionally.

Miss Brenda gave me a tour of the facility and explained how they operated and who they helped. Most of the clients that came for food assistance came a very short distance to get there. They were all from the nearby neighborhoods. It was clear that Miss Brenda's Christian faith inspired her to feed those around her facing hunger, and I could tell that she did this work with kindness and compassion for her fellow man.

I asked how many people they served every Saturday morning. She looked at her clipboard, and said, "Today we served just over forty households, which is about average. Do you know how many people that is?"

I took a guess and said, "Eighty people."

"Nope" she said, "the average household that we serve is four, so it's closer to one hundred sixty people every week. Some households have seven or eight people, and some are just one person, but it averages four people." She smiled, and I could see how happy she was about that.

I asked Miss Brenda lots of questions about the history of Avery Creek Road, about Gilbert's mom Clementh and about her husband Avery, if she had known them, where she went to school, and where she taught school. We had a very pleasant conversation for about an hour, and before I went to leave, I asked what she does with the old vegetables that go bad. I knew the shelf life was already very short when she got them from MANNA.

She replied, excited, "Oh, do you have pigs? We never know what to do with old produce, and I hate to throw it in the dumpster."

I said, "We'd love to take whatever you have for our composting bin. Melissa could really put it to good use in the garden to help recycle the minerals and nutrients and build up the soil. It's her thing."

When I finally said goodbye and left the church, I had two boxes of old produce in my car. Here I had come to talk about bringing them produce, and I was leaving with a bunch of it, but Melissa loved the fact that we would be helping to close the food-to-waste-to-food cycle at this food bank. And for the rest of the summer, we would be bringing fresh, hyper-local food every Friday to the food pantry at the Avery Creek United Methodist Church in Arden, North Carolina. Every week Melissa would also put several copies of quick, simple recipes in the boxes for how to cook and prepare the vegetables that were in there. Miss Brenda loved that she did that.

Most food banks welcome fresh produce from wherever they can get it, and they often get it from home gardeners. Many people have a large backyard garden just for the purpose of growing food for the food insecure. It's a hobby that they love that also has some real benefit to the community. And simply doing things that are beyond your own self-interest (helping others) builds self-esteem which improves personal happiness and well-being. That has health benefits.

BUILDING COMMUNITY AT CREEKSIDE FARM

Some groups within a neighborhood or development have organized and made it easier for their neighbors to find ways to get involved. Members of groups like this have discovered that getting involved and helping others is a key to life satisfaction and fulfillment.

Neighbors at the Cliffs at Walnut Cove have organized one member-run nonprofit that supports several other nonprofit organizations in the region. The Walnut Cove Members Association (WCMA) is a community group that raises funding for many different charitable groups around Asheville. It was started and is managed by residents and led by a board of members. In 2017, the WCMA donated a whopping $180,000 to local nonprofits (which is a considerable amount since there are only 250 homes currently in the Cliffs and less than half are full time residents). In 2018 that number jumped up to over $300,000. To date the WCMA at the Cliffs at Walnut Cove has donated over 300 grants worth well over $1.3 million dollars.

The WCMA was featured in a December 28, 2017 Wall

Street Journal article on community giving. Donna Bailey, the past president of the Cliffs member group and a retired software marketer, said in the article, "What else would you do with your life if you didn't get involved." That pretty much sums it up nicely.

The Walnut Cove Members Association collects its funds from membership dues, which is voluntary and not related to any Cliffs membership or benefit, and through various fundraising events for members that they schedule throughout the year. In 2017, the WCMA awarded grants to over 31 nonprofits who serve Western North Carolina. These included the Avery's Creek Elementary Library, Meals on Wheels, The Mission Hospital Foundation Epilepsy Unit, YWCA Mother Love program, Arts for Life at Mission Children's Hospital, and a lot more.

One grant recipient that I was familiar with was a program at the University of North Carolina Asheville called 'Good Food For All', run by Sonia Marcus, the Director of Sustainability at UNC Asheville. Sonia took me on a campus tour of UNC Asheville in the summer of 2017 to show me how various vegetable gardens were maintained by student volunteers all around campus, and to talk about what was growing and how the food was used. I'd never seen a plot of heirloom tomatoes or cucumbers growing in the middle of a college campus, and the gardens were well kept and very productive. It was quite impressive, this edible campus, and the food grown there helps feed hungry students. Sonia loves to show people around the gardens and tell this story to visitors on campus.

Sonia is a remarkable person and another great teacher, and her students seem to love her. She's currently teaching a popular sustainability class using *The Omnivore's Dilemma* as course material. UNC Asheville takes sustainability very seriously in its buildings and infrastructure, in the energy it uses, pollution it generates, and how its grounds are kept. Administrative staff get around campus in small electric vehicles. The main campus quad isn't watered or sprayed with chemicals, and it won't always look dark green and lush like some campus quads. But that's OK, everyone understands what a little brown grass on the quad means when the hot summer days come. It tells the story that we're a sustainable campus, and we wait for the rain.

The grant donated by the Cliffs members will go to support a healthy food pantry that was set up on campus for struggling college students who don't always have the money to eat regular, healthy meals. The donation will help build awareness and fund fresh healthy food for students living closer to the economic edge, and there's a lot of them. The program has a story behind it; poor college students shouldn't go hungry, and they need to eat healthier foods. And when the story spreads and people begin to participate in it, the story becomes transformative. This is the power of the story.

Cliffs member supported programs like Good Food for All and the CSA shares dedicated to MANNA tell another important story. The story is always important because stories can change perceptions and even transform culture. These programs (and the stories behind them) attempt to increase understanding of the healthy and nutritious benefits of fresh, organic food, and the goal is to help people make healthier food choices by developing a stronger culture of "good food" in communities, schools, and at home.

Farmers Markets, CSA Programs and organizations like ASAP and Organic Grower's School are creating a new narrative for what our food culture can be. They tell the story that is helping to bring the change. And there's a moral to the story –

Eat better and you'll be healthier, and might even live a longer, more active and fulfilling life.

Food is becoming a cultural product again, and the story behind local food is a way for people to identify with and connect to a regional culture. A traveler might stop in a restaurant and read a short story about the farmer who grew the food. The stories behind the food, the type of food, where it came from and the farmer who grew it, how she grew it within the local environment and the climate, all these things are a part of the story and a way to engage people and build cultural connections. The local farm story, often told by growers at the farmer's market when they tell customers about their farms, creates emotional bonds and connection points that people will remember, and these become the bonds of local culture. The farm story also contributes to a changing cultural narrative about the values we care about; land stewardship and healthy food for all. There is a transformative power in the story of food.

The Creekside Farm Education Center is beginning to write its own story. It has become a place to gather, prepare and cook food, and to celebrate it with others. It's the social hub of a new farm community where people gather regularly to share and celebrate a new kind of food web and listen to stories from the farm. The stories and events help to build our own community food culture.

Below is the calendar of events for our CSA members during the 2018 season. Because there were other Cliffs organized events planned within the larger wellness community, including many golf, tennis and charitable events, plus a healthy social calendar, we squeezed the farm events in where we could. I must admit that these retirees have a better social life than I did in college.

Creekside Farm CSA 2018 Calendar of Events

All events held at the Creekside Farm Education Center

May 5 – Spring Food Drive for MANNA FoodBank

May 10 – Gardening Class –backyard herb gardens

May 31 – Cooking Class – Early Summer Greens

June 7 – Honey Bee Class

June 15 – Farm-to-Table Dinner circa 1900

June 22 – Flower Arrangement Class – guest florist

July 13 – Farm to Table Dinner, Annual Pig Roast

August 2 – Cooking Class, Great Vegetarian Meals

August 25 – Farm to Table Dinner, MANNA Benefit

August 31 – Fall Canning Class

September 6 – Wine and Speaker Event

September 22 – Fall Harvest Festival

September 29 – Fall Food Drive for MANNA

October 4 – Wine and Speaker Event

November 16 – Holiday Tree Festival

These were just the formally announced events for CSA members at the education center, but a good number of informal events also happened throughout the year and filled in the farm calendar. That included teachers and students from local schools coming out for classroom and field instruction. Other events were held by and for Organic Grower's School and ASAP. We allowed and encouraged other local food organizations like these to use our facility for some of their own meetings and smaller events.

The cooking and canning classes were a big hit and made a big mess in the kitchen, and the Honey Bee and gardening classes were fun and interesting. Kara ran the bee class and showed up in her bee suit, which looks like a moon suit, and brought in some of her bees on a frame in a viewable glass box so we could all see them busy at work. I learned some very interesting things about bees, like worker bees are all female and do all the work, and all the male bees are called 'drones' and are very lazy. They don't even have a stinger. The drones just eat honey (and don't collect any) and fly around at about 40 feet above the ground waiting to mate with a queen. That's it, just hanging out at 40 feet looking for a good time. The female worker bees will fly up to five miles away looking for nectar to make into honey back at the hive. The hive is one big, living organism, with worker bees doing different jobs that includes feeding the young, feeding the queen, making the cones, taking out the trash (and dead bees) and guarding the hive. The lazy male bees are kicked out of the hive in winter (and die) to save honey for the hive in the winter months. Serves 'em right, lazy drones, I thought. I couldn't help but think also that there was a message in this bee class, a message from the natural world, that was meant for me. I'm not sure why, just a feeling, and then the thought suddenly occurred to me that I never really offered to help Kara with her bee hives over the summer, and maybe she would be considering kicking me out of the house this winter? Maybe I deserve that? But surely, I thought, I do enough work around the farm to be a valuable asset to the overall farming operation.

Classes like this have been helpful in getting more people to come out to the farm on a regular basis, and some started coming to help in the garden because they all felt a little more at home there. The most popular events were the farm-to-table meals cooked by a guest chef, which helped to build his celebrity status in the community. Most of the food prepared for these meals came right from the farm and gardens. All the farm to table meals over the summer were a lot of fun, but the "Appalachian Dinner circa 1900" probably drew the most attention and recognition from our members, so I'll describe that event in a little detail here.

What did people right here in this mountain region of Appalachia eat for supper in the year 1900? That's a fun question. Our chef for the evening, Jerami Jones, had most of the information stored away on notecards and recipes he gleaned from conversations and family meals at his grandmother and great-grandmother's home. Jerami grew up here and grew up eating homemade cornbread and all the other wonderful Appalachian dishes that his family shared at the dinner table. Jerami told me that his great-grandparents pulled most of the food they ate from their own gardens and kept and slaughtered their own animals, and family meals were big events. So was this one, with most of the food pulled right out of our garden the day we ate it. Jerami cooked several pork roasts and made chow-chow as a condiment for the meat that he presented in mason jars on the tables. Chow-chow is an old Appalachian dish made by fermenting vegetables, and it was such a big hit that many people kept asking for the recipe, but Jerami just side-stepped the request all evening. Then people started asking if he could make more and sell mason jars of it. He said he'd think about it. Really, I think he just wanted to ask his grandmother first if it was OK that he shared her recipe or sold jars of it. It was, after all, a secret family recipe that went back over 100 years.

The meal included deviled eggs, potatoes, and a hearty salad, all pulled from the garden and the chicken coop. We served it family style at larger tables, like the old days, and people passed dishes around the tables and helped each other by holding plates and serving each other. It made for a real communal meal, much different than buffet style or having waiters bring individual plates. On the invite we said we'd have wine and beer, but people could also bring a bottle to share with neighbors if they wanted to, and most did like old time neighborhood gatherings. We fed 60 people that night in the main dining hall.

I invited Asheville music icon Wayne Erbsen to play music and tell old time stories about food in Appalachia during the event. He brought his daughter and another player, who were also accomplished musicians on several instruments, and they took turns singing and playing the fiddle, banjo and guitar. Wayne's program included songs, stories, history and humor mixed with old-time, bluegrass, and Appalachian music. For the past thirty years, Wayne has had his own radio show called "Country Roots" on Asheville's public radio station, WCQS. He knew how to entertain our group, and his lively songs and instrumentals filled the dining hall all evening. The food and old-time music let us all step back in time to a food culture that has lasted in Appalachia for hundreds of years, and people like Chef Jerami and Wayne have been key to keeping it all alive, so it isn't forgotten.

Other farm to table meal events included a pig roast with more bluegrass music. In August we put on a farm to table Tapas dinner (with classical Spanish music) to benefit Manna FoodBank. That event raised enough money to provide over 12,000 meals for MANNA. MANNA is so efficient with food distribution that they can stretch every dollar to provide three and a half meals. Later in the Fall we had our second annual Fall Harvest Festival with tents out in the garden, soups and salads from the fields, local hard apple cider, local beer, local fresh baked pies, and local fun.

What all these events did over the course of the summer was build bonds and networks and friendships, and in the end, community. It's what they were designed to do; build community around the sharing and celebration of food. And there's one other benefit from these events – it can help to prevent CSA member burnout and improve shareholder retention year after year, which is important to sustainability. The CSA model asks its members to keep eating fresh vegetables every week, it really forces you to, because the boxes keep coming every week, which might become a burden to some members who don't necessarily like to cook all the time. It's important to keep stressing that the CSA program is not just about fresh veggies. It's about a lot of other important values and principles, education and knowledge. It's about supporting local farmers and giving them a job. It's about keeping farms in farming. It's about food security, sustainability and community resilience, and we need to keep stressing that, reminding people, at every opportunity (and I do). And if they do take a break from cooking and eating healthy food for a week, and don't pick up their box, that's OK. The food will certainly go to good use at the food bank just down the road.

Something else happened that summer. We sold our first lot in the agrihood. It wasn't long after we listed the lots in the agrihood before we had a buyer. A couple from California somehow found us on the internet and flew out to take a look. She wanted to garden, and he wanted a wellness community focused on a healthier lifestyle, including some golf. What surprised me was that once this couple fully learned about what we were doing, and because they had their own strong Christian beliefs, they started talking about buying a second lot next to them just to grow more food for MANNA and other food security organizations, and they asked if we could cause it to be farmed for that purpose. It wasn't really necessary for them to do that, we already had excess capacity, I explained, but what a relief it was to know someone got it and was even willing to go a step further. The agrihood concept was perfect for this couple, and it was exactly what they were looking for without them even knowing it. They loved the whole idea, and she couldn't wait to get their new home built and start gardening herself. It was a fluke google search from Southern California that found us the first time, but Kara and I could begin to rest easy now as more people kept coming out to learn about the project and sales continued to happen. Maybe I wasn't crazy after all.

The Creekside Farm Education Center became, in a very short time, much more than a venue and a kitchen for events and classes; it became a hub for the gathering and dissemination of information related to community sustainability and resilience in Appalachia and beyond. We developed the web site www.eatyourview.com and a social media campaign including Facebook and Instagram (follow them both also at Eat Your View) as primary vehicles to disseminate as much information as we could about the importance of the local food movement and community resilience. Some people just like to follow what's happening at the farm and check in on the animals, and our miniature donkeys Pedro and Darla have started to become regional celebrities with all the social media attention. We've distributed t-shirts, shopping totes, and thousands of window decals and bumper stickers with the "Eat Your View" slogan printed on them. We hired a couple interns for research and brought together successful business and finance people from the neighborhood to look at developing the different programs we wanted to start, like the 'market stamps' program (food stamps redeemable only at farmers markets), financing a large-scale hydroponics operation, and the potential financing and feasibility for a bio-fuels operation.

The farm and the education center are becoming a local connection point in a network of scientists, chefs, business people, activists, farmers, and educators that are trying to promote research and education in sustainable agriculture, building more resilient communities, and creating opportunities for small farmers and growers.

So far we've done a pretty good job of building community support for the farm and the education center. We brought in outside partners and organizations that supported common goals in the local food network. We started to build community education through speakers that came to talk about their organizations, like ASAP, Organic Growers School and MANNA. And we learned where we had to go with this whole thing to really help build the local food infrastructure. We needed to find more ways to help new, young growers get into the business if local food and farming were going to be sustainable long into the future.

THE FARMER INCUBATOR PROGRAM

This book has tried to focus on the business side of the local food movement, and it's time to ask the question, is it profitable? I know the growers at the farmers market aren't getting rich doing this work, but are they really making any money at all. Organic growers have different values, principles and motivations than most start-ups, and many are not necessarily focused on profit, but the question remains, are many of these growers practicing a form of self-exploitation in the process? Are some making less than minimum wage for all their efforts? And how do we improve the profitability of small, local farms so that famers don't burn out and they're sustainable for the long term?

Launching a farm business requires significant capital, as we've discussed, which is the major barrier to starting a farming operation. At Creekside Farm, we believed that we needed to help new farmers learn the trade by providing low cost land and training so they can begin or expand an agricultural business, and we needed to help them understand the business side of the operation early on. If it's not profitable, it can't last. They needed to really understand the business side of farming, not just growing food, but how to find customers and distribution channels for their products and how to market their goods. If we were to try to help, a business incubator model, like those in the tech industry, seemed like a good place to start. Participants in a farmer incubator program might spend a few years in a program like this growing food on land that would be very inexpensive for them to lease and that would give them access to greenhouses, hoop houses, a barn for storage, a tractor, water and electricity. But it would also give them a way to start small, without a lot of up-front costs, and begin to develop a customer base.

A farmer incubator program would help aspiring farmers to build their farming business from the ground up. A farm incubator setting would offer affordable access to land and some of the basic resources and infrastructure that these new farmers need, including access to an experienced mentor farmer like Melissa. As I started looking into it, I discovered that there are other similar programs across the country and they usually offer short term leases for organic farm land in smaller increments, usually starting at about a half-acre parcel, and that allows new growers to gradually scale up their farm business.

I learned that the farm at the Southern Appalachian Highlands Conservancy already has a program like this up and running, and they were fairly close by, so I went for a visit. The farm manager there, Chris Link, gets applicants thinking about a business plan early on, and he'll even help them run the numbers and discuss the profitability of the plan (often in terms of dollars per square foot of growing space). The target, says Chris, is $50 per square foot of growing space in gross revenue per year. That's a hefty goal, but I found it very interesting how Chris puts a dollar amount to a such a small piece of earth, just one square foot, because he knows the unit costs of labor and supplies, and like any business, he wants these new farmers to think in business terms and units of production. And he stresses that you can't just grow what you want to grow, you must grow what the market wants and needs, the market demands, and you must know what your competition is already growing and supplying to your target customer base. That's good business.

New farmers for our incubator program need to send in an application that looks a lot like a business plan, including vegetables they plan to grow, and the customer base they plan to go after and attract, which gets them thinking about the business side of their operation early on and before the tiller even hits the ground. If they plan to sell to restaurants, who are those restaurants and what type of products are they looking for, specifically? If they want to grow for a CSA, then how will they acquire their shareholders? What's the marketing plan to attract them?

I also believed that they needed some skin in the game. We wrestled with the question of how much to charge a young, cash strapped new farmer to lease land at Creekside Farm for their new farming operation, and what to charge for access to greenhouses and equipment. But having some skin in the game, some financial investment in the operation, no matter how small that was, would make it less likely that someone might give up mid-season. It would require a financial commitment, however small and affordable that we could make it, but still a commitment that all farmers make every growing season. It's an incentive that might add determination to get through difficult and challenging times. We would certainly be there to help with advice, encouragement and moral support. But from my own experience in business and financial risk, becoming financially vested in something is a great motivator and driver of success. Fear, I've also found, is a great motivator.

I put some skin in this game. I didn't have a background in farming or food production, but I threw my hat in the ring anyway to see what would happen. I had one foot in the dirt and one foot out, and I think the one foot out has been important. I never really knew exactly what I was doing. I shot from the hip mostly. I came into this whole thing completely ignorant, and luckily, I received a lot of help from other farms and farmers.

There are many organizations and academic institutions out there today, including many brilliant researchers and scientists, that are on the cutting edge of research in sustainable food production, and I know that I've just scratched the surface in this subject matter. But I am grateful that I had a chance to see this local food movement from a farmer's perspective. It hasn't been the purely academic or analytical perspective of a scientist. It hasn't been the straight economic perspective of a developer or business man, or strictly the viewpoint of an environmentalist. The whole learning process has been a little dirty, messy, confusing and scary – Kind of like life.

But the rewards of seeing people come together at a table, at a table to share food grown very nearby; to celebrate the harvest and know what it means, to know the hard work that went into growing the food; and to toast and give cheers to the farmer who grew it, as she just shyly smiles and sets a dish on the table; that has made it all worth-while. It is a celebration of food, and a celebration of life, that comes from a garden.

While this book has been focused on the agrihood and a new type of farming community, many of the ideas and principles can be applied to any neighborhood or community. All it takes is a good community organizer to get something started. A community organizer can work with a neighborhood homeowner's association or local government to identify a good spot of land for a community garden. She can reach out to others within the community to promote the benefits of local food and attract other stakeholders and potential members of a Community Supported Agriculture Program. She can run an ad on Craigslist or reach out to farmers at the local farmers market to find local growers in the area that might farm the land and run the CSA.

A farming operation can be run on a smaller scale, with a walk behind tiller and a part-time farmer, if you just have access to a small plot of land and water. Just 35 members in a CSA program might be enough to support a farmer for the summer, but she'd have to find other work come winter. If the CSA charged 35 members $750 for the growing season, that comes to $26,250 in revenue, which might cover supplies and transplants and pay a decent living wage to the farmer for full-time work over the summer. With some help in the garden from members, it becomes even more cost effective and financially achievable. The numbers can be worked out if you have enough people interested in supporting the program. You can build your own agricultural community that supports a farmer with a small piece of land and some customers. You just need to get others involved and start organizing.

The simplest way to build a more sustainable and resilient community is to get your neighbors to shop at the local farmer's market. The next step is to start a CSA program in your neighborhood, or join an existing one, because that gives a farmer the support she needs in the spring and for the entire growing season. The smaller steps include shopping for and buying locally grown food at your grocery store (and convincing your grocer to carry locally grown food) and eating at restaurants that promote locally grown food (and convincing other restaurants and chefs to do the same). If you've got the neighborhood and your community behind you, then you wield power and influence with many types of food businesses, including institutional buyers at hospitals and schools. Remember that if you do nothing, you resign yourself to live at the mercy of the industrial food complex and take no responsibility for feeding yourself and your community. You'll get your food from unknown sources in far-away places. That's risky business in a changing world, and that should be motivation enough to get you started.

So, Mr. Developer, sitting on your yacht in Miami, who's your customer for the new agricultural neighborhood that you're going to build? Who are the people that might want to live there in this new sustainable and resilient community that, surprisingly, protects farm land and gives a farmer a job?

They're the same people leading the environmental movement, working at food banks, shopping the farmer's markets, and joining CSA programs. They want healthier food without all the chemicals, but they are also people just trying to live up to their own self-chosen commitments. They want food justice. They want justice for farm animals and for nature and the environment. They want to tread lightly upon the earth. And they want to feel connected with others in a very real sense of community.

They are people willing to learn and teach the facts about the environment, climate change and sustainability. They understand the reasons for the farm to table movement, for agrihoods, agri-tourism and organic, local food at restaurants, and they understand the need for agricultural sustainability.

They are often blessed with a deeper, spiritual connection to the land and have the unique ability to stand in awe and wonder at its natural systems and beauty. They believe in the preservation of pastoral views and natural landscapes and protecting the bounty of the earth.

They can see the destructive behavior in mass consumption. With the mantra of "everything in moderation," they believe it is prudent behavior to use our resources wisely, and to temper our emotions, desires and wants for the long-term health of the planet.

They appreciate the hard working, self-reliant people out in the fields of the organic and sustainable food movement. They understand the failings of our industrial food complex and our misguided but complete dependence on it, and they understand the flaws of sprawling suburbia. They believe in local food from local farms, and sustainability to the point of self-sufficiency.

They stand by the brave farmers risking it all every season, and those honest and brave individuals with the strength to fight against injustice in the food web wherever they encounter it, whether it's in small town Asheville or inner-city Detroit. They care about others, and work towards building stronger, more resilient communities, and they believe healthy food is a natural right for all human beings.

There are motivating factors that drive people to do things and which in turn give their lives meaning, and whether it's helping the environment or helping people, there's no cash reward for the effort. But these acts have their own reward, and that reward is personal self-esteem and ultimately, happiness.

So many Americans build their lives around pursuing pleasure when social engagement and meaning are much more important. Finding ways of making their life feel more engaged and meaningful is probably the biggest reason people volunteer or get involved in service or community organizations in the first place. It's why some people might volunteer at MANNA FoodBank, shop at a farmer's market, join a CSA, or even take up the occupation of farming. It's also why some people might want to move to an agrihood.

The agrihood can be a model for the future that builds community sustainability and resilience, supports farms and farmers, and promotes healthier eating habits. The agrihood is a place where local food and the 'eat your view' movement intersect with the land and real estate. Here's one final story at the intersection of food and real estate. You should definitely tell this one at your next farm to table dinner party.

RUN FOR MANHATTAN

In the introduction to this book, I described an island called Run in the Spice Islands. It was at first the rumored home of headhunters and cannibals, and so the island's name was perhaps used as a noun and a verb at various times by the early spice traders. That was until the intrepid explorer and spice trader Nathaniel Courthope established an alliance with the natives and built a fort there.

Run played an important role in world history that goes unnoticed by most of the world. The Dutch East India Company and the British East India Company both made claims to the island and fought over it in the early 17th century because of the valuable nutmeg grown on the island. England believed that it was the rightful "owner" of the island because it was first, under Courthope, to form a treaty with the natives and to construct a fort and warehouse on the island. The Dutch later captured the island and so held their claim to it. As retaliation for Dutch aggressions and the taking of Run, the brother of King Charles II, the impetuous James, Duke of York, ordered four ships to cross the Atlantic to attack and capture the island of Manhattan from the Dutch in what was then New Netherland (now of course, New York, after the Duke of York). The English ships captured Fort Manhattan and the island in September 1664, after a brief skirmish, and war was on once again between the two countries.

The war dragged on across the high seas for a few more years until it was agreed that the two countries should meet at Breda in the Netherlands in March 1667 to negotiate a resolution. Commissioners for the British East India Company first offered to return Manhattan in exchange for the return of their captured sugar plantations and factories in Suriname on the Northeast coast of South America, but the Dutch refused. As talks began to break down, peace negotiators suggested that in return for the Dutch keeping the island of Run, the English should be allowed to keep Manhattan. In what became known as the Treaty of Breda, both sides agreed to the trade, and the British gained Manhattan, and the Dutch kept Run.

The demand for nutmeg faded, and so did the riches of Run, until it became just an obscure backwater island in the middle of nowhere. It takes several days to reach the island now, with no regular air service, and travel there includes an eight-hour ferry ride from the Indonesian island of Amboyna to the Banda Islands, and then another smaller boat ride to Run. That's of course after you get to the other side of the planet in the first place. You really have to want to go there, if you want to get there, because it's not easy. There are no cars on Run, and electricity comes from a private provider for only a few hours in the evening. Two miles long and half a mile wide, this sleepy little island has just a few hundred residents. But at one time it played a significant role in one of the most unbelievable real estate deals in world history, when Manhattan was traded for nutmeg. The Dutch gave up a valuable piece of real estate and a foothold on the continent. They probably wish they could take that deal back.

ENDNOTES

1   USDA-AMS-Local Food Research & Development Division. 2016. "National Count of Farmers Market Directory Listings." www.ams.usda.gov/sites/default/files/media/National%20Count%20of%20Operating%20Farmers%20Markets%201994-2016.jpg.

2   Pollan, Michael. *The Omnivore's Dilemma* (New York, 2006). The brilliant writing of Michael Pollan first opened my eyes to the modern, industrialized agriculture complex and his work remains the best account of the problems our society faces in relation to food production.

3   Gamerman, Amy. "Upscale Farm Living (You don't have to get your hands dirty)" Wall Street Journal. March, 2018

4   Thomas Vilsack. "Statement by Thomas Vilsack, Secretary of Agriculture, Before the House Committee on Agriculture, February 24, 2016." http://agriculture.house.gov/uploadedfiles/vilsack_testimony_022416.pdf.

5   National Restaurant Association. 2016. "2016 Restaurant Industry Forecast." www.restaurant.org/News-Research/Research/Forecast-2016.

6   National Restaurant Association. 2016. "What's Hot Culinary Forecast." www.restaurant.org/News-Research/Research/What-s-Hot.

7   Chris Hardman. 2015. "How One Visionary Changed School Food in Detroit." Civil Eats. http://civileats.com/2015/04/06/how-one-visionary-changed-school-food-in-detroit/.

8   National Gardening Association. 2014. "Food Gardening in the U.S. at the Highest Levels in More Than a Decade According to New Report by the National Gardening Association." www.garden.org/learn/articles/view/3819/.

9   Dennis Jerke. 2008. *Urban Design and the Bottom Line*. Washington, DC: Urban Land Institute.

10   American Farmland Trust, June 2018 Report

11   Dave Merrill and Lauren Leatherby, 2018 "How America Uses Its Land," Bloomberg, July 31, 2018.

12   Urban Land Institute. *Cultivating Development: Trends and Opportunities at the Intersection of Food and Real Estate*. Washington, D.C.: Urban Land Institute, 2016. Provides an excellent overview of the connections between food and real estate

13   USDA-AMS-Local Food Research & Development Division. 2016. "National Count of Farmers Market Directory Listings." www.ams.usda.gov/sites/default/files/media/National%20Count%20of%20Operating%20Farmers%20Markets%201994-2016.jpg.

14   Bendix Anderson. 2016. "Food Adds Flavor (and Value) to Real Estate: 'Agrihoods' and Other Food-Based Concepts." *UrbanLand*, June 28. http://urbanland.uli.org/sustainability/food-adds-flavor-value-real-estateagrihoods-food-halls-food-based-concepts/.

15   Organic Trade Association. 2016. "U.S. Organic Sales Post New Record of $43.3 Billion in 2015." www.ota.com/news/press-releases/19031

16   Duany, Andres and DPZ. *Garden Cities: Theory & Practice of Agrarian Urbanism* (London, 2011). My understanding and interpretation of the agricultural neighborhood was greatly influenced by Duany and the DPZ firm. Published by the Princes Foundation for the Built Environment, the book describes community plans and management that enables the interaction between agriculture, development and modern society.

17   Ibid The descriptions of the "environmentalist", "trendsetter", "opportunist", "survivalist" come from Duany.

18   ibid

19   ibid

20   Global Wellness Institute, *Build Well to Live Well: Wellness Lifestyle Real Estate and Communities*, January 2018. A wonderful overview of the wellness real estate trend, and a big influence on my thinking of the subject.

21   ibid

22   ibid

23   ibid

24   Cynthia L. Ogden, Margaret D. Carroll, Brian K. Kit, and Katherine M. Flegal. 2014. "Prevalence of Childhood and Adult Obesity in the United States 2011–2012." *JAMA* 311: 806–14. doi:10.1001/jama.2014.732.

25   Centers for Disease Control and Prevention. n.d. "Healthy Schools, Childhood Obesity Facts." U.S. Department of Health and Human Services. www.cdc.gov/healthyschools/obesity/facts.htm.

26   U.S. Department of Agriculture, Economic Research Service. n.d. "Food Security in the U.S." www.ers.usda.gov/topics/food-nutritionassistance/food-security-in-the-us.aspx.

27   Anne-Marie Hamelin, Jean-Pierre Habicht, and Micheline Beaudry. 1999. "Food Insecurity: Consequences for the Household and Broader Social Implications." *Journal of Nutrition* 129: 525S–528S. http://jn.nutrition.org/content/129/2/525.long.

28   RTI International Center for Health and Environmental Modeling. 2014. "Current and Prospective Scope of Hunger and Food Security in America: A Review of Current Research." www.rti.org/sites/default/files/resources/full_hunger_report_final_07-24-14.pdf.

29   Robert Wood Johnson Foundation. 2013. "Metro Map: New Orleans, Louisiana." www.rwjf.org/en/library/infographics/new-orleans-map.html.

30   PolicyLink and the Food Trust. 2013. *Access to Healthy Food and Why It Matters: A Review of the Research.* http://thefoodtrust.org/uploads/media_items/access-to-healthy-food.original.pdf.

31   U.S. Department of Agriculture, Economic Research Service. 2009. *Access to Affordable and Nutritious Food: Measuring and Understanding Food Deserts and Their Consequences.* www.ers.usda.gov/media/242675/ap036_1_.pdf.

32 Kelley E. Borradaile, Sandy Sherman, Stephanie S. Vander Veur, Tara McCoy, Brianna Sandoval, Joan Nachmani, Allison Karpyn, and Gary D. Foster. 2009. "Snacking in Children: The Role of Urban Corner Stores." *Pediatrics* 124: 1293–1298.

33 Dave Merrill and Lauren Leatherby. 2018. "How America Uses Its Land," Bloomberg, July 31, 2018. https://www.bloomberg.com/graphics/2018-us-land-use/ Merrill and Leatherby present an excellent map of land use in the U.S. in the online Bloomberg article. Several facts in the next few paragraphs are based on interpretations from the map and my understanding of their research behind it.

34 Berry, Wendell. 1977. *The Unsettling of America: Culture and Agriculture*. I used the 2015 Counterpoint Press Edition, Berkeley, CA. Original copyright and publication in 1977, this work has become a classic in the sustainable agriculture movement.

35 Natural Resources Defense Council. 2007. "Food Miles: How Far Your Food Travels Has Serious Consequences for Your Health and the Climate." http://food-hub.org/files/resources/Food%20Miles.pdf.

36 Sarah DeWeerdt. 2009. "Is Local Food Better?" Worldwatch Institute. www.worldwatch.org/node/6064.

37 Philpott, Tom. 2015. "Invasion of the Hedge Fund Almonds" Mother Jones. https://www.motherjones.com/environment/2015/01/california-drought-almonds-water-use/

38 Christopher L. Weber and H. Scott Matthews. 2008. "Food-Miles and the Relative Climate Impacts of Food Choices in the United States." *Environmental Science & Technology* 42: 3508–3513. doi: 10.1021/es702969f.

39 Global Agriculture. n.d. "Agriculture at a Crossroads: Findings and Recommendations for Future Farming." www.globalagriculture.org/report-topics/meat-and-animal-feed.html.

40 Food and Agriculture Organization of the United Nations. 2013. *Food Wastage Footprint: Impacts on Natural Resources*. www.fao.org/docrep/018/i3347e/i3347e.pdf.

41 John M. Mandyck and Eric B. Schultz. 2015. *Food Foolish: The Hidden Connection between Food Waste, Hunger and Climate Change*. Syracuse, NY: Pinckney Hugo Group.

42 Dana Gunders. 2012. "Wasted: How America Is Losing Up to 40 Percent of Its Food from Farm to Fork to Landfill." National Resources Defense Council. www.nrdc.org/sites/default/files/wasted-food-IP.pdf.

43 ibid

44 Christopher Peterson and Martin Seligman, et al. *Character Strengths and Virtues* (New York: Oxford University Press, 2004). Peterson, Seligman et al wrote the textbook on the subject of human character strengths and virtue, now used in positive psychology courses at colleges and universities across the United States. It is an insightful and illuminating work in the growing field of positive psychology and a great influence on my thinking and interpretation of human values and strengths.

45 ibid. The page reference was used for humor and dramatic affect. The virtue of justice is actually discussed starting on page 355.

46 Ibid.

47 Farmers Market Coalition web site. n.d. "Supplemental Nutrition Assistance Program (SNAP)." https://farmersmarketcoalition.org/advocacy/snap/.

48 Christopher Peterson and Martin Seligman, Character Strengths and Virtues (New York: Oxford University Press, 2004). An inspiring description of Citizenship pg. 355

49 Pirog, Rich, et al. 2001. "Food, Fuel and Freeways: An Iowa perspective on how far food travels, fuel usage, and greenhouse gas emissions". Leopold Center for Sustainable Agriculture, Iowa State University. http://ngfn.org/resources/ngfn-database/knowledge/food_mil.pdf

50 ibid

51 ibid

52 ibid

53 Peter Diamandis and Steven Kotler. Abundance: The Future is Better Than You Might Think. Free Press, New York, 2012. Diamandis and Kotler give an excellent account of the new technologies that will have a positive effect on the future of our planet, and the world and our future is not all doom and gloom as the media often portrays (to sell advertising- it keeps us glued to the TV and our smart phones). Diamandis and Kotler greatly influenced my thinking in this chapter.

54 Wikipedia. https://en.wikipedia.org/wiki/Victory_garden

55 Kallen, Stuart A. The War at Home. San Diego, Lucent Books. 2000

56 Wikipedia. https://en.wikipedia.org/wiki/Victory_garden

57 Schumm, Laura. 2014 "America's Patriotic Victory Gardens". History.com. https://www.history.com/news/americas-patriotic-victory-gardens

58 USDA Agricultural Projections to 2027. Office of the Chief Economist, World Agricultural Outlook Board, U.S. Department of Agriculture. Prepared by the Interagency Agricultural Projections Committee. Long-term Projections Report OCE-2018-1, 117 pp.

59 Volpe, Richard, Edward Roeger, and Ephraim Leibtag. "How Transportation Costs Affect Fresh Fruit and Vegetable Prices", ERR-160, U.S. Department of Agriculture, Economic Research Service, November 2013.

60 Pollan, Michael The Omnivore's Dilemma (New York, 2006). Here again, I am greatly indebted to Pollan's work. Pollan has greatly influenced my thinking as a farmer and a writer.

61 Bingham, Sam. 2007. "Agricultural Development Protection Plan" compiled by Sam Bingham for Buncombe County. https://www.farmlandinfo.org/sites/default/files/BC_FarmPlan.pdf

62 Christopher Peterson and Martin Seligman, et al. Character Strengths and Virtues (New York: Oxford University Press, 2004). See page 520 for a wonderful description of spirituality and transcendence, based on scientific research.

63 ibid. Peterson et all give a brilliant account of research that shows how human beings can build and improve character strengths and virtue.

64 "Letter from George Washington to Richard Henderson, 19 June 1788," *Founders Online*, National Archives, last modified June 29, 2017, http://founders.archives.gov/documents/Washington/04-06-02-0304. [Original source: *The Papers of George Washington*, Confederation Series, vol. 6, *1 January 1788–23 September 1788*, ed. W. W. Abbot. Charlottesville: University Press of Virginia, 1997, pp. 339–342.]

65 "Letter from Thomas Jefferson to James Madison, 20 December 1787," *Founders Online*, National Archives, last modified June 29, 2017, http://founders.archives.gov/documents/Jefferson/01-12-02-0454. [Original source: *The Papers of Thomas Jefferson*, vol. 12, *7 August 1787–31 March 1788*, ed. Julian P. Boyd. Princeton: Princeton University Press, 1955, pp. 438–443.]

66 "Letter from Thomas Jefferson to Abbe Salimankis" The Thomas Jefferson Papers, Library of Congress, Monticello, 1810

67 "Letter from Thomas Jefferson to Edward Everett, 24 February 1823," *Founders Online*, National Archives, last modified June 29, 2017, http://founders.archives.gov/documents/Jefferson/98-01-02-3355

68 L. Lengnick, M. Miller and G. Marten. 2015. "Metropolitan Foodsheds: A Resilient Response to the Climate Change Challenge." Journal of Environmental Studies and Sciences 5(4): 573-592.

69 New York City Economic Development Corporation. 2015. "Mayor de Blasio Announces $150 Million Investment in Hunts Point Food Distribution Center." www.nycedc.com/blogentry/mayor-deblasio-announces-150-million-investment-hunts-point-fooddistribution-center.

70 New York City Produce Terminal Market. n.d. "NYC Produce Terminal Market in Hunts Point." www.terminalmarkets.com/huntspoint.htm

71 Sandy Dall'erba and Francina Domínguez. 2015. "The Impact of Climate Change on Agriculture in the Southwestern United States: The Ricardian Approach Revisited." *Spatial Economic Analysis* 11 (1): 46–66. doi.org/10.1080/17421772.2015.1076574.

72 U.S. Department of Agriculture. 2016. "Farmland Value." www.ers.usda.gov/topics/farm-economy/land-use,-land-value-tenure/farmlandvalue.aspx.

73 Nishat Tasnim, et al, "Linking the Gut Microbial Ecosystem with the Environment: Does Gut Health Depend on Where We Live?" Frontiers in Microbiology, October 6, 2017

https://www.ncbi.nlm.nih.gov/pmc/articles/PMC5635058/

74 Mike Amaranthus and Bruce Allyn. 2013. "Healthy Soil Microbes, Healthy People: The microbial community in the ground is as important as the one in our guts." The Atlantic. https://www.theatlantic.com/health/archive/2013/06/healthy-soil-microbes-healthy-people/276710/

75 Jackson, Charlie and Allison Perrett. 2018. "The End of Tobacco and the Rise of Local Food in Western North Carolina". Local Food Research Center, Appalachian Sustainable Agriculture Project, March 2018

76 Campbell, Elliot. "Most Americans Could Eat Locally, Research Shows" 2015 https://www.ucmerced.edu/news/2015/most-americans-could-eat-locally-research-shows

77 U.S. Department of Agriculture, National Agricultural Statistics Service. 2015. "2012 Census of Agriculture Highlights: Family Farms." www.agcensus.usda.gov/Publications/2012/Online_Resources/Highlights/NASS%20Family%20Farmer/Family_Farms_ Highlights.pdf.

78 Malleret, Thierry. 2018. "Eco-Anxiety: The Rising Psychological Toll of Climate Change". Global Wellness Institute. https://globalwellnessinstitute.org/global-wellness-institute-blog/2018/11/19/eco-anxiety-the-rising-psychological-toll-of-climate-change/